Confidentiality in International Commercial Arbitration

Kyriaki Noussia

Confidentiality in International Commercial Arbitration

A Comparative Analysis of the Position under English, US, German and French Law

Springer

Dr. Kyriaki Noussia
University of Hamburg
Faculty of Law
Schlüterstraße 28
D-20146 Hamburg, Germany
Max Planck Institute for Comparative and
International Private Law Mittelweg 187
D-20148 Hamburg, Germany
noussia@gmail.com

Printed with the support of Alexander von Humboldt-Stiftung

ISBN 978-3-642-10223-3 e-ISBN 978-3-642-10224-0
DOI 10.1007/978-3-642-10224-0
Springer Heidelberg Dordrecht London New York

Library of Congress Control Number: 2010921318

Cover design: WMXDesign GmbH, Heidelberg, Germany

Printed on acid-free paper

Springer is part of Springer Science+Business Media (www.springer.com)

Στη μνήμη του πατέρα μου, Γεωργίου Ηρ. Νούσια

Preface

Arbitration is the most popular form of alternative dispute resolution. Of the reasons for arbitration's leading position as a means of alternative dispute resolution, at least in an international commercial context, is the presumption of the principle of confidentiality entailed in it.

This monograph is a comparative study of the doctrine of confidentiality in international commercial arbitration in the legal systems of England, the USA, Germany and France. The undertaking of the current work has been considered essential due to the central role of confidentiality in arbitration, alongside the fact that confidentiality is not always preserved and the fact that its protection is often problematic in many respects and in many stages throughout the arbitration proceedings. The purpose of this book is to analyse comparatively, critically discuss and assess the role and the problematic areas of confidentiality in international commercial arbitration, in the legal systems of England, the USA, Germany and France, and to propose ways to overcome the problems encountered in the light of the wider spread and strengthening of the role of arbitration worldwide as a powerful means of alternative dispute resolution.

I would like to acknowledge the Alexander von Humboldt Foundation for awarding me the prestigious Alexander von Humboldt Research Fellowship which enabled me to research and write this monograph. I am also grateful for the financial assistance provided by the Alexander von Humboldt Foundation for the printing costs connected with the publication.

In addition, I am indebted to various academic institutions and people in Germany. On the one hand I am indebted to the Georg-August University of Göttingen, Faculty of Law, Institute of Procedural Law, and Prof. Joachim Münch for agreeing to host me and provide me with guest readership status so as to use the library of the Institute of Procedural Law for the four months period between October 2007 and January 2008, during which I was following also intensive German language courses.

I am also indebted to the University of Hamburg, Faculty of Law, Institute of Procedural and Private Law for hosting me for the time period of the research fellowship (Feb. 2008 – Jan. 2010) and for all the assistance provided.

Special thanks are also due to the Max Planck Institute of Comparative and Private International Law in Hamburg, for allowing me to be a guest reader and thus facilitating my research during the same period.

I am deeply grateful to my host professor (*Betreuer*) Herr. Prof. Dr. iur., RiOLG Ulrich Magnus for hosting me and mostly for his overall support, encouragement and appraisal of my work whilst an Alexander von Humboldt Research Fellow in Hamburg.

I am also grateful to Frau Dr. Brigitte Reschke Executive Editor for Law in Springer Verlag, Heidelberg for all the publishing support provided.

I would like to thank all academic colleagues at the Max Planck Institute of Comparative and Private International Law in Hamburg for the constructive academic discussions we have had, which have helped enrich my thinking and writing.

I would also like to thank all of the administrative colleagues at the Max Planck Institute of Comparative and Private International Law in Hamburg for the administrative support provided.

I am also grateful to Mr. Keith Uff, Visiting Lecturer in Law at the B'ham Law School for the constructive discussions we have had on civil procedural law and arbitration and for offering to undertake the arduous task of proof-reading the present manuscript.

Not least, I should acknowledge my family who, as ever, have stood by me during the process of completing this work.

The law stands as on 30 September 2009.

Hamburg
30 September 2009

Kyriaki Noussia

Contents

Abbreviations

ADR	Alternative Dispute Resolution
CCI	Chambre de Commerce Internationale
CPR	Civil Procedure Rules
DAC	Departmental Advisory Committee
DIS	Deutsche Institution für Schiedsgerichtsbarkeit
ECHR	European Convention on Human Rights
ECJ	European Court of Justice
EU	European Union
IBA	International Bar Association
ICC	International Chamber of Commerce
LCIA	London Court of International Arbitration
OLG	Oberlandesgericht
UNCITRAL	United Nations Commission on International Trade Law
UNIDROIT	Institute for the Unification of Private Law Institut pour l' Unification du Droit Privé
WIPO	World Intellectual Property Organisation

Chapter 1
Introduction

1.1 General

Confidentiality is perhaps one of the fundamental, if not the most compelling, of reasons for which parties choose to arbitrate. Arbitration proceedings are not conducted in public. Thus, unlike public trial court proceedings, arbitration proceedings are private and documents which are prepared for the purpose of arbitrations and copied to the arbitrators and the other party, as well as the award itself, are protected by a duty of confidentiality. However, the private character of the arbitration proceedings has not always implied that the concepts of confidentiality and privacy are identical. Confidentiality of arbitral proceedings, as opposed to privacy, does not refer to the ability of third parties to access and observe the proceedings without the consent of the disputing parties and possibly the arbitrator, but to the ability of the parties arbitrating, as well as others, to disclose documents and information used or related to the arbitration.[1]

At least in England, the original distinction between privacy and confidentiality is not as strong nowadays as it has been in the past. In effect, the concepts of confidentiality and privacy, though in principle distinct, have in recent years moved closer together. In English law, there has long been a tort of breach of confidence which permits the claimant to restrain the publication of information which has been obtained under a duty of confidence. The root decision establishing that is *Prince Albert v Strange*.[2] That tort, as subsequently developed by the courts, rested upon three conditions, i.e. first, that the information possesses the necessary quality of confidence, which may relate to personal affairs or to business secrets, secondly that the information was obtained under an express or implied duty of confidentiality and thirdly that the publication of the information would be detrimental. Equally, although no independent tort exists to protect the privacy of an individual,[3]

[1] Merkin (2004, § 17.26–17.34.7).

[2] *Prince Albert v Strange* (1849) 1 Mac & G 25.

[3] *Wainwright v Home Office* [2003] 4 All ER 969; *Campbell v MGN Ltd* [2004] 2 All ER 995.

K. Noussia, *Confidentiality in International Commercial Arbitration*,
DOI 10.1007/978-3-642-10224-0_1,

nevertheless the English courts, on the basis of the right of privacy which is set out in article 8 of the European Convention on Human Rights, have developed the tort of breach of confidence by all but eliminating the need for a pre-existing relationship of confidence between the parties, so that the tort has become upon the misuse of private information.[4]

However, the above-stated distinction between confidentiality and privacy does not operate in the current context in the same way as it has done in the past.

Moreover, in spite of the fact that the distinction between the two concepts was drawn in the Australian case of *Esso Australia Resources Ltd v Minister for Energy and Minerals*,[5] the existence of any duty of confidentiality in arbitration was denied and it was stated that the fact that arbitration proceedings were private did not also entail that there was any duty of confidentiality attaching to the documents thereby generated – thus departing from the general trend followed by English law.[6]

As this monograph will demonstrate, there are many cases which allow us to reach the above conclusion.[7] To name but a few in this section, in the case of *Associated Electric & Gas Insurance Services Ltd v European Reinsurance Co of Zurich*[8] reference was made to the distinction between confidentiality and privacy and a warning was made against any elision of the two, but the point does not appear to have had any significance other than in distinguishing between the award and the documents produced in the arbitration leading up to the award.

Most recently, in *Emmott v Michael Wilson & Partners Ltd*[9] the issue of the distinction between confidentiality and privacy was raised again by Lawrence Collins LJ who commented[10] that an arbitration was private "in the sense that because arbitration is private, that privacy would be violated by the publication or dissemination of documents deployed in the arbitration" and that it was confidential in the senses of the "inherent confidentiality in the information in documents, such as trade secrets or other confidential information generated or deployed in an arbitration" and of "an implied agreement that documents disclosed or generated in arbitration can only be used for the purposes of the arbitration." Confidentiality in the first sense was subsumed by confidentiality in the second sense, in that arbitration documents remain confidential whether or not they contain trade secrets and the like.[11]

---

[4]*Campbell v MGN Ltd* [2004] 2 All ER 995.

[5]*Esso Australia Resources Ltd v Minister for Energy and Minerals* (1995) 128 ALR 391.

[6]Merkin (2004, § 17.26–17.34.7).

[7]That the above-stated distinction between confidentiality and privacy does not operate in the current context in the same way as it has done in the past.

[8]*Associated Electric & Gas Insurance Services Ltd v European Reinsurance Co of Zurich* [2003] 1 All ER (Comm) 253.

[9]*Emmott v Michael Wilson & Partners Ltd* [2008] EWCA Civ 184.

[10]*Emmott v Michael Wilson & Partners Ltd* [2008] EWCA Civ 184, at para 79.

[11]Merkin (2004, § 17.26–17.34.7).

Notwithstanding the statements of Lawrence Collins LJ[12] in *Emmott v Michael Wilson & Partners Ltd*,[13] the confidentiality rule has always been regarded as ultimately vital to the arbitral process in England where the general assumption is that confidentiality takes effect as an implied term in the arbitration agreement between the parties. As also noted by Lawrence Collins LJ[14] parties arbitrating in England expect that the hearing will be in private, and that confidentiality and privacy are implicit in the parties decision to arbitrate instead of litigate in state courts. His Lordship stated also that all of the above is underlined by CPR 62.10 (3)(b), CPR 62.2.(1) and CPR.PD62.5.1 all of which encapsulate the starting point that the parties wish for confidentiality in their arbitral proceedings and went on to refer in particular to the confidentiality principle set out in and recognised almost universally by institutional rules, such as the Rules of the London Court of International Arbitration (LCIA) articles 19(4), 30(1) and 30(3), the Rules of the Court of Arbitration of the International Chamber of Commerce (ICC) articles 21(3) and 28(2), the Arbitration Rules of the World Intellectual Property Organisation (WIPO) article 53(c) and the UNCITRAL Rules, articles 25(4) and 32(5).[15]

As it will be demonstrated in this monograph, at least as far as English law is concerned but not restrictively within English law, this was further recognised in many cases,[16] all of which encapsulate the general assumption that confidentiality takes effect as an implied term in the arbitration agreement between the parties. This implied term approach remains the one favoured by most of the authorities and was again restated in *Emmott v Michael Wilson & Partners Ltd*[17] wherein it was also ventured that the implied agreement is really a rule of substantive law masquerading as an implied term.

However, the duty of confidentiality is not absolute and there are situations in which the duty may be overridden by wider considerations or waived by the parties.[18]

1.2 Aims, Outline and Scope

1.2.1 General

This monograph is on confidentiality in international commercial arbitration in a comparative perspective. Although confidentiality is perceived as one of the main

---

[12] *Emmott v Michael Wilson & Partners Ltd* [2008] EWCA Civ 184, at para 79.

[13] *Emmott v Michael Wilson & Partners Ltd* [2008] EWCA Civ 184.

[14] *Emmott v Michael Wilson & Partners Ltd* [2008] EWCA Civ 184, at paras 62 onwards.

[15] Merkin (2004, § 17.26–17.34.7).

[16] Such as *Mitchell Construction Kinnear Moodie Group v East Anglia Regional Hospital Board* [1971] CLY 375, *Dolling-Baker v Merrett* [1991] 2 All ER 891, at 899.

[17] *Emmott v Michael Wilson & Partners Ltd* [2008] EWCA Civ 184.

[18] Merkin (2004, § 17.26–17.34.7).

advantages of arbitration as a dispute resolution system and mechanism, yet different jurisdictions recognise confidentiality differently, i.e. to varying extents, in spite of the fact that arbitration is a private agreement of parties to submit their dispute to it and as such it should be confidential in many of its aspects, i.e. for example in terms of the documents produced, or in terms of the award rendered, or in terms of the process of the arbitral hearing, etc.

In light of the above observation regarding the different levels of protection and the different aspects and treatment of the concept of confidentiality in international commercial arbitration, this comparative research will examine all of the above in the legal systems of Germany, France, England and the USA. The above legal systems have been chosen because they constitute three of the most representative legal families, i.e. Common law, Continental/Romanic law, Continental/Germanic law. It is believed that their examination will help better understand how confidentiality operates within arbitration, better address its problematic areas and propose ways to overcome those as well as lead the way forward, all in an effort to further promote arbitration.

1.2.2 Aims

The monograph has the following aims:

(1) To study, identify and reflect on the main differences between state courts and arbitration tribunals/proceedings, i.e. the fact that when submitting themselves to the adjudication of the former, the parties succumb to the public character embodied in their nature, in sharp contrast with the case where they submit themselves to arbitral tribunals/proceedings, which by their nature have a private character and – are at least perceived to – entail the element of confidentiality, as well as the extent to which such differences affect arbitration and the role that confidentiality asserts in relation to all that
(2) To investigate the reason why national courts and legislation assume that confidentiality is not to be preserved in national court proceedings on issues related to arbitrations, whether actually confidentiality is or should be preserved and if yes, how far it should be preserved
(3) To study the problem of confidentiality in arbitration proceedings
(4) To study, compare and contrast the way in which confidentiality in international commercial arbitrations is addressed, i.e. whether it is protected or not, in the chosen jurisdictions, the extent to which it is being preserved and the factors affecting this extent
(5) To discuss the extent to which this varying level of protection affects the wider European and global context and status quo that arbitration enjoys
(6) To discuss critically and analyse the advantages and disadvantages of confidentiality in arbitration and the desired level of confidentiality that arbitration should afford

(7) To answer the question of the purpose of arbitration and its interplay with confidentiality
(8) To address the impact of transnational law in the area of arbitration and its interplay with confidentiality
(9) To analyse comparatively the effect that confidentiality in arbitration, in each of the chosen jurisdictions, has on the promotion of arbitration in terms of the globalisation that this field enjoys
(10) To help detect the problems that may impede such flourish of arbitration in view of problems related to confidentiality
(11) To promote the future development of international commercial arbitration by analysing this important aspect/factor of it
(12) To draw conclusions, provide critique and in discussing the various aspects and problems entailed and also to establish the main trends imposed in law in terms of confidentiality in arbitration

1.2.3 Background Justification

England has traditionally been a major arbitral centre attracting even today the conduct of a vast number of international commercial arbitrations. In addition, France, and to a lesser extent Germany, have also been established as big arbitral centres. This is attributable, amidst other factors, to the fact that rules such as the LCIA, or the ICC rules are widely used. To a large extent, the same has occurred in the USA, i.e. there has been large growth also in the USA due to factors such as globalisation and the volume of international commercial trade which have contributed to an attempt to change the scenery and promote arbitration.

Arbitration asserts, more and more, a European-global perspective, due to the fact that the concept of engaging alternative dispute resolution mechanisms is getting even more important than ever nowadays, both at national and international levels. Consequently, confidentiality in arbitration also asserts,[19] a pivotal role. In spite of the considerable growth of arbitration, there are still many difficulties to overcome. Although various uniform legislative frameworks exist, such as the UNCITRAL Model Law, there are no uniform rules widely established, adopted and followed regarding confidentiality in arbitration. Given those impediments in relation to the confidentiality factor in arbitration, it is natural to wonder about the following: Does the large growth and increase in the use of arbitration also presume and guarantee a further continuous flourishing of international commercial arbitration? Does the fact that confidentiality exists as a judicially established doctrine in arbitration, entrenched in it and perceived as an advantage of its character as a means of alternative dispute resolution, presume also the observance of confidentiality

[19] More than ever nowadays.

nowadays? This research will not only seek to answer the above questions but also to investigate the way in which confidentiality in terms of international commercial arbitrations is preserved nowadays and the effect it has on parties in cases where it is not observed, as well as the extent of court intervention, the socio-legal factors that impede or promote confidentiality and the future prospects for arbitration in light of the great importance of the feature of confidentiality.

1.2.4 Research Purpose

The currently proposed research concerns confidentiality in international commercial arbitrations in different jurisdictions. The purpose is not only to research in a comparative way and to comment from a legal angle on the different procedural rules/aspects but also to explore other issues which embody sociological features and aspects.[20] The approach to be taken will be both legal and sociological and it will aim to draw conclusions regarding the prospect of further flourish of arbitration and the positive or negative role of confidentiality in relation to all that.

1.2.5 General Outline

The monograph discusses the advantages and disadvantages entailed within the aspect of confidentiality in international commercial arbitration, the *status quo* of confidentiality in international commercial arbitrations in the chosen jurisdictions, the socio-legal aspects involved within the notion of confidentiality in international commercial arbitrations, the question of the purpose of arbitration and the purpose of confidentiality within it in terms also of the wider European – global context and *status quo* that international commercial arbitration enjoys. It provides some food for thought via the critical analysis which is being conducted and it investigates the results of the interplay of confidentiality within arbitration in light of the globalisation and Europeanisation of arbitration and in view also of the trend to resort to alternative dispute resolution mechanisms rather than to national court proceedings.

The discussion can be categorised in three main sections which discuss the main problems and questions on confidentiality in arbitration, the *status quo* of confidentiality in arbitration in the various jurisdictions and the outcomes of the proposed research on confidentiality in arbitration.

---

[20] For example, questions such as the reasons why in some jurisdictions the level of protection of confidentiality differs, the effect this has on arbitration and the socio-legal reasons entailed behind this difference on the level of protection.

1.2.6 Detailed Outline

Chapter 1 discusses the general and detailed outline of the issues within the present monograph. It also attempts to address the aims of the monograph, the reasons why the discussion does not deal in depth with the other forms of alternative dispute resolution as well as the grounds for specifically dealing with confidentiality within international commercial arbitrations.

Chapter 2 discusses the history of arbitration, the importance of arbitration as well as the modern and increased use it enjoys. More specifically, it discusses the eminence of alternative dispute resolution over state court litigation and the eminence of arbitration over other means of alternative dispute resolution, the pros and cons of arbitration and mediation as the main forms of alternative dispute resolution, the eminence of arbitration over other methods to resolve disputes, the importance and use of confidentiality in the various forms of alternative dispute resolution, and more specifically in arbitration, mediation and Med-Arb, the role of arbitration as a central part of transnational law, i.e. the need for a transnational legal system in terms of international commercial arbitration, the role of transnational law in arbitration and the way arbitral law, international legal instruments and national laws function as transnational law applied to arbitration.

Chapter 3 discusses the main problems and questions encountered in relation to confidentiality in arbitration. In doing so, it addresses issues such as the advantages and disadvantages of arbitration, the desired levels of confidentiality in arbitrations, the main differences between state courts and arbitration tribunals and proceedings, the relation between the transnational character of arbitration and confidentiality, the various problems of confidentiality within arbitral proceedings at the various stages of it, the ways to address and preserve confidentiality in the various jurisdictions and the effect that the varying level of adherence to confidentiality affects the European-global context and *status quo* of international commercial arbitration, the socio-legal factors affecting international commercial arbitration and confidentiality within it, the various issues and case law arising from the examination of article 6 of the European Convention on Human Rights in relation always to confidentiality in international commercial arbitration as well as the correlation of the latter with issues of professional privilege, and last but not least the prospects of arbitration to further flourish as a means of alternative dispute resolution and the role of confidentiality within it.

Chapter 4 discusses the present status of confidentiality in international commercial arbitration in the various chosen jurisdictions, i.e. the way in which confidentiality is perceived and treated at a judicial level, what the examination of the most representative case law so far is able to show us and what conclusions and critique we can derive from all the above.

Chapter 5 attempts a critical analysis and overall assessment on the basis of the examined case law, i.e. the position nowadays and the various problems which are being detected, the possible solutions and the way that the encountered problems may affect arbitration in all or in some of the examined jurisdictions. It also attempts the same critical analysis and overall assessment on the basis of arbitration and of confidentiality within it, i.e. it draws a critical profile of the purpose of arbitration and of its interplay with confidentiality, of the advantages and disadvantages of arbitration and confidentiality within it, of the desired level of confidentiality and of the justification of the reasoning for observing such a level of protection, of the attempt of the courts to create a safety net and achieve a balance between their needs for clarity in terms of the public sphere and the needs of the individuals for confidentiality and sensitive information and of their reasoning at times to permit the non observance of confidentiality when public interest needs detect so. It also discusses the way in which the various and different levels of the modern European and global character of arbitration are affected by the different levels of protection of confidentiality.

Chapter 6 discusses the impact of transnational law on international commercial arbitration and its interconnection with confidentiality, in particular the modern European and global character of arbitration and the way in which the various levels of protection of confidentiality affect it.

Chapter 7 discusses the advantages and disadvantages as well as the possibility of achieving a uniform transnational arbitration law, in the light of a "new *lex mercatoria*" which appears to be emerging in international commercial arbitration.

Chapter 8 attempts to draw overall conclusions. In doing so it also suggests future routes and directions that may be followed as to the position and treatment of confidentiality within arbitration and the overall future of arbitration as a means of alternative dispute resolution.

1.3 Arbitration, as Opposed to Other Means of Alternative Dispute Resolution, and Confidentiality Within It

Arbitration is the most traditional and well-known form of alternative dispute resolution. It arises mostly, though not exclusively, from pre-dispute contracts in which the parties agree that if a dispute arises, it will be resolved by arbitration. There are many reasons why arbitration, as opposed to other means of alternative dispute resolution such as mediation or Med-Arb, especially in an international commercial context, is perceived as having and has rightly won a leading position as the most eminent form of alternative dispute resolution. To name but a few, alternative dispute resolution means such as mediation or Med-Arb may raise concerns about the enforceability of the agreements reached under their auspices and may prove incapable of preserving certain principles, such as the principle of confidentiality, due to the less formal character it has as opposed to arbitration.

For such reasons, in terms of our study we will examine the concept and function of confidentiality in relation only to arbitration and not in all forms of alternative dispute resolution. In particular, we have chosen to examine comparatively in the legal systems of the UK, USA, France and Germany, the concept of confidentiality within arbitration because there is a given assumption of confidentiality in arbitration and, moreover, because arbitration – alongside with the elements of speed and efficacy that it entails as well as the fact that it creates no binding precedent – is mostly chosen because of the confidentiality feature that it is presumed to assume and guarantee within its nature.

Moreover confidentiality is important in relation to arbitration from a functional point of view, as it denotes the extent of the ability of the arbitrating and other parties to disclose documents and information used in or related to the arbitration. However, confidentiality is not always preserved and its protection is often problematic in many stages. Thus, it is essential that we address and discuss all of these problems at the various stages of arbitration, i.e. at the proceedings stage in relation to it *per se*, and in relation to the award. In short, the pivotal and key role that confidentiality plays in the successful practice of alternative dispute resolution is one of the main reasons for arbitrating and this alone urges the full examination of the concept.

The English Arbitration Act 1996 makes no reference to the obligation of confidentiality.

However, this omission was no indication that confidentiality was not regarded as being important. It was the difficulty of reaching a statutory formulation, in the light of the many exceptions and qualifications that would have to follow, that led the Departmental Advisory Committee to conclude that the courts should be left to continue to work out its implications on a pragmatic case by case basis.[21]

Arbitration is an important vehicle for the resolution of disputes, supported by a strong national policy favouring the arbitration of disputes. One of the potential advantages of the process is that it is private. Third parties can be prevented from observing the proceedings. Parties to the arbitration can contract to prevent each other from disclosing arbitration communications to third parties. In addition, arbitrators are ethically bound to preserve this confidentiality unless otherwise required by law. Less clear is whether the law can require the disclosure of those arbitration communications for purposes of discovery and admission in other legal proceedings. The emerging view of the courts appears to be that such disclosures may be compelled – a position that would undermine legislative and other intents to endorse a private alternative to public adjudication, because – once they are introduced – such communications would become public records that may be disseminated freely as a general matter. The continuation of this trend would undermine the national policy favouring arbitration by frustrating the parties' reasonable expectations with respect to the confidentiality of arbitration, ultimately chilling the use of the arbitration process. The law's expectation of access to these materials is not trivial, however, and proper legal policy must reflect a balance of these competing public and private interests. This balance may be struck by raising the burden of proof for the admission of evidence sought from arbitration proceedings by requiring the proponent of such evidence to demonstrate that it is otherwise

[21]Robb (2004).

unavailable and necessary for the resolution of the case. The adoption of an elevated standard will not resolve all questions regarding the confidentiality of arbitration communications. Legitimate questions may be raised, such as for example the questions of who has the power to prevent a third party from attending an arbitration hearing and how far it may be exercised. Can the media, for example, be barred from an arbitration hearing? What if the government is a party? On these questions, there is, again, little statutory or common law at present, and the few court rulings on the question have suggested that there are circumstances under which the media's interest in attending and reporting on an arbitration may trump a confidentiality clause to arbitrate or internal organisational rules calling for the confidentiality of arbitration.

Such issues merit closer attention. As arbitration continues to expand as a fixture on the landscape of civil justice, it becomes more important for participants in the process to be aware of the contours of arbitration's relationship with the law, of the limitations of arbitration as well as its strengths. As with the discovery and admissibility of mediation communications, a rigorous inquiry is a necessary foundation for good legal policy with respect to arbitration communications. Like any alternative dispute resolution process, arbitration does not stand apart from the law, and when the two come into contact, wise policy requires a careful balancing of the needs, interests, and concerns of both institutions.[22]

[22]Reuben (2006, pp. 1299–1300).

Chapter 2
The History, Importance and Modern Use of Arbitration

2.1 The History of Arbitration

Once men begin to live and trade together, inevitably various forms of adjudication emerge. It follows from the above that the submission of disputes to independent adjudication is a form of ordering human society as old as society itself.

Why did arbitration develop as a means of alternative dispute resolution? In order to answer this question, one needs look at the history of arbitration.

2.1.1 England

In England merchants have resorted to adjudication outside the Royal Courts from the first development of national and international trade. Already in the later middle ages, a solid connection between finance and commerce existed. Commercial transactions were commonly done on credit terms, such as bills of exchange, widely accepted at the seasonal fairs which brought together the trading community and provided the basis of this credit system. The character of the Royal Courts was not adapted initially to serve the needs of this trade and traders, firstly because the early courts were primarily interested in disputes over land and conduct detrimental to the King's peace, secondly because contracts, commercial credits and debts incurred abroad and owed by and to foreigners were almost wholly unenforceable, thirdly because the traditional court procedure lacked the much needed expedition that merchants, passing from fair to fair and so often changing jurisdiction, needed and fourthly because jurisdiction was ousted by the necessity of proving venue in England. Thus, the trading communities relied on special tribunals, i.e. the Courts of the Boroughs, of the Fair and of the Staple, in order to solve the controversies arising in the world of local and international trade. These courts were the predecessors of today's modern arbitral tribunals in that a predominant feature of their character was that law should be speedily administered in commercial causes, which

K. Noussia, *Confidentiality in International Commercial Arbitration*,
DOI 10.1007/978-3-642-10224-0_2, © Springer-Verlag Berlin Heidelberg 2010

in effect led also to a relaxation of the strict procedure in these Courts, and in that, according also to the nature of the dispute, commercial men were also elected to form part of the tribunal. Thus, the Middle Ages saw a diverse system of tribunals dealing with commercial disputes, where it was already acknowledged that people with special knowledge to the related trade would be on some disputes better assessors to arbitrate on it and that the settlement of the commercial cases should be speedy.

Following the discovery of the New World, the international society of the Middle Ages dissolved into nation states and, in this new age, men of commerce begun to look for new institutions to refer their disputes. However, although the habit for arbitration and the desire for its use continued to exist, nevertheless the adjudication of commercial disputes were not anymore exclusively reserved to it for reasons such as the fact that the common law courts developed by the mid-sixteenth century a general remedy in contract and thus gave themselves also jurisdiction over causes involving foreign elements by recognising a notional venue in England, and because at the same time the Admiralty court expanded a jurisdiction over cases in which a foreign merchant was a party. However, the assertion by the traditional courts of a role in the settlement of business disputes was not entirely to the liking of the commercial community, who liked the idea of tribunals in which they also had some share, not least because the predominant notion was that lawyers did not understand commercial problems as well as the notion that the technical and time-consuming character of litigation did not accord with their desire for speed in the resolution of their disputes. In effect, a solution was found in that charters were drafted which tended to incorporate the privilege for company merchants to settle potential disputes between themselves.[1] By the eighteenth century arbitration was solidly entrenched as a means of alternative dispute resolution within which judicial intervention now extensively occurs because of the natural desire of the courts to keep all adjudications within their sphere, or the fear of the growth of a new system of law, but most importantly due to the fact that litigants in arbitrations needed the assistance of the courts who in turn exacted a price for the assistance offered.[2] In the nineteenth century comes the final fruition in the growth of satisfactory judicial and arbitral modes of resolving commercial disputes. The zenith of the work of absorption and growth which transmuted the practice of commerce into an effective part of the ordinary law and brought the commercial arbitral tribunal under the control of the ordinary courts, is the Common Law Procedure Act 1854 via which, for the first time, the courts were given the power to stay proceedings whenever a person, having agreed that a person's dispute should be referred to arbitration, nevertheless commenced an action in respect of the matters referred. Secondly, statutory provisions as to the appointment of arbitrators and umpires were formulated to solve difficulties arising on default and, thirdly, the courts were given power to remit an award back to the arbitrator, who was able to state a question of law for the determination of the court.

[1]Lord Parker of Waddington (1959, pp. 5–12).

[2]Lord Parker of Waddington (1959, pp. 12–14).

Commercial arbitrations were made subject to a systematic code of law by the Arbitration Act 1889 which amended and consolidated all previous practices. Since 1900, the general position has been that a commercial dispute can be speedily and efficiently determined in the courts as well as by arbitration, depending on its nature and what common practice in the particular sector requires, and that the two systems ought indeed to be properly regarded as coordinate rather than rival.[3]

The Arbitration Acts 1950, 1975, 1979 and 1996 all encapsulate the need for party autonomy as opposed to the previous tradition of judicial intervention. More specifically, the Arbitration Act 1979 was the first legislative instrument to abolish the long-established case stated procedure, whereby the courts were free to review an award if an error of law or fact appeared on the face of the award, and in its place established a structure under which errors of fact could not be the subject of an appeal and errors of law could be appealed only under stringent conditions. The Arbitration Act 1996 is a combination of consolidation and reform of the legal principles enshrined in the previous Arbitration Acts and the common law. It is the closest thing to a definitive code of arbitration law which has ever been enacted in England, although both the common law and decisions on earlier legislation still remain significant, not least as a guide to the interpretation of its provisions. It has managed to move English law far closer to the UNCITRAL Model Law than it was originally anticipated to do.[4]

2.1.2 USA

In the USA, already from the time of the American colonies, arbitration among merchants was common, since it proved more efficient and effective than the courts during that period. The first US president George Washington himself also served as an arbiter of private disputes before the Revolution.[5] However, in the late nineteenth and early twentieth centuries, arbitration enjoyed a not particularly favourable position, as there was some mistrust by the legal establishment on arbitration's capacity to produce fair results. Moreover it was feared that arbitration, if it proved too successful, could jeopardise the livelihood of all those who relied on the court system. Nowadays the scenery is totally different and arbitration is embraced as a viable alternative to litigating disputes. The tide of hostility towards arbitration began to turn in America with the enactment of modern state and federal arbitration acts and the creation of the American Arbitration Association. In 1920, New York reformed its arbitration law so as to enforce agreements to arbitrate future disputes. The American Bar Association in 1921 developed a draft of a Federal Arbitration Act patterned on the then-existing New York law. The American Bar Association draft was introduced in Congress the

[3]Lord Parker of Waddington (1959, pp. 18–24).

[4]Merkin (2000, pp. 1–10).

[5]Folberg et al. (2005, p. 454).

following year and, with minor revisions, became law in 1925. During the same decade the American Arbitration Association was also instrumental in advancing arbitration, as it sought to promote the arbitral process – via the development of uniform rules – and it also secured qualified individuals to act as arbitrators. However, there was still some negativity towards state level arbitration which was eradicated by the late twentieth century via the adoption of arbitration statutes in all 50 states, as well as by broad federal court jurisdictional interpretations of "interstate commerce" under the Federal Arbitration Act.[6]

2.1.3 France

In France, arbitration always played an important role. Already from the sixteenth century, the Decree of the Moulins of 1566 made arbitration the sole and obligatory means of dispute resolution for commercial disputes. Not least, there was in France a notable mistrust of the capacity of the state's courts to resolve such disputes with the same effectiveness as arbitration. This trend is reflected in article 1 of the Decree of 16–24 August 1790 which stated that arbitration was to be considered the most reasonable means of dispute resolution between citizens.[7] In the nineteenth century arbitration in France declined and only really revived in the 1960s. The establishment of institutions such as the Chambre de Commerce Internationale (CCI) was important in this development. In the modern era, the French law of arbitration is characterised by the existence of both a domestic and an international procedural system, with domestic arbitrations being regulated by Titles I–IV of Part IV (articles 1442–1491) of the Civil Code and with international arbitrations being regulated by Titles V–VI of Part IV (articles 1492–1507) of the Civil Code.[8]

2.1.4 Germany

In Germany arbitration was from early on practised and recognised as an effective means of alternative dispute resolution. Prior to the enactment of the German Arbitration Act 1998, the law was considered anachronistic. The German Arbitration Act 1998, which came into force on 1 January 1998, was therefore adopted to better facilitate domestic and international arbitration proceedings in Germany. It is codified in the German Code of Civil Procedure (Zivilprozessordnung or ZPO) §§ 1025–1066 and applies on all agreements to arbitrate concluded on or after 1 January 1998. The German Arbitration Act 1998 was modelled after the

---

[6]Bruner and O'Connor Jr (2002, Chap. 20, § 20:2).

[7]Guyon (1995, pp. 7–8).

[8]Devolvé (1982).

UNCITRAL Model Law on International Commercial Arbitration in order to create an arbitration-friendly jurisdiction that would be also attractive to foreign practitioners. The rationale of the German legislation was to favour the creation of a legal structure that would be familiar to the arbitration community as an already accepted international standard.[9]

2.2 The Importance and Modern Use of Arbitration

In explaining the growth and modern use of arbitration, one need take into account factors such as the desire for secrecy, the attraction of moving to a custom of using industry experts as arbitrators rather than traditional state court judges and therefore also more flexible procedures, the option of selecting trade norms as the rules of decision[10] and the economy, speed, secrecy and certainty of the process, as well as the ability given to parties to settle a dispute whilst maintaining business relations.[11]

2.2.1 The Eminence of Arbitration Over Other Means of Alternative Dispute Resolution

2.2.1.1 In General

Given the increasing importance of arbitration as an alternative to costly litigation, it is critical to understand the role that arbitration plays in encouraging self-negotiated settlements in different settings[12] and the reasons why it is more effective, especially in an international commercial context as opposed to other widely used means of alternative dispute resolution, such as mediation and Med-Arb.

Mediation constitutes a process of assisted negotiation in which a neutral person helps the parties to reach agreement. It differs from arbitration in that it is rather more consensual and does not always lead to a final settlement of the dispute. It is cheaper than arbitration and assists the parties to find their own solution to the dispute. Even if no final solution is found it may help them to decide the best further steps for the resolution of the dispute. Although litigants may in some circumstances be compelled to enter mediation – or at least be put under heavy pressure to do so – it is only effective and successful to the extent that disputants find it effective. All the above, and other factors such as the fact that this means of alternative dispute resolution does not fit cases where a disputant is not capable

9 Rützel et al. (2005, p. 110).

10 Brunet et al. (2006, p. 25).

11 Bonn (1972, p. 257).

12 Deck and Farmer (2007, p. 549).

of negotiating, or feels the need to establish a legal precedent, or requires a court order to control the conduct of an adversary,[13] have resulted in arbitration being more popular and more often chosen and used as a means of alternative dispute resolution.

In the case of Med-Arb, which is an interim form of alternative dispute resolution in that it entails features from both arbitration and mediation, parties may choose, and arbitral institutions may offer, it in order to resolve contractual disputes. In some cases having a single neutral person serving in both the role of arbitrator and mediator saves time and money and may encourage parties to resolve their dispute at the mediation stage, because they know that their mediator will finally render a final and binding decision if disputes are not settled at the mediation stage. Nevertheless, this form of alternative dispute resolution has not evolved and is not used as much as arbitration. There is hostility towards the mixing of the roles of arbitrator and mediator for many reasons. Firstly, the roles are considered distinct and incompatible. Secondly and in contrast with what is used as an argument in favour of Med-Arb, parties may be less candid in communicating with the mediator and, thus, undermine a vivid feature of mediation, if they know that their mediator will in any case decide the dispute should mediation fail. Thirdly, the possibility that the mediator-turned-arbitrator's view of the issues concerned may have been affected by information imparted confidentially in *ex parte* discussions, is also a negative factor that may deter the use of this form of alternative dispute resolution. Fourthly, a negative factor that may deter the use of this form of alternative dispute resolution is the fact that many mediators have little or no experience conducting an arbitration hearing and may not be competent to take on the other role. Lastly, there is also the chance, unless there is an express waiver of such a right, for the arbitral award to be challenged on grounds of *ex parte* communication at the mediation stage.[14]

2.2.1.2 In Relation to Confidentiality

Confidentiality is vital to mediation because effective mediation requires a certain level of candour, secondly because fairness to the disputants requires its preservation, thirdly because it constitutes one of the incentives for choosing to mediate, fourthly because it helps preserve the process and character of mediation as a means of alternative dispute resolution and finally because it helps the preservation of neutrality of the mediator, especially if the latter is involved in a subsequent legal proceeding. However, the preservation of confidentiality in mediation has, for many reasons, proved problematic. Firstly, because the most usual means of protecting it

[13] Folberg et al. (2005, pp. 223–231).

[14] See *Township of Aberdeen v Patrolmen's Benevolent Association*, 669 A.2d 291 (N.J.S. Ct., App. Div. 1996) where the arbitral award rendered was struck down by the Court on the basis that the arbitrator had improperly relied on information gained during the course of mediation and not presented during the arbitration process; Folberg et al. (2005, pp. 643–646).

is via a rule of evidence which nonetheless does not always extend this level of protection to all aspects and facets of mediation but is only a valid means of mandatory protection of confidentiality mostly in relation to state courts proceedings. Secondly, because confidentiality is often only impliedly protected or, even where it is protected via a confidentiality provision, still the extent of this protection remains vague and even where confidentiality rules are contained in statutes in the form of legal privileges, the form of such privileges and the subsequent protection of confidentiality under them may differ. Thirdly, even if there are mediation agreements covering confidentiality these bind only the parties entering those agreements and not third-parties that may enter the process of mediation. Fourthly, public policy issues may detect the lifting of the veil of confidentiality.[15] Likewise, the protection of confidentiality may also prove problematic in the case of Med-Arb, for all the above stated reasons, as well as because of the possibility of having *ex parte* communication at the mediation stage which, as stated above, may put the whole Med-Arb process at stake as the arbitral award can be challenged on such a ground.

2.3 Tentative Observations

It is generally thought that an expectation of confidentiality on the part of participants is critical to the successful conduct of a mediation or Med-Arb process and, as already stated above, candour by the parties can be crucial to a successful mediation or Med-Arb process. Despite its important role, the issue of confidentiality in mediation, which continues to be a hotly debated topic in the courts and among academia, remains still wide open, considering the difficulties of precisely defining such a rule together with all the possible legitimate exceptions and the fact that its protection may depend on several and variable parameters such as the terms of the mediation agreement, the applicable institutional rules, the law governing the mediation agreement, the nature of the information to be disclosed, the extent of allowance of such disclosure and the factors determining the extent of protection of confidentiality even in cases where the latter exists.

However, in contrast to the above, and irrespective of the fact that no final formulation of the confidentiality obligation can be found in case law, it is generally recognised that there is, at least in common law, an enforceable and implied duty of confidentiality arising out of the nature of arbitration whereby the arbitral proceeding must be privately conducted and subject to the duty of confidentiality.[16]

For all the above reasons, we support the argument that arbitration is a much more preferred and widely used means of alternative dispute resolution.

[15] Folberg et al. (2005, pp. 307–414).

[16] Zamboni (2003, pp. 178–179).

Chapter 3
Problems and Questions Encountered in Relation to Confidentiality in Arbitration

3.1 The Main Problems and Questions on Confidentiality in Arbitration

3.1.1 General

When one reflects on the concept of confidentiality in arbitration, there are many parameters and questions to be considered prior to reaching any conclusions.

The main questions to be posed and answered can be grouped as follows:

What are the advantages and disadvantages of arbitration? Is confidentiality an advantage of arbitration or not and for which reasons? What is the main purpose of arbitration? How does confidentiality relate to the purpose of arbitration?

Is there a desired level of confidentiality in arbitration? What are the standards that affect the setting of such a level, and depending on which factors and at which stages of arbitration does this level fluctuate? How do privacy and confidentiality interact nowadays? Are they distinct or identical? What are the problems of confidentiality in arbitral proceedings? Is confidentiality preserved and respected as a general principle? Are there any limits and exceptions imposed and are there any factors affecting those limits and exceptions? What are the difficulties related to confidentiality when collecting evidence, whether in the course of acquiring oral evidence, discovery of documents or in other stages of the arbitral proceedings?

How does the varying level of adherence to confidentiality affect the European – global context and face of arbitration?

What are the main differences between state courts and arbitration proceedings? How do those differences relate to confidentiality and how do they affect arbitration as a means of alternative dispute resolution? Are national court proceedings initiated in relation to arbitration issues of a public or private character? Is confidentiality preserved or should it be preserved, and to what extent, in such national court proceedings? When state courts have to decide on issues such as the recognition and enforcement of arbitral awards, how does the fact that such decisions are

K. Noussia, *Confidentiality in International Commercial Arbitration*,
DOI 10.1007/978-3-642-10224-0_3, © Springer-Verlag Berlin Heidelberg 2010

taken in publicly held proceedings affect arbitration? If there is an issue of confidentiality involved in such a case, what are its consequences and how can they be addressed?

Given that arbitration has developed to be a transnational system of law, how does this latter aspect of arbitration relate to confidentiality?

What are the limits imposed upon confidentiality by article 6 of the ECHR and professional privilege?

This chapter will address these and any other relevant issues.

3.1.2 The Advantages and Disadvantages of Arbitration as Opposed to State Court Litigation and the Interplay with Confidentiality

Arbitration entails many advantages and disadvantages. Among its advantages are the moderate cost of the proceedings and time-saving, when compared to state court litigation, the less formal character of the procedure as opposed to the procedural rules in state court litigation and the subsequent relaxation of rules of evidence in arbitration in some jurisdictions, as opposed to those employed in state court litigation. Other advantages include the confidentiality and privacy elements of the arbitral proceedings, the ability of the parties to control the procedure. The parties may also make certain decisions regarding the arbitration processes and procedures in advance, and they can not only select an arbitrator but also choose one with a particular expertise, to adjudicate on their matter, as opposed to state court litigation where the latter is a state appointed judge. The finality of the arbitrator's award has the same force as that of a judgment of a state court but the award does not create a binding precedent, while the parties may choose the legal forum for the resolution of their dispute. Among its disadvantages are the lack of a full range of discovery and the limited availability of cross-examination of witnesses, the impossibility – or extreme difficulty – in appealing the arbitral award and the lack of a guarantee of the preservation of confidentiality in all cases.

Arbitrations have generally been more secretive than litigation because arbitral decisions have traditionally been unpublished. In other words, many parties choose to arbitrate rather than to litigate precisely because they do not want the subject matter of their dispute to become public. However, the perception and preservation of confidentiality is not guaranteed as often, and in most jurisdictions, it is only an implied obligation not expressly provided for and protected by law. Some common law jurisdictions[1] recognize the confidentiality of arbitration[2]

---

[1] Such as, for example, the UK or Malaysia.

[2] See, for example, rule 9 of the Rules for Arbitration of the Kuala Lumpur Regional Centre for Arbitration.

whilst others,[3] have rejected the concept that arbitration is subject to a confidentiality privilege.[4]

Nevertheless, the reason why parties enter into a confidentiality agreement is to ensure greater protection, for via such agreements they agree to keep the existence of the proceedings, all documents and communications related to the arbitration and the award, private. The sole fact that parties enter into such agreements does not, nevertheless, guarantee the observance of such agreements. Confidentiality agreements can also be breached, because no absolute guarantee exists for the preservation of confidentiality and because arbitration proceedings between private parties – although private proceedings not open to the public, as opposed to the court proceedings[5] – constitute proceedings whose private and confidential character can be prone to various threats.[6] To name but a few, the tradition of confidentiality which is embedded in arbitration can also be threatened by local media or attract other kinds of attention. In addition, to the extent that parties to an arbitration clause agree to keep the subject matter of their potential dispute confidential, this agreement would not apply to non-signatories who are later compelled to arbitrate alongside the contracting parties. The participation of non-signatories in arbitral disputes is not in itself a factor destroying confidentiality as arbitrators routinely ensure that such non-signatories honour any confidentiality clauses contained in the original agreement by simply requiring them upon entering the arbitration to sign an order to observe confidentiality. However it is not always feasible to compel all non signatory parties to enter into such agreements. Factors such as those described above could cause parties to abandon arbitration as a dispute-resolution device.

The privacy of arbitral proceedings has also always been subject to factors outside of the arbitration itself. Courts may appoint the same arbitrator to two or more similar cases, in an effort to ensure consistent results, and thereby make all of the relevant documents and transcripts from one proceeding available in the next.[7] Courts also play an important role in challenging or enforcing arbitral awards, and any decision that a court makes may become a matter of public record.[8]

The fact that statutory laws alongside with some arbitration rules[9] do not impose confidentiality, together with the fact that a general contractual obligation of confidentiality in case of legal proceedings does not automatically cover arbitration, make it prudent to explicitly address arbitration and confidentiality in arbitration clauses.

---

[3]Such as, for example, Australia and the United States.

[4]*Esso Australia Resources Ltd. & Others v. Plowman*, 183 C.L.R. 10, 128 A.L.R. 391 (1995); *United States v. Panhandle Eastern Corp.*, 118 F.R.D. 346 (D. Del. 1988).

[5]Article 34 of the International Arbitration Rules of the International Centre for Dispute Resolution (ICDR), a division of the American Arbitration Association, calls for the arbitrator and the administrator to maintain the confidentiality of arbitration proceedings and the award.

[6]Laeuchli (2007, p. 84).

[7]*Abu Dhabi Gas Liquefaction Co. v. E. Bechtel Corp.*, (1982) 2 Lloyd's Rep. 425, 427.

[8]Daly (2007, pp. 124–125).

[9]Such as for example the Rules of Arbitration of the International Chamber of Commerce (ICC).

There are also other good reasons for explicitly imposing confidentiality in arbitration. The International Bar Association (IBA) 1999 Rules on the Taking of Evidence in International Commercial Arbitration intend to govern in an efficient and economical manner the taking of evidence in international commercial arbitrations, particularly those between parties from different legal traditions. When parties elect to use these International Bar Association (IBA) rules of evidence, a party can request the arbitral tribunal to exclude certain information from evidence, production of documents or oral testimony, on compelling technical and commercial confidentiality grounds.[10] Thus, an existing nondisclosure obligation will facilitate the task of the requesting party to convince the arbitral tribunal to exclude such information.[11] Further, in case of public tenders and pre-qualifications governmental administrations often ask for detailed data about current or past arbitrations. A confidentiality obligation allows a party to restrict such reporting about the arbitration cases and the involved parties to very basic information.[12]

A number of competing values must be reconciled if any general principles are to be established. A fundamental basis for agreeing to arbitration rather than to litigation in public courts is to preserve privacy and confidentiality to the greatest extent possible. Arbitration is a private dispute resolution process in which the arbitrators and rules are selected by the parties. In principle, there is no reason why business people should not be able to resolve their commercial disputes in a private and confidential manner. However, a concurrent and sometimes overriding public interest sometimes has to be recognised which would require to lift the cloak of confidentiality in a number of circumstances, including the following: (1) where the subject matter or the existence of the dispute and/or its outcome must be publicly reported because it may be material to the financial condition of a public company; (2) where the disclosure of the dispute and the surrounding circumstances or outcome may be required by shareholders, partners, creditors or others having a legitimate business interest in the affairs of one of the parties to the dispute, (3) where one of the parties may conclude that its commercial interests and the interests of shareholders and potential shareholders would be enhanced by publicly disclosing information about the dispute and any resulting award and, accordingly, has a duty to make such disclosure, (4) where one or both of the parties may be subject to obligations[13] to disclose information in spite of any express or implied term to the contrary in the arbitration agreement, (5) where it may not be possible or proper to shield the company's auditors and outside advisors from the fact and nature of the dispute and the surrounding circumstances and the ultimate award – whether confidential or not – (6) where the parties have duties of disclosure to insurers, (7) where the parties must be free to present the award and relevant surrounding

[10]International Bar Association (IBA) 1999 Rules on the Taking of Evidence in International Commercial Arbitration, Article 9.

[11]Buhler (2002, p. 380).

[12]Stouthuysen (2006, pp. 146–147).

[13]For example as a fiduciary.

circumstances in a public court to either enforce or appeal the award or use it as evidence in another related proceeding, (8) where the parties may be obliged to disclose evidence from the arbitration in another proceeding, (9) where the evidence of illegal or criminal conduct that should be reported to public authorities may be uncovered during the course of the proceedings.

The amount of competing values entailed makes it difficult for any legislated solution to be effective enough to resolve the issue of confidentiality in all circumstances. However, a number of arbitral institutions have enacted rules dealing with confidentiality[14] which are generally intended to ensure the privacy and confidentiality of the proceedings, subject to the consent of the parties and the application of any overriding legal duty of disclosure. Nevertheless, not all arbitration rules refer to confidentiality.[15]

The question of confidentiality is best left to the parties in their commercial agreement or arbitration agreement and, in this respect, it is always preferable to negotiate a written arbitration agreement before a dispute arises, because it is often difficult to reach a consensual agreement once a dispute occurs. The appropriate terms of a confidentiality agreement will differ depending on the circumstances of each transaction or dispute. If the arbitration agreement does not address the issue of confidentiality, the parties may address that issue during an administrative conference with the tribunal at a preliminary stage of the proceeding.

In short, because of the legal inconsistencies across jurisdictions and different treatment by institutional arbitration rules, parties to arbitration should not assume that the existence of arbitration presupposes that the evidence and the award will be kept confidential. Thus, at most, and in an effort to preserve confidentiality, parties should incorporate express confidentiality provisions in their arbitration agreement

[14]For instance see: Rules of Arbitration of the International Chamber of Commerce, Appendix I, Article 6 and Appendix II, Article 1; Rules of the London Court of International Arbitration, Article 30; International Centre for Dispute Resolution (American Arbitration Association) International Arbitration Rules, Article 34; World International Property Organization Arbitration Rules, Articles 73–76; Swiss Rules of International Arbitration, adopted by the Chamber of Commerce and Industry of Zurich in 2004, Article 43; Swiss Rules of International Arbitration, adopted by the Chamber of Commerce and Industry of Geneva in 2004, Article 43; Arbitration Rules of the German Institution of Arbitration (DIS), Section 43; Arbitration Rules of the Singapore International Arbitration Centre, Rule 34.6; Hong Kong International Arbitration Centre Domestic Arbitration Rules, Article 26; Rules of the International Commercial Arbitration Court that the Chamber of Commerce and Industry of the Russian Federation, Article 11; ACICA Arbitration Rules, Article 18.

[15]A number of institutions have rules that do not refer to confidentiality. For instance: the United Nations Commission on International Trade Law International Arbitration Rules; the Arbitration Rules of the International Centre for Settlement Investment Disputes (ICSID); the ICSID Rules of Procedure for the Institution of Conciliation and Arbitration Proceedings (Institution Rules); the Rules of the Arbitration Institute of the Stockholm Chamber of Commerce; the International Arbitral Centre of the Austrian Federal Economic Chamber's Rules of Arbitration (Vienna Rules); the China International Economic and Trade Arbitration Commission (CIETAC) Arbitration Rules.

and address the issue by stipulating to confidentiality terms in the arbitrator's procedural directions or in an order from the arbitral tribunal.[16]

3.2 Factors and Standards Affecting the Level of Protection of the Duty of Confidentiality in Arbitration

3.2.1 The Distinction Between Privacy and Confidentiality in Arbitration as Opposed to State Court Proceedings

Arbitration is private but not confidential. This is a paradox to the extent that it is seemingly contradictory, but states a truth. Arbitration is private in that it is a closed process, but it is not necessarily confidential because information revealed during the process may become public. This has caused misperceptions and confusion regarding the arbitration process.[17] It is true that arbitration proceedings generally are private and do not produce published opinions comparable to the judgments of courts. It is not correct, however, to assume that information revealed in arbitration is automatically confidential.[18] As stated above, in many jurisdictions, arbitration laws do not guarantee such secrecy of arbitration information and, moreover, institutional rules which parties may incorporate in their arbitration agreements

[16]Scholars such as Thomson CR and Finn AMK; See Thompson and Finn (2007, pp. 78–79) who have suggested a form of confidentiality clause that can serve as a basis for discussion and negotiation when confidentiality is important to the parties. Their starting point is that any confidentiality clause must comply with the applicable law in the relevant jurisdiction. The general part of the proposed text of such a confidentiality clause is as follows: *Draft Confidentiality Agreement*: Subject to any applicable and overriding law and duty, the parties agree for themselves and any persons or companies under their control and direction that any arbitration conducted under the authority of this agreement will be private and confidential, and all documents, evidence, orders and awards, whether electronic or otherwise, will be kept private and secret and will not be disclosed to persons who are not participating in the arbitration proceeding. This obligation continues during the course of the proceeding and thereafter unless all parties otherwise agree. If a party concludes that its legal duty requires disclosure of such material, it will give the opposing party notice of its intention to disclose before making any such disclosure. If the opposing party will not consent to the disclosure, the parties agree that the question of whether there is any applicable and overriding law and duty in relation to the material under consideration will be presented for decision to the arbitrator who is appointed under this agreement. The parties agree to be bound by the ruling of the arbitrator whose decision will be final and binding. The arbitrator may determine the timing, nature and extent of disclosure. The parties agree that any failure to abide by the decision of the arbitrator may give rise to a claim for an injunction.

[17]Contracting parties often assume that arbitration's privacy denies the public access not only to arbitration hearings, but also information revealed during the hearings. These parties may then accept arbitration agreements without contracting for confidentiality. This, in turn, may negatively impact corporate parties expecting arbitration to shield their business information, as well as individuals who assume that personal information revealed in arbitration will remain secret.

[18]Buys (2003, pp. 129–131); Schmitz (2006, p. 1211).

generally do not provide broad confidentiality protections. Furthermore, third party participants who do not agree to any confidentiality agreement or rules remain free to talk about the arbitration proceedings.[19] Privacy thus does not ensure confidentiality of arbitration proceedings and arbitration is not entirely secret, as information about arbitrations may become public unless the parties contractually require that this information remain confidential.[20]

3.2.1.1 Privacy

Arbitration developed as a means for providing self-contained dispute resolution that culminates in a third-party determination, but may be more efficient and flexible than litigation because it is not subject to judicial constraints. In addition, western world models of arbitration are generally private in that only the parties to the arbitration agreement and other invitees may attend the proceedings. Arbitration also is private to the extent that arbitrators do not publish reasoned opinions that provide information to the public regarding arbitrated cases and further development of the law. Arbitration may therefore "privatise" the law.[21]

Arbitration's private process limits its transparency by precluding the public's observation of and participation in the process, so that the public has access to little information regarding the conduct and outcomes in arbitration proceedings. This privacy provides a more "cosy" atmosphere as opposed to that of a state court hearing in that only the arbitrators, the parties, their attorneys and any witnesses are present.[22] Disputants usually sit across the table from one another at fairly close quarters without the physical and procedural protections of a court. The formality and degree of privacy of an arbitration proceeding depends on the parties' agreement, on the rules they decide to incorporate in their agreement, and on the norms that exist in the given context or *forum*.[23]

Arbitration is moreover private to the extent that arbitration awards generally are not published. This affects the transparency of arbitrated cases, as well as the "law" they produce. Parties' arbitration agreements set forth required procedures, and define the arbitrators' authority in determining the parties' disputes. Although arbitrators must remain unbiased and ensure fundamentally fair hearings, their first priority is to obey the scope of their authority under a given arbitration agreement. This generally allows arbitrators to decide disputes based on flexible conglomerations of law, equity, practicalities, and applicable norms and standards. In this way, arbitration's privacy essentially allows parties to contract out of, or

[19]Schmitz (2006, p. 1211).

[20]Goldhaber (2005); Schmitz (2006, p. 1214).

[21]Ware (1999, pp. 706–726) distinguishing between private and government adjudication; Schmitz (2006, pp. 1214–1215).

[22]Mentschikoff (1961, p. 846).

[23]Schmitz (2006, pp. 1215–1216).

privatise, law.[24] Arbitrators do not necessarily apply the law in deciding disputes whereas courts will confirm arbitral awards save in the cases where the arbitrators have clearly exceeded their authority in reaching their results.[25]

3.2.1.2 Confidentiality

Confidentiality transcends privacy as it involves also the element of secrecy. Such confidentiality should preclude disclosure of any evidence, communications, or other information in relation to arbitration proceedings or the disclosure and use of the arbitral award in other arbitrations or state court proceedings, thus making public access impossible. However, in reality such level of confidentiality generally does not exist in arbitration. In practice underlying information may at various stages come to the public eye. This is further exemplified by the fact that arbitral laws in various jurisdictions do not expressly address the need to preserve arbitral confidentiality[26] and therefore courts permit discovery of arbitration materials in later cases, or the use of the arbitral proceedings *per se* in further proceedings – for purposes of consolidation of proceedings – or the use of arbitral awards in further proceedings.[27]

Institutional arbitration rules generally preserve privacy but do not ensure confidentiality of arbitration proceedings.[28] However, even when institutional

[24] Sturges (1960, pp. 1032–1033); see also Schmitz (2006, pp. 1215–1216).

[25] For example, the Supreme Court of the United States has emphasized this finality, and most other federal and state courts have followed suit. Courts have looked to the goals and functions of arbitration to guide them in reinforcing arbitration's finality as necessary to guard its privacy, flexibility, and efficiency; See *Brennan v. King*, 139 F.3d 258, 266 n.7 (1st Cir. 1998); See Schmitz (2006, pp. 1217–1218); However, as far as English law is concerned, this last point is only true to a limited extent.

[26] For example the English Arbitration Act 1996 only impliedly refers to the duty to observe and protect confidentiality.

[27] Kouris (2005, pp. 134–135).

[28] The commonly used American Arbitration Association (AAA) Commercial Arbitration Rules and Mediation Procedures, for example, do not address confidentiality of general arbitration proceedings. At most, some domestic arbitration rules require that arbitrators and administrators refrain from disclosing certain information or otherwise maintain some level of confidentiality. Similarly, international arbitration rules often go no further than requiring that arbitrators maintain limited levels of confidentiality in the processes they administer. The American Arbitration Association's International Arbitration Rules, for example, provide for a presumption that hearings remain private, but that selected awards may be publicly available unless the parties agree otherwise. They also require the arbitrators, but not the parties, to maintain the confidentiality of arbitration proceedings and awards. The Internal Rules of the International Chamber of Commerce (ICC) similarly require arbitrators and administrators to maintain the "confidential nature" of their arbitral tribunals' internal operations by refraining from disclosing evidence or information they learn through their participation in arbitration. These rules generally do not, however, restrict the parties' rights to disclose such information. Moreover, most rules leave the meaning of "confidential nature" unclear; see Schmitz (2006, pp. 1219–1220).

rules or agreements require that arbitrations remain confidential, parties are often left wondering whether courts will enforce the confidentiality provisions. Some courts have found confidentiality provisions invalid or waived by parties.[29] They also have pierced confidentiality provisions when a compelling public interest need or statutory mandate makes disclosure of information or materials necessary because the public's interest overrides the disputants' contractual freedom to opt for confidentiality.[30] Additionally, confidentiality agreements precluding disclosure of evidence and testimony may not bar parties, witnesses and other third-party attendees from publicly revealing underlying information unless they have signed binding confidentiality agreements.[31]

3.2.2 *The Judicial Attitude*

Courts will not always or easily accept the non-disclosure of information used in arbitral processes. For example in the USA, the leading cases of *United States v. Panhandle Eastern Corp.*[32] and *Cont'ship Containerlines, Ltd. v. PPG Industries, Inc.*[33] reflect this tendency of the courts to allow the disclosure of documents and information used in arbitrations. In *United States v. Panhandle Eastern Corp.*[34] it was held that arbitration communications are discoverable and admissible and refused to grant an order protecting them under the Federal Rule of Civil Procedure 26(c). The argument that domestic or else said "internal arbitration rules" require confidentiality was specifically rejected. What was also rejected were general assertions of economic harm that might be caused by disclosure as inadequate to establish good cause. In *Cont'ship Containerlines, Ltd. v. PPG Industries, Inc.*[35] the discovery of arbitration communications from an international commercial arbitration held in London was compelled and the argument that confidentiality is somehow implied at law as a part of the agreement to arbitrate was rejected, contrary to the holdings of English decisions that the duty of confidentiality is implied at law – from the agreement to arbitrate – as a necessary predicate of the arbitration process. It was also noted that the lack of external constraints on the disclosure of arbitration

[29]*AT&T Corp. v. Pub. Serv. Enters.*, Nos. CIV. A. 99-4975, CIV. A. 99-6099, 2000 WL 387738, at *2 (E.D. Pa. Apr. 12, 2000).

[30]*Omaha Indem. Co. v. Royal Am. Managers, Inc.*, 140 F.R.D. 398, 400 (W.D. Mo. 1991); *City of Newark v. Law Dep't*, 760 N.Y.S.2d 431, 436–437 (N.Y. App. Div. 2003).

[31]Schmitz (2006, p. 1222).

[32]*United States v. Panhandle Eastern Corp.* 118 F.R.D. 346 (D. Del. 1988).

[33]*Cont'ship Containerlines, Ltd. v. PPG Industries, Inc.* No. 00 Civ. 0194 RCCH BP, 2003 WL 1948807 (S.D.N.Y. Apr. 23, 2003).

[34]*United States v. Panhandle Eastern Corp.* 118 F.R.D. 346 (D. Del. 1988).

[35]*Cont'ship Containerlines, Ltd. v. PPG Industries, Inc.* No. 00 Civ. 0194 RCCH BP, 2003 WL 1948807 (S.D.N.Y. Apr. 23, 2003).

communications by the parties, such as a contractual confidentiality agreement between the parties, or the rule of an arbitral body prohibit such disclosures.

Neither *United States v. Panhandle Eastern Corp.*[36] nor *Cont'ship Containerlines, Ltd. v. PPG Industries, Inc.*[37] dealt with situations in which the parties had executed a confidentiality agreement. However, in *Lawrence E. Jaffee Pension Plan v. Household International, Inc.*,[38] the parties had an explicit confidentiality provision in the arbitration agreement, and the court still compelled the production of arbitration communications as evidence. Similarly, in *Urban Box Office Network v. Interfase Managers,*[39] the Federal District Court for the Southern District of New York looked beyond the confidentiality provision in an arbitration clause when it upheld the discovery of documents produced at an arbitration and when it rejected arguments in a later case that they were shielded by attorney-client privilege and by a confidentiality provision in the arbitration clause. The court in *Urban Box Office Network v. Interfase Managers*[40] found that there was a valid confidentiality agreement in the arbitration clause. However, it also found that the confidentiality agreement did not trump the party's waiver of the attorney-client privilege with respect to certain documents when it disclosed them at the prior arbitration. Again, the demonstrated expectations of the parties were significant to the court, which noted that the parties took no affirmative steps to invoke the confidentiality provisions of the arbitration clause, such as stamping the documents "confidential". We, therefore, note the unwillingness of the American courts to grant protective orders that prevent the introduction of arbitration communications, consistently with the longstanding judicial policy generally favouring the admissibility of evidence.[41]

In England, in *Dolling-Baker v Merrett,*[42] it was stated that, as between parties to an arbitration, its very nature is such that there must be some implied obligation on both parties not to disclose or use for any other purpose, any documents prepared for and used in the arbitration.[43] In *Hassneh Ins. Co. of Israel v Mew*[44] it was stated that an obligation of confidentiality attaching to documents can exist only because it is implied in the agreement to arbitrate[45] and similarly *Ali Shipping Corp. v.*

[36]*United States v. Panhandle Eastern Corp.* 118 F.R.D. 346 (D. Del. 1988).

[37]*Cont'ship Containerlines, Ltd. v. PPG Industries, Inc.* No. 00 Civ. 0194 RCCH BP, 2003 WL 1948807 (S.D.N.Y. Apr. 23, 2003).

[38]*Lawrence E. Jaffee Pension Plan v. Household International, Inc.* No. Civ. A. 04-N-1228 (CBS, 04-X-0057), 2004 WL 1821968 (D. Colo. Aug. 13, 2004).

[39]*Urban Box Office Network v. Interfase Managers* No. 01 Civ. 8854 (LTS) (THK), 2004 WL 2375819 (S.D.N.Y. Oct. 21, 2004).

[40]*Urban Box Office Network v. Interfase Managers* No. 01 Civ. 8854 (LTS) (THK), 2004 WL 2375819 (S.D.N.Y. Oct. 21, 2004).

[41]Reuben (2006, pp. 1260–1268).

[42]*Dolling-Baker v Merrett*, 1 W.L.R. 1205.

[43]*Dolling-Baker v Merrett*, 1 W.L.R. 1205, at 1213.

[44]*Hassneh Ins. Co. of Israel v. Mew*, 2 Lloyd's Rep. 243.

[45]*Hassneh Ins. Co. of Israel v. Mew*, 2 Lloyd's Rep. 243, at 246.

Shipyard "Trogir"[46] discussed the holdings in *Dolling-Baker v Merrett*[47] and in *Hassneh Ins. Co. of Israel v Mew*[48] on the implied duty of confidentiality created by arbitration agreements.

The normative question of whether arbitration communications evidence should be discoverable and admissible is complex, raising fundamental questions about the relationship between arbitration and the law. Court proceedings and arbitration, often perceived as public and private adjudication respectively, are similar in that both are processes in which a third-party adjudicator decides how a dispute will be resolved. Arbitration and court proceedings differ, however, in two important respects that have important implications for the confidentiality of evidence of communications concerning the arbitration and the level of formality of the process and the public/private character of the process. A characteristic of court proceedings is their formality. Arbitration, by contrast, is an informal process that does not rely upon formal rules of law and procedure as these decisional standards are not necessarily applied, absent the agreement of the parties. Moreover, the awards of arbitrators are generally final and binding without judicial review for correctness. Even though it is informal, the arbitration process has certain needs to operate effectively, efficiently, and legitimately in the sense that it is consistent with principles of procedural justice and democratic values. Court proceedings are often called public adjudication because of their public character. Arbitration, on the other hand, is a private process. The parties assume the preservation of confidentiality in relation to the arbitration hearings and awards. All the above do not favour the availability of disclosure of the arbitration material. The private character of arbitration provides the justification for the adoption of such a position. Simply put, the promise of a dispute resolution process that operates apart from, but is supported by, the public system of law would prove illusory if communications made in that process were readily subject to discovery and admissibility in other formal proceedings.[49]

3.2.3 *The Scope and Limits for the Observance of the Duty to Confidentiality in Arbitration*

Exceptions to observe confidentiality are variously justified, if agreed by the parties or if they are established by trade usages and practices or on account of express or implied duties, or due to public policy reasons.[50] However, there is no straightforward answer as regards the extent to which confidentiality may be waived and

[46] *Ali Shipping Corp. v. Shipyard "Trogir"*, 1 Lloyd's Rep. 643.

[47] *Dolling-Baker v Merrett*, 1 W.L.R. 1205.

[48] *Hassneh Ins. Co. of Israel v. Mew*, 2 Lloyd's Rep. 243.

[49] Reuben (2006, pp. 1260, 1274–1281).

[50] Trackman (2002, p. 16).

the issue needs to be addressed in relation to various circumstances, categories of documents and stages of the arbitration proceedings.

3.2.3.1 With Regards to the Arbitration Proceedings Themselves

With regards to confidentiality in relation to the arbitral proceedings, and more specifically with regards to the course of the proceedings themselves, arbitral tribunals have no power to consolidate proceedings[51] – if parties have not expressly opted for it – except in cases where earlier awards of a competent court could be used to bind subsequent arbitrations. There are, however, no set rules to determine such a usage or not, and, therefore, general principles of law should be applied to determine the issue.

3.2.3.2 With Regards to Documents Relating to Discovery or Evidence

Discovery or evidence is, and more particularly requests for it are, often given by reference to a category or class of documents. When giving discovery the purpose of listing is two-fold, i.e. firstly to record what has been discovered should that become relevant and, secondly, to enable the other parties to determine what they require copies of. In general, documents produced during or in preparation for an arbitration as well as evidence introduced during the arbitration, are protected by the duty to observe confidentiality.[52]

3.2.3.3 With Regards to the Award

Considerations different to those relating to the restrictions on the use of material obtained in arbitration proceedings apply in relation to the award itself. Confidentiality clauses should not be interpreted in an unrestricted way because this could preclude disclosing an award to state courts in order to have it enforced and this would go against the right of the parties to enforce an award, as well as against the essential purpose of arbitration to determine disputes between parties.[53] In general,

---

[51] *Sacor Maritima SA v. Repsol Petroleo SA* [1998] 1 Lloyd's Rep. 518 (QBD (Comm)).

[52] *Ali Shipping Corp. v. Shipyard "Trogir"*, 1 Lloyd's Rep. 643 (A.C. 1998), *Dolling-Baker v. Merrett* [1991] 2 All E.R. 890. Following *Dolling-Baker v. Merrett* [1991] 2 All E.R. 890 the decisions in *Hassneh Insurance Co. of Israel v. Mew* [1993] 2 Lloyd's Rep. 243, *Insurance Co v. Lloyd's Syndicate* [1995]1 Lloyd's Rep. 272 and in *Ali Shipping Corporation v. Shipyard Trogir* [1998] 1 Lloyd's Rep. 643 reaffirmed the existence of an implied duty of confidentiality but recognised that it was subject to exceptions.

[53] Nappert and Cooke (2003, pp. 43–44).

arbitral awards are protected by the implied duty to observe confidentiality[54] unless the disclosure is characterised as reasonably necessary.[55] The term "reasonably necessary" covers only the case where the right in question can not be enforced or protected unless the award and reasons are disclosed to a stranger to the arbitration and where the making of an award is a necessary element in the establishment of the party's legal rights against a stranger.[56] In the case of arbitral awards, as opposed to that of other documents in the arbitration proceedings, the veil of strict confidentiality needs to be lifted so that the award produces the results which are pertinent to its nature, i.e. its recognition and enforcement.

In *Associated Electric & Gas Insurance Services Limited v European Reinsurance Company of Zurich*[57] the Judicial Committee of the Privy Council, on appeal from the Court of Appeal of Bermuda, examined, *inter alia*, questions of confidentiality in the context of the enforcement of an arbitral award. The confidentiality clause in one of the two disputes involved in the case was particularly detailed and entailed that the arbitration result would not be disclosed at any time, to any individual or entity, in whole or in part, who was not a party to the arbitration. During the adjudication of the second dispute by a differently constituted panel, European Re asserted that the same dispute had been raised in the second arbitration as had been decided by the first arbitration panel and sought to rely on the first arbitration award. Aegis obtained an *ex parte* injunction to prevent the first arbitration result from being disclosed "at any time to any individual or entity, in whole or in part, which is not a party to the arbitration", pursuant to the confidentiality clause. European Re successfully appealed to the Bermudan Court of Appeal and the injunction was discharged. The Privy Council's approach placed emphasis on "the essential purpose of arbitration" and on different types of confidentiality which attach to different types of documents. Following *Ali Shipping Corporation v Shipyard Trogir*[58] and *Dolling-Baker v Merrett*,[59] where the principle of privacy in arbitration proceedings and the duty of confidentiality as an implied term in an arbitration agreement were affirmed, and where also exceptions to the duty of confidentiality were formulated, the Privy Council stated that considerations different to those relating to the restrictions on the use of material obtained in arbitration proceedings apply in relation to an arbitral award, because documents used in proceedings and in a subsequent award constitute different classes of documents and are subject to different rules of confidentiality. An award was confidential as

[54]*Department of Economic Policy & Development of the City of Moscow (DEPD) v. Bankers Trust Co.* [2003] EWHC 1337; [2003] 1 W.L.R. 2885; *Insurance Co v. Lloyd's Syndicate*[1995]1 Lloyd's Rep. 272.

[55]*Hassneh Insurance Co of Israel v. Stuart J Mew* [1993] 2 Lloyd's Rep. 243.

[56]*Insurance Co v. Lloyd's Syndicate*[1995]1 Lloyd's Rep. 272; *Ali Shipping Corporation v. Shipyard Trogir* [1998] 1 Lloyd's Rep. 643.

[57]*Associated Electric & Gas Insurance Services Limited v European Reinsurance Company of Zurich* [2003] UKPC 11, The Times, January 30, 2003.

[58]*Ali Shipping Corporation v Shipyard Trogir* [1999] 1 W.L.R. 314.

[59]*Dolling-Baker v Merrett* [1990] 1 W.L.R. 1205.

between the parties and as between the parties and the arbitrators. However, an award should be capable of enforcement, notwithstanding its confidential nature. The Privy Council construed the confidentiality agreement so as to give effect to the fundamental purpose of arbitration, namely to determine disputes between the parties. If the confidentiality clause was applied in an unrestricted way, it would preclude the disclosure of the award in terms of enforcement. Given the essential character and purpose of arbitration, which was to determine disputes between parties, European Re was entitled to enforce the decision in the first award where the same issue was raised by Aegis for consideration in the second arbitration.[60]

When state courts have to decide issues such as the recognition and enforcement of arbitral awards, the fact that such decisions are taken in publicly held proceedings understandably affects arbitration and the element of the duty to preserve confidentiality which is therein entailed. It is submitted, however, that the role of the courts in assisting the parties at the recognition and enforcement stage supersedes the issue of confidentiality. The most vital factor is that the arbitral award should be recognised and enforced so that it produces the desired results.

3.2.3.4 Legal Professional Privilege

Because international commercial arbitration will often involve parties, witnesses and documents from potentially a number of different countries, each having its own system of law, problems relating to discovery or production of evidence will often relate to issues of legal professional privilege, the latter being a rule that entitles a party during the course of legal proceedings to withhold from his opponent and from the court evidence of whatever form within the scope of the privilege.[61]

In so far as the position under English law is concerned, although a privileged communication can be withheld from opponents and from the court in proceedings before English courts, or before arbitral tribunals where English law is applied, it does not follow that it will be accorded the same treatment in proceedings before a foreign court or a tribunal applying foreign law. However, the approach of an arbitral tribunal applying English law is that all communications falling within the scope of legal professional privilege will be protected irrespective of how a foreign court would treat them. Moreover, it is now well-established that written or oral communications made as part of negotiations genuinely aimed at, but not resulting in, settlement of a dispute are not generally admissible in evidence in litigation (or arbitration) between the parties over that dispute and are described as "privileged". The underlying philosophy is that parties should be encouraged to settle their disputes without recourse to national courts or arbitration as appropriate. They should not be discouraged from doing so by the fear that whatever they might

---

[60]Nappert and Cooke (2003, pp. 43–44).

[61]Ashford (2006, pp. 90–92).

say could be used against them in whatever tribunal ultimately had to adjudicate upon the dispute. The use of the words "without prejudice" may indicate whether the communications in question attract the privilege, but it is not necessarily determinative on the point. The basis for the "without prejudice" rule is said to be part contract and part public policy. The contractual element arises from a notional implied agreement between the parties that what is said in negotiations cannot be used before the appropriate tribunal. The public policy element is also founded on encouraging parties to settle, but not only prevents the usage of the communication before the appropriate tribunal but also prevents a party from having to produce the communication to another.[62]

3.2.3.5 The Limitations Imposed by the European Convention on Human Rights

The traditional view that the procedural right to a fair trial, which is enshrined in article 6 of the European Convention on Human Rights ("ECHR") is not applicable in arbitration proceedings has lately been superseded by the view that article 6 of the ECHR may apply in the context of arbitration proceedings, albeit in limited circumstances.[63]

It was confirmed by the European Court of Human Rights in *Suovaniemi v Finland*[64] that parties who voluntarily submit their disputes to arbitration are generally considered to have waived their right of access to an article 6 protected court, in other words that parties by agreeing to arbitration also agree that any dispute will be resolved before an arbitration tribunal and cannot subsequently argue that they have a right under the Convention to have the dispute heard before a court. This reflects the private nature of the proceedings and the well-recognised principle of confidentiality in arbitration proceedings.[65] However, the parties' rights under article 6 of the ECHR are not entirely extinguished by their voluntary submission to arbitration.[66] Although many of the article 6 rights are waived by an agreement to arbitrate, recent developments suggest that at least one aspect of article 6 remains important, namely the requirement that a tribunal must be "independent and impartial". The meaning of this requirement was summarised by the European Court of Human Rights in *Findlay v United Kingdom*[67] whereby it was stated that:

---

[62]Ashford (2006, p. 116).

[63]Hodges (2007, p. 163).

[64]*Suovaniemi v Finland* (Case No. 31737/96, February 23, 1999, European Court of Human Rights).

[65]Hodges (2007, p. 164).

[66]Hodges (2007, p. 163).

[67]*Findlay v United Kingdom* [1997] 24 E.H.R.R. 221.

> in order to establish whether a tribunal can be considered as 'independent', regard must be had inter alia to the manner of appointment of its members and the term of office, the existence of guarantees against outside pressures and the question of whether the party presents an appearance of independence. As to the question of "impartiality", there are two aspects to this requirement. First, the tribunal must be subjectively free from judicial bias. Secondly, it must also be impartial from an objective view point, that is, it must offer sufficient guarantees to exclude any legitimate doubt in this respect.[68]

Section 24(1) of the English Arbitration Act provides that a party to arbitral proceedings may apply to the court to remove an arbitrator on any of a number of grounds, including the fact that "circumstances exist which give rise to justifiable doubts as to his impartiality". This wording was not expressly intended to reflect the requirements of the ECHR. However, the English courts have traditionally approached the issue of bias in arbitration proceedings in the same way as for judges in court proceedings. In practice this has meant that, although the article 6 requirement of independence and impartiality may not apply directly to proceedings before an arbitral tribunal, nevertheless the "legal test for bias" under section 24(1) of the Arbitration Act mirrors the test for bias in English court proceedings which has been influenced by European case law on article 6 of the ECHR. In *ASM Shipping Ltd of India v TTMI Ltd of England*[69] the Court held that this modified test of bias should also apply to questions of bias arising in the context of arbitration tribunals. Article 6 of the ECHR was considered in the context of impartiality and fairness in *Paul Stretford v Football Association Ltd*[70] where the Court of Appeal noted that by voluntarily agreeing to arbitrate, the parties had waived their rights under it. However, the Court also noted that this waiver of rights was actually relatively limited in extent, as the mandatory provisions of the Arbitration Act still provided protection against serious irregularities such as impartiality and unfairness. The Court noted the link between independence and impartiality, but was not required to address the issue directly as the arbitration clause itself included a requirement that an arbitrator must be independent.[71]

Although the extent to which the rights under article 6 of the ECHR apply to the proceedings before the tribunal itself has been approached in a restrictive way, some of the article 6 rights remain protected by the English Arbitration Act. Thus, article 6 of the ECHR remains relevant, for example, to questions about the impartiality of the arbitrators and any allegations of bias. It is submitted, however, that the English courts should resist any pressure to extend the application of article 6 of the ECHR any further within the arbitration arena.

In conclusion, the special status and nature of international commercial arbitration as a voluntary system of private dispute resolution – which takes disputes largely outside of the judicial system by agreement of the parties – should remain an

[68] Hodges (2007, p. 164).

[69] *ASM Shipping Ltd of India v TTMI Ltd of England* [2006] 1 Lloyd's Rep. 375.

[70] *Paul Stretford v Football Association Ltd* [2007] EWCA Civ 238 (March 21, 2007, CA).

[71] Hodges (2007, pp. 168–169).

important consideration if arbitration is to remain an efficient and effective alternative to litigation.[72]

3.2.4 Confidentiality and Its Correlation with the European: Global Context of Arbitration

The impact of transnational law on international commercial arbitration and its interconnection with confidentiality are correlated concepts. In discussing them, we address the modern European and global character of arbitration and the way in which the various levels of protection of confidentiality affect it.

The impact of transnational law on international commercial arbitration has a great interconnection with confidentiality, in the variety of the rules and practices used in the process of evidence and in the different legal systems and traditions of the arbitrating, all of which will display diverse attitudes in relation to confidentiality and the extent of the duty of its preservation.

Transnational rules which apply to arbitration will also affect confidentiality in arbitration, most often in terms of third-party intervention in the arbitration. Although different levels of confidentiality affect the European and global character of arbitration, nevertheless the use of transnational rules in arbitration promote the duty to preserve confidentiality as they encourage uniformity and consistency at a European-global level.

3.3 The Way Forward?

In arbitration third parties can be prevented from observing the proceedings and arbitral parties can contract to prevent each other from disclosing arbitration communications to third parties.

The position of the law and the boundaries regarding the disclosure of arbitration communications for purposes of discovery and admission in another legal proceeding are unclear. The emerging view of the courts appears to be that such disclosures may be compelled. Such a position however is likely to undermine any intent to endorse a private alternative to public adjudication because, once they are introduced, such communications are likely to become public records that may be disseminated freely as a general matter.

The continuation of this trend would undermine the national policy favouring arbitration by frustrating the parties' reasonable expectations with respect to the confidentiality of arbitration, and would ultimately chill the use of the arbitration process. The law's expectation of access to these materials is not trivial, however,

---

[72]Hodges (2007, p. 169).

and proper legal policy must reflect a balance of these competing public and private interests. This balance may be struck by raising the burden of proof for the admission of evidence sought from arbitration proceedings by requiring the proponent of such evidence to demonstrate that it is otherwise unavailable and necessary for the resolution of the case. However, the adoption of an elevated standard will not necessarily resolve all questions regarding the confidentiality of arbitration communications.[73]

[73]Reuben (2006, pp. 1260, 1299–1300).

Chapter 4
The Present Status of Confidentiality in International Commercial Arbitration in the Various Jurisdictions

4.1 Setting the Scene

4.1.1 General Observations on Confidentiality in International Commercial Arbitration

4.1.1.1 The Distinction Between Privacy and Confidentiality

By its nature, arbitration is a private proceeding in which the parties are able to conduct their dispute without being publicly exposed. The privacy and the confidentiality of arbitration are two of its major advantages. However, though correlated, the two concepts differ, significantly, in their nature.

Arbitration is private in that it is a closed process, but it is not confidential because information revealed in its processes may become public. This has often caused misconceptions and misinterpretations, as parties often assume that arbitration's privacy denies the public access to arbitration hearings and all information revealed during them. Thus, corporate or private contracting parties often enter arbitration agreements without contracting for confidentiality because they expect arbitration to shield their business or personal information and guard it as secret.

The fact that arbitration proceedings are generally private and do not result in published opinions which will be considered by courts in later cases, does not presuppose or guarantee that any information revealed in arbitration is automatically confidential.[1] Arbitral laws in various jurisdictions[2] do not guarantee the secrecy of arbitration information and the institutional rules, which parties may have incorporated into their arbitration agreements generally do not provide broad confidentiality protections. In addition, third party participants who do not agree to any confidentiality agreement or rules, remain free to talk about the arbitration

[1]Buys (2003, pp. 129–131); Schmitz (2006, p. 1211).

[2]For example the English Arbitration Act 1996 as well as the US federal Arbitration Act 1925.

K. Noussia, *Confidentiality in International Commercial Arbitration*,
DOI 10.1007/978-3-642-10224-0_4,

proceedings. Furthermore, this confusion regarding privacy and confidentiality in arbitration fosters misguided contracting, as well as simplistic assumptions, regarding the value of secrecy in the arbitration process.[3] Thus, in order to ensure that confidentiality is preserved in the best way throughout the proceedings, it is increasingly necessary to rely on an express provision of relevant statutory rules or to enter into a specific confidentiality agreement.[4]

Privacy and confidentiality have varied meanings. There is no single definition of the term "privacy" and its various meanings differ according to time, place, culture or society. However, the various definitions share some common ground. Privacy can refer to seclusion, or the right to be left alone, or the right to informational privacy. Within informational privacy a further distinction exists between secrecy, anonymity and control of information. Secrecy is the confidentiality of the content of information. Anonymity relates to the identities of the persons communicating information, and can exist between the original parties to a communication or between them and any future recipients of the information. Control of information, refers to the ability of an individual, with privacy rights over certain communications, to determine who can gain access to certain information and on what terms.[5]

In arbitration, privacy generally refers to the closed and non public character of the arbitration process, which prevents public access to hearings or published opinions that would aid the development of public law. Confidentiality, in arbitration, refers to the secrecy of information regarding or revealed during the arbitration process. Privacy reasons are a concern for confidentiality. Confidentiality is impossible without privacy and privacy is meaningless without confidentiality.[6] However, privacy does not ensure confidentiality of the arbitral proceedings and, thus, to a certain extent, arbitration, is not entirely secret.[7]

The need to protect informational privacy and confidentiality is a recent development that reflects growing social concern. However, legal counter-measures to protect informational privacy and confidentiality have been minimal or non-existent at all,[8] as there is no explicit authority for protecting confidentiality.[9] It is precisely this lack of explicit authority, that makes confidentiality and privacy issues problematic in international commercial arbitration. In effect, although parties may assume that courts will honour confidentiality agreements, this is not always the case. Thus, parties' expectations about the privacy and confidentiality of their arbitral proceedings are often disappointed or negated by the courts, because

[3]Schmitz (2006, pp. 1211–1212).

[4]Uff and Noussia (2009, pp. 1428–1449).

[5]Rabinovitch-Einy (2002, pp. 6–8).

[6]Brown (2001, pp. 972–975).

[7]Schmitz (2006, pp. 1211–1214).

[8]Rabinovitch-Einy (2002, p. 9).

[9]Brown (2001, p. 974).

there has been no consensus of doctrinal views and there have been differing judicial attitudes shown.[10]

Privacy

Arbitration has developed as a means for providing dispute resolution that may be more efficient and flexible than litigation, because it is not subject to the strictness of judicial processes. Moreover, western models of arbitration are generally private, in that only the parties to the arbitration agreements and their invitees may attend the proceedings. Arbitration is also private, to the extent that arbitrators do not publish reasoned opinions. Arbitration's private process limits its transparency by precluding the public's observation of and participation in the process. Arbitration is also private to the extent that arbitral awards are generally not published.[11]

Institutional arbitration rules commonly provide that arbitrations conducted under those particular rules shall be held in private. Unless the provision in question goes further than merely to restate a right of privacy, it adds nothing to the position that would obtain as a matter of law.[12]

The right to privacy is recognised in English law as an implied right which attaches to all agreements to arbitrate as an incident of such a contract, unless it is expressly excluded by agreement of the parties.

This position was also adopted in Australia, in *Esso/BHP v Plowman*,[13] where Mr Justice Brookings stated:[14] "... I think we should recognise a rule of law that is an implied term of arbitration agreements – which the parties may exclude if they choose – that arbitrations should be heard in private in the sense of the absence of strangers as just defined unless the parties consent to the presence of a stranger."[15]

In *Esso/BHP v Plowman*,[16] strangers were defined as "persons whose presence is not necessary or expedient for the proper conduct of [the] proceedings". However, merely excluding persons from the proceedings, does not necessarily imply or guarantee that the general public will not learn of what went on at the arbitration hearing, or that documents prepared for or used as evidence at the hearing will never be used for a purpose unrelated to the arbitration itself.[17]

An obvious consequence of an implied right to privacy arises in the case of related disputes between several different parties, which have so many common

---

[10]Brown (2001, pp. 974–975).

[11]Schmitz (2006, pp. 1214–1216).

[12]For example, English law has for centuries recognised that arbitrations take place in private; Collins (1995, p. 322).

[13]*Esso/BHP v Plowman* (1995) 128 A.L.R. 391, High Court of Australia.

[14]*Esso/BHP v Plowman* (1995) 128 A.L.R. 391, High Court of Australia at 402–403.

[15]Collins (1995, p. 323).

[16]*Esso/BHP v Plowman* (1995) 128 A.L.R. 391, High Court of Australia, at 402.

[17]Collins (1995, p. 323).

features that there would be considerable practical advantages in hearing them together.[18] However, the most important consideration against the above, is the danger of inconsistent results. English law has stated this danger in *Oxford Shipping Co v Nippon Yesen Kaisha [The "Eastern Saga"]*[19] in which it was held that privacy, albeit implied, was, nevertheless, a substantive and core element of arbitration.[20]

Confidentiality

Confidentiality, in arbitration, goes further than privacy, and connotes a certain amount of secrecy which precludes disclosure of any evidence, communication or other information about arbitration proceedings. In reality, however, confidentiality is generally not guaranteed because underlying information in arbitral proceedings may become public.

The English Arbitration Act 1996 does not explicitly protect confidentiality. In the USA, the Federal Arbitration Act does not address arbitral confidentiality, nor does US law otherwise ensure secrecy of information disclosed in arbitration. In addition, many American courts permit discovery of arbitration materials in later cases.[21] As far as institutional rules are concerned, they generally preserve privacy but do not ensure confidentiality of arbitration proceedings, as they often do not go further than requiring that arbitrators maintain limited levels of confidentiality in the process they administer.[22] Even where institutional rules or agreements require that arbitrations remain confidential, parties are often left wondering whether courts will enforce the confidentiality provisions, and courts have often found confidentiality provisions unconscionable,[23] or that parties have waived confidentiality

[18]For example, disputes arising out of a head-charter and sub-charter of a vessel, or multiple party disputes arising out of string contracts in the context of commodities, where the same documents will commonly be relevant to both disputes, or the same witnesses will be required to give evidence. Collins (1995, p. 323).

[19]*Oxford Shipping Co v Nippon Yesen Kaisha [The "Eastern Saga"]* [1984] 2 Lloyd's Rep. 373 (QB).

[20]Collins (1995, pp. 323–327).

[21]See, e.g. *Princeton Ins. Co. v Vergano*, 883 A. 2d 44, 61–67 (Del. Ch. 2005); Schmitz (2006, pp. 1214–1218).

[22]The AAA International Arbitration Rules, provide for a presumption that hearings remain private, but that selected awards may be publicly available, unless the parties agree otherwise and require the arbitrators, but not the parties, to maintain the confidentiality of arbitration proceedings and awards. The Internal rules of the ICC, similarly require arbitrators and administrators to maintain the confidential nature of their arbitral tribunal's internal operations, by refraining from disclosing evidence or information they learn through their participation in the arbitration, Schmitz (2006, pp. 1219–1220).

[23]*Plaskett v Bechtel Int'l*, 243 F. Supp. 2d 334, 340–345 (D.V.I. 2003) finding arbitration agreements with a confidentiality provision unconscionable; Schmitz (2006, p. 1220).

requirements,[24] or that statutory mandates, public interest or governmental needs dictate the disclosure of information and material.[25]

Although common understandings of privacy lull individuals into assuming, that personal information revealed in arbitration may not become public, and that privacy and confidentiality are synonymous, in reality the paradox is that what is private in arbitration does not necessarily remain also confidential. This privacy paradox connotes short sighted contracting and simplistic assumptions about arbitral justice. Although the axiom of privacy in arbitration, i.e. the acceptance of the fact that, unless otherwise agreed, strangers are to be excluded from arbitration, would prompt us to deduce that parties should also be under an explicit duty not to disclose to strangers what has occurred in arbitrations, the stark reality is that there exist vast exceptions to the rule of privacy.[26]

In conclusion, contracting parties should draft their arbitration contracts more carefully, and policymakers should promote policy reforms that consider the tensions that are created by the privacy paradox.[27]

4.1.2 Arbitration and Human Rights

The ECHR, via its articles 33, 34, enables contracting states and any person or group of individuals claiming to be the victim of a violation of the rights set forth in the Convention to file directly their application with the Court. Article 6 of the ECHR contains a number of essential principles which together guarantee the right to a fair trial.[28] More specifically, when an action relates to disputes concerning rights and obligations of a civil nature, article 6 of the ECHR provides that each

---

[24] *AT&T Corp. v Pub. Serv. Enters.*, Nos. CIV. A. 99-4975, CIV. A. 99-6099 2000 WL 387738, at *2 (E.D. Pa. Apr. 12, 2000) dismissing breach of a confidentiality contract claim, on grounds that the claimant waived the confidentiality provision to the extent it sought to use that provision in the same litigation; Schmitz (2006, p. 1220).

[25] *Omaha Indem. Co. v Royal Am. Managers, Inc.* 140 F.R.D. 398, 400 (W.D.Mo. 1991) finding that federal prosecutors could use arbitration testimony transcripts, subject to the arbitrating parties' stipulation of confidentiality for impeachment in a criminal trial involving these parties; *City of Newark v Law Dep't*, 760 N.Y.S. 2d 431, 431–437 (N.Y. App. Div. 2003) finding that an arbitration panel's confidentiality order was ineffectual, to the extent it conflicted with the public's access to such information under the Freedom of Information Law; Schmitz (2006, p. 1220).

[26] For example, with regard to documents and information produced during the arbitration, a different approach may be warranted for different types of material; and, consequently, the award, and the reasons, underlying it, may be treated differently from the transcript of evidence taken during the hearing, witness statements, expert reports, written counsel summaries and legal arguments. Also, documents disclosed during the hearing, form another category which calls for different treatment. Also, the extent of any obligation of confidentiality may depend upon the intended use of the material in question. Collins (1995, pp. 326–327).

[27] Schmitz (2006, p. 1253).

[28] Briner and von Schlabrendorff (2001, p. 89).

party has the right to have its case decided by an impartial and independent tribunal instituted by law. The Convention goes further than simply proclaiming theoretical principles and sets out to protect "practical and effective" rights.[29] The European Court of Human Rights has, in many instances, also stated the paramount position of a fair trial in today's democratic modern society.[30]

Article 6, of the ECHR, lays down guarantees, for the proper administration of justice in court proceedings. There is nothing in the ECHR prohibiting parties from renouncing some of their rights, as set forth in Article 6 of the ECHR. Thus, private parties are not prevented from submitting their disputes to settlement by arbitration. In addition, the European Court has always viewed the choice by the parties to use arbitration, instead of court proceedings, as a means of settling their dispute, as within the Convention. In 1999 the European Court in *Osmo Suovaniemi & Others v Finland*[31] stated that a waiver of court proceedings in favour of arbitration is in principle acceptable from the point of view of article 6 of the ECHR. At the same time, the Convention authorities have always held that a waiver of the right of access to a court, as reflected in an arbitration agreement, should not be considered as amounting to a waiver of all rights under article 6 of the ECHR, but that it should only imply a partial waiver of the guarantees set forth in Article 6 of the ECHR.[32]

Some of the rights protected under article 6 ECHR are so fundamental and important in a democratic society that no person should be deprived of them even if acting voluntarily and free from coercion.[33] Thus, it follows that the Convention authorities, view arbitration proceedings as a special case where special rules apply. In *Nordström-Janzon* and *Nordström-Lehtinen v The Netherlands*[34] the Commission pointed out that it cannot be required under the ECHR that national courts must ensure that arbitration proceedings have been in conformity with article 6 of the ECHR. However, there are certain procedural rights that are of such a fundamental nature, that they constitute international procedural public policy and must be complied with. While no specific accepted definition of international public policy

---

[29]*Airey v Ireland*, Application No. 6289/1973, Decision of 9 October 1979, A. no. 32 § 24, *Artico v Italy*, Application No. 6694/1974, Decision of 13 May 1980, A. no. 37, § 33.

[30]For example in *Delcourt v Belgium*, Application No. 2689/1965, Decision of 17 January 1970 or in *De Cubber v Belgium*, Application No. 9186/1980, Decision of 26 October 1984.

[31]*Osmo Suovaniemi & Others v Finland*, Application No. 31737/1996, Decision of 23 February 1999.

[32]*X v Germany*, Application No. 1197/1961, Decision of 5 March 1962, *Dewer v Belgium*, Application No. 6903/1975, Decision of 27 February 1980, *R v Switzerland*, Application No. 10881/1984, Decision of 4 March 1987, *Nordström-Janzon* and *Nordström-Lehtinen v The Netherlands*, Application No. 28101/1995, Decision of 27 November 1966.

[33]*Albert & Le Compte v Belgium*, Application Nos 7299/1975 and 7496/1976, Decision of 10 February 1983, Series A-58, § 35.

[34]*Nordström-Janzon* and *Nordström-Lehtinen v The Netherlands* Application No. 28101/1995, Decision of 27 November 1966.

exists, it is agreed that the concept covers the basic requirements of due process, such as the equal treatment of the parties, the constitution of a fair, impartial and independent tribunal and the fair opportunity to present one's case.

4.1.2.1 Impartial and Independent Tribunal

The impartiality and independence of the arbitral tribunal are fundamental requirements of international commercial arbitration. However, if parties by their conduct refrain from challenging the arbitrator, this represents a valid waiver of their right to an impartial and independent arbitrator. In *Osmo Suovaniemi & Others v Finland*[35] the European Court inferred the waiver of the right to an impartial and independent arbitrator from the fact that the party concerned did not make use of its right to challenge the arbitrator during the proceedings.[36]

In spite of the fact that many of the rights entailed in article 6 of the ECHR are waived by an agreement to arbitrate, or by conduct, nevertheless recent developments suggest that at least one aspect of article 6 of the ECHR remains important, namely the requirement that a tribunal must be "independent and impartial". In *Findlay v United Kingdom*[37] the European Court of Human Rights stated that:

> . . . in order to establish whether a tribunal can be considered as 'independent', regard must be had inter alia to the manner of appointment of its members and the term of office, the existence of guarantees against outside pressures and the question of whether the party presents an appearance of independence. As to the question of 'impartiality', there are two aspects to this requirement. First, the tribunal must be subjectively free from judicial bias. Secondly, it must also be impartial from an objective view point, that is, it must offer sufficient guarantees to exclude any legitimate doubt in this respect.

Section 24(1) of the English Arbitration Act 1996 provides that a party to arbitral proceedings may apply to the court to remove an arbitrator on any one of a number of grounds, including the fact that "circumstances exist which give rise to justifiable doubts as to his impartiality". This wording was not expressly intended to reflect the requirements of the Convention, and there is no explicit additional requirement of independence. Nevertheless, most of the well-known institutional rules provide for the independence of arbitrators, either expressly, or by requiring a potential arbitrator to disclose any possible conflicts of which he or she is aware.[38]

However, the English courts have traditionally approached the issue of bias in arbitration proceedings, in the same way as with regards to judges in court proceedings. In practice this has meant that although the article 6 of the ECHR requirement

[35]*Osmo Suovaniemi & Others v Finland*, Application No. 31737/1996, Decision of 23 February 1999.

[36]Briner and von Schlabrendorff (2001, pp. 91–94).

[37]*Findlay v United Kingdom* [1997] 24 EHRR 221.

[38]See for example Arts 9(2) and 11 of the ICC Rules, Arts 5.2, 5.3 and 10.3 of the LCIA Rules, Arts 9 and 10 of the UNCITRAL Rules, and Arts 22 and 24 of the WIPO Rules.

of independence and impartiality may not apply directly to proceedings before an arbitral tribunal, the legal "test" for bias under s. 24(1) of the English Arbitration Act 1996 mirrors the test for bias in English court proceedings, which has been influenced by European case law on article 6 of the ECHR.

Prior to the entry into force of the Human Rights Act the test applied to questions of bias was the one established in *R. v Gough*,[39] i.e. the test of a real danger of actual bias, rather than simply an appearance of bias. However, this formulation was modified in *Porter v Magill*[40] so as to bring it in line with the decision in *Findlay v United Kingdom.*[41] Following this decision the test for bias applied to judges in court proceedings became whether the fair-minded and informed observer, having considered the relevant facts, would conclude that there was a real possibility that the tribunal was biased.[42] In *ASM Shipping Ltd of India v TTMI Ltd of England*,[43] the Court held that this modified test of bias should also apply to questions of bias arising in the context of arbitration tribunals.[44] In *Norbrook Laboratories v Tank Ltd*[45] the application of the modified test, in the context of arbitration tribunals was also upheld. Most recently, in *Sukuman Ltd v Commonwealth Secretariat*[46] it was stated that a waiver of the right to an impartial tribunal without knowledge of the

[39] *R. v Gough* [1993] AC 646.

[40] *Porter v Magill* [2002] 2 AC 357.

[41] *Findlay v United Kingdom* [1997] 24 EHRR 221. The case concerned the independence and the impartiality of a court-martial (Army Act 1955). Pending the proceedings before the Court the United Kingdom had made changes to the legislation at issue. With respect to the new legislation the Court held that it could not rule on legislation *in abstracto*, but it noted with satisfaction the changes made to the court-martial system by the Armed Forces Act 1996. With respect the applicability of Article 6(1) the Court concluded that this article was clearly applicable since the proceedings involved the determination of a sentence following a guilty plea. On the compliance with the requirements of Article 6(1) the Court held that the convening officer was central to the prosecution and was closely linked to the prosecuting authorities. Inter alia, he decided which charges should be brought, he convened the court-martial, he appointed members of prosecuting and defending officers. The members of the court-martial were all military personnel subordinate in rank to the convening officer who, as confirming officer, could vary the sentence imposed. The defects could not be corrected by subsequent review proceedings since the applicant was entitled to the first instance tribunal meeting requirements of Article 6(1). The Court concluded that there had been a violation.

[42] *Porter v Magill* [2002] 2 A.C. 357 at 359; Hodges (2007, p. 164).

[43] *ASM Shipping Ltd of India v TTMI Ltd of England* [2006] 1 Lloyd's Rep. 375.

[44] In *ASM Shipping Ltd of India v TTMI Ltd of England* [2006] 1 Lloyd's Rep. 375, the chairman of the tribunal had previously been instructed as counsel by the defendant's solicitors in another case, in which serious allegations of impropriety had been made against the claimant's main witness. The Court held, that the chairman should have declined to sit on the panel, because an objective and independent observer, considering the facts, would have shared the feeling of discomfort, expressed by the claimant's main witness, about the chairman's impartiality, and would have concluded that there was a real possibility of bias.

[45] *Norbrook Laboratories v Tank Ltd* [2006] EWHC 1055.

[46] *Sukuman Ltd v Commonwealth Secretariat* [2007] EWHC 188 (February 14, 2007, Comm).

relevant facts should not occur, as it would constitute an unjust and disproportionate restriction of the right to be protected by article 6 of the ECHR.[47]

The case law examined indicates that the impartiality and fairness provisions contained in article 6 of the ECHR remain relevant to arbitration, and that the waiver of the rights entailed in article 6 of the ECHR is limited by the protections contained within the English Arbitration Act 1996. As such, article 6 of the ECHR remains relevant to arbitration proceedings themselves.[48]

4.1.2.2 Fair Trial

The first sentence of article 6(1) of the ECHR, provides that "... in the determination of his civil rights and obligations or of any criminal charge against him everyone is entitled to a fair and public hearing within a reasonable time by an independent and impartial tribunal." Fair trial, as referred to in article 6 of the ECHR, is a composite concept comprising a number of procedural elements. There is a general agreement, that amongst the major components of a fair trial are the principles that a party must be given reasonable time to present its case, i.e. he must be able to exercise the right to be heard (the right to adversarial proceedings) and the principle that the parties must have an equal chance to argue their cases, i.e. so-called, equality of arms, must apply.[49]

To what extent is the procedural right to a fair trial, enshrined in article 6 of the ECHR, applicable in arbitration proceedings? The view traditionally supported by scholars has been that arbitration proceedings are private proceedings between individuals, to which the Convention has no application.[50] However, this approach has now been superseded by the view that article 6 of the Convention may apply in the context of arbitration proceedings, albeit in limited circumstances. More specifically, in relation to arbitration proceedings, the fair trial requirement laid down in article 6 ECHR must be seen as a standard which, perhaps more clearly than that of article V of the 1958 New York Convention, reflects the criterion of international, rather than national, public policy. In other words, it is a standard that imposes only the very basic requirements of due process, such as equal treatment of the parties, fair notice of the proceedings and a fair opportunity to present the case involved, the right to obtain a decision within a reasonable time, and, to a certain extent and with specific limitations, the right to a public hearing.

In England, the entry into force of the Human Rights Act 1998, augmented the profile of the Convention and the number of cases in which the English courts have

---

[47]*Sukuman Ltd v Commonwealth Secretariat* [2007] EWHC 188 (February 14, 2007, Comm) [80].

[48]Hodges (2007, pp. 164–166).

[49]Briner and von Schlabrendorff (2001, p. 96); Van Dijk and Van Hoof (1990, p. 318); Art. 6; *Stran Greek Refineries and Stratis Andreatis v Greece*, Application No 13427/1987, Decision of 9 Dec. 1994, § 46.

[50]Such as Jarosson and Jacot-Guillarmond; Jarrosson (1989, p. 573); Jacot-Guillarmond (1988).

been asked to apply it. Since then, the courts have considered on a number of occasions the interface between the procedural rights embodied, explicitly or implicitly, in article 6 of the ECHR and the right of commercial parties to agree to settle disputes via arbitration, pursuant to the English Arbitration Act 1996.[51]

4.1.2.3 Decision Within a Reasonable Time

The Convention authorities have interpreted this requirement of article 6 ECHR as prohibiting any abusive or dilatory behaviour by the judicial authorities. In terms of arbitration proceedings, the latter do not raise any particular issues with regard to the time they require. The Convention authorities have also repeatedly emphasised that it is up to the parties to proceed with due diligence. Thus, the reasonable time requirement of article 6 of the ECHR can only be justified in cases of delays for which national courts, reviewing arbitration proceedings, are responsible for.[52]

4.1.2.4 Public Hearing and Confidentiality

The Convention authorities have also stated that the right to a public hearing can be validly waived in court as well as in arbitration proceedings. This reflects the private nature of the proceedings, and the well-recognised principle of confidentiality in arbitration proceedings.[53]

In *Nordström-Janzon* and *Nordström-Lehtinen v The Netherlands*,[54] the Commission pointed out that, in relation to the public access to hearings, arbitration proceedings are in theory not intended to be in conformity with article 6 of the ECHR. The European Court of Human Rights has also in other cases such as *Le Compte, Van Leuven and De Meyere v Belgium*[55] and *H v Belgium*,[56] repeatedly decided that a party may renounce the right to a public hearing, when the waiver is unequivocal and not in conflict with public interest issues.

---

[51]*Paul Stretford v Football Association Ltd* [2007] EWCA Civ 238 (March 21, 2007, CA); *Sukuman Ltd v Commonwealth Secretariat* [2007] EWCA Civ 243 (March 21, 2007, Comm), [2007] EWHC 188 (February 14, 2007, Comm); *North Range Shipping v Seatrans Shipping Corp* [2002] 1 W.L.R. 2397; *ASM Shipping Ltd of India v TTMI Ltd of England* [2006] 1 Lloyd's Rep. 375 (Comm) and [2006] EWCA Civ 1341 (CA); *CGU International Insurance Plc v AstraZeneca Insurance Co Ltd* [2006] EWCA Civ 1340; *Norbrook Laboratories v Tank Ltd* [2006] EWHC 1055; Hodges (2007, p. 163).

[52]Briner and von Schlabrendorff (2001, p. 97).

[53]Hodges (2007, pp. 163–164).

[54]*Nordström-Janzon* and *Nordström-Lehtinen v The Netherlands* Application No. 28101/1995, Decision of 27 November 1966.

[55]*Le Compte, Van Leuven and De Meyere v Belgium*, Application Nos. 687/1975 and 7238/1975, Decision of 23 June 1981, § 59.

[56]*H v Belgium*, Application No. 11855/1985, Decision of 21 February 1990, § 66.

Although the Australian decision in *Esso Australian Resources Lzd et al. v Plowman et al*[57] raised doubts, as to whether the confidentiality of arbitrations proceedings can still be taken for granted in cases where the parties have not specifically agreed for it, there can be little doubt that in most cases parties engaged in arbitration proceedings wish confidentiality to be respected, at least as a matter of principle, in order to prevent possibly sensitive information from reaching unauthorised parties.[58]

In *Department of Economic Policy and Development of the City of Moscow v Bankers Trust Co*,[59] where two of the parties applied under s. 68 of the English Arbitration Act 1996 to challenge an award in private arbitration proceedings, the judge dismissed the application, and a summary of his judgment was prepared by Lawtel and sent to customers via the internet. The government and a department of the city of Moscow sought publication of the judgment, or of the Lawtel summary, in order to demonstrate to the international financial community, via the arbitral holding, that it had not committed any financial default and had been the subject of detailed and careful scrutiny by the court. The judge decided that neither his judgment nor the summary should be published. After reviewing the rules relating to arbitration, in the light of common law principles, and of the requirements of article 6 of the ECHR, and after having taken into account the parties' expectations, the importance of arbitration in commercial life, and the fact that a judgment on a point of law or practice should be made known for future guidance, he concluded that there was a valid argument for his judgment not to be made available for publication, but that Moscow should be permitted to publish generally the summary, given the fact that it did not disclose any sensitive or confidential information, and because there were no other grounds for precluding its publication.[60]

In *Ali Shipping v Trogir*,[61] the Court of Appeal held that an obligation of confidentiality should be "implied into arbitration agreements as a matter of law since it was an essential corollary of the privacy of arbitration proceedings and thus a term which the nature of the agreement implicitly required".[62] In that case, the Court concluded that arbitration proceedings and documents, or other information generated during the course of the arbitration, should be treated as confidential, subject to the exceptional cases where there is consent or an order of the court, or leave by the court, or circumstances where disclosure is reasonably necessary to protect or establish the legal right of a party, or of a third party, or because of

---

[57] *Esso Australian Resources Lzd et al. v Plowman et al* 183 CLR 10, 128 ALR 391 (1995).

[58] Briner and von Schlabrendorff (2001, p. 98).

[59] *Department of Economic Policy and Development of the City of Moscow v Bankers Trust Co* [2004] EWCA Civ 314; [2005] Q.B. 207 (CA (Civ Div)).

[60] Case Comment, *Department of Economic Policy and Development of the City of Moscow v Bankers Trust Co*, [2004] EWCA Civ 314; [2005] Q.B. 207 (CA (Civ Div)), P.L. 2005, SPR, 176.

[61] *Ali Shipping v Trogir* [1999] 1 W.L.R. 314.

[62] *Ali Shipping v Trogir* [1999] 1 W.L.R. 314, 316.

interests of justice.[63] The extent of these exceptions was subsequently considered in *Glidepath v Thompson*[64] in the context of an application by a non-party for copies of documents held on the court file, in proceedings which had been stayed pursuant to section 9 of the English Arbitration Act. It was held that copies could only be supplied where the parties would have consented to it, or where there was an overriding "interest of justice".

Thus, insofar as the proceedings before the tribunal itself are concerned, the principle of confidentiality in arbitration will usually mean that the parties are considered to have waived their right to a public hearing under article 6 of the ECHR.[65]

4.1.2.5 Other Cases of Necessary Compliance with Article 6 of the ECHR

Although *Suovaniemi v Finland*[66] judicially confirmed that parties who voluntarily submit their disputes to arbitration are generally considered to have waived their right of access to an article 6 of the ECHR protected court,[67] nevertheless the parties' rights under Art. 6 of the ECHR are not entirely extinguished by their voluntary submission to arbitration. For example, if an appeal is brought against an arbitral award, under sections 67–69 of the English Arbitration Act 1996, the decision of the English court to grant or refuse leave to appeal, and the decision reached on the substantive appeal itself – should leave be granted – must still comply with article 6 of the ECHR.[68]

According to sections 67–69 of the English Arbitration Act 1996, any challenge of an arbitral award must be based on the following grounds: challenging the substantive jurisdiction of the tribunal;[69] or a serious irregularity affecting the tribunal, the proceedings, or the award;[70] or the existence of a question of law which the tribunal was asked to determine – and which substantially affects the rights of one or more of the parties – in a context where the decision of the tribunal on the question was obviously wrong; or when the question is one of general public importance and the decision of the tribunal is open to serious doubt; as well as, in circumstances where it is just and proper for the court to determine the question.[71]

---

[63] *Ali Shipping v Trogir* [1999] 1 W.L.R. 314, 326–327.

[64] *Glidepath v Thompson* [2005] EWHC 818 (Comm).

[65] Hodges (2007, pp. 164–165).

[66] *Suovaniemi v Finland* Application No.31737/96, Decision of February 23, 1999.

[67] *Suovaniemi v Finland* Application No.31737/96, Decision of February 23, 1999; See also *Paul Stretford v Football Association Ltd* [2007] EWCA Civ 238 (March 21, 2007, CA); Hodges (2007, p. 163).

[68] Hodges (2007, p. 163).

[69] Section 67 of the English Arbitration Act 1996.

[70] Section 68 of the English Arbitration Act 1996.

[71] Section 69 of the English Arbitration Act 1996.

However, article 6 of the ECHR does not guarantee a right of appeal, and where a right of appeal is given to the parties under national laws restrictions on the exercise of that right – such as those contained in sections 67–69 of the English Arbitration Act 1996 – are not considered as incompatible with the rights of the Convention.[72]

Likewise, the exclusion by parties, within their arbitration agreement of the right of appeal is not incompatible with the ECHR.

In *Sukuman Ltd v Commonwealth Secretariat*[73] it was held that there was no reason, in principle, why at least certain ECHR article 6 rights, including the right to appeal on a point of law,[74] may not be waived.[75]

Case law such as *Hiro Balani v Spain*[76] has also established that the right to a reasoned decision is fundamental to the right to a fair trial. In *Mousaka Inc v Golden Seagull Maritime Inc*,[77] and in *North Range Shipping v Seatrans Shipping Corp*,[78] the impact of the requirement on decisions to grant or refuse leave to appeal against arbitral awards has been considered by the courts. In the former case it was stated that the practice of not giving a fully reasoned decision when refusing an application for leave to appeal against an arbitral award was not inconsistent with Art. 6 of the ECHR, or with any other duty to give reasons.[79]

Litigation and arbitration centre on two different objectives. Litigation focuses on the principle of correctness, whereas arbitration, on the other hand, lives primarily according to the principle of finality. The choice of objective made for arbitration is, to a certain extent, respected by litigation. This explains why arbitration is, in principle, not open to a proper appeal, though setting-aside actions, based on a limited number of specific grounds, are possible in most countries.[80]

4.1.2.6 Tentative Observations

The impact of human rights, and more particularly of the ECHR, on arbitral proceedings is increasingly important.

Article 6(1) of the ECHR is applicable in terms of arbitration proceedings as well as in court proceedings related to arbitration. However the extent and format of this

---

[72]See *Tolstoy v United Kingdom* [1995] 20 E.H.R.R. 442 at [59]; *North Range Shipping v Seatrans Shipping Corp* [2002] All E.R. (D) 409.

[73]*Sukuman Ltd v Commonwealth Secretariat* [2007] EWCA Civ 243 (March 21, 2007, Comm).

[74]Hodges (2007, p. 166).

[75]*Sukuman Ltd v Commonwealth Secretariat* [2007] EWCA Civ 243 (March 21, 2007, Comm), at [57].

[76]*Hiro Balani v Spain* [1994] 19 EHRR 566.

[77]*Mousaka Inc v Golden Seagull Maritime Inc* [2002] 1 WLR 395.

[78]*North Range Shipping v Seatrans Shipping Corp* [2002] 1 W.L.R. 2397.

[79]Hodges (2007, p. 166).

[80]Schultz (2006, p. 23).

application varies. Nonetheless, the scope of Article 6(1) of the ECHR may be very broad, and this provision can no longer be ignored by arbitration practitioners.

The main provisions of article 6 of the ECHR, especially the right to an independent judge/arbitrator and the right to a fair trial, are obligations which must be observed also in arbitral proceedings. At the same time, as far as arbitration is concerned and with regards to the right to a public hearing, arbitration dictates the right of the parties to abide by confidentiality. Thus, in that sense, the scope of the application of the right to a public hearing, embodied in article 6 of the ECHR, is limited and parties can renounce the right to a public hearing when the waiver is unequivocal and not in conflict with public interest issues.[81] Likewise, parties may decide to waive the right to the appeal of an award. However, if an appeal is brought against an arbitral award, the decision on the appeal has to comply with article 6 of the ECHR.[82]

4.1.3 Legal Privilege, Arbitration and the Issue of Confidentiality

One of the reasons why parties choose to arbitrate is the flexibility relating to evidentiary rules applied in arbitration, which may be chosen by the arbitration agreement.

However, this fact, alone, does not necessarily automatically waive the parties' right to claim the benefit of evidentiary privilege according to which parties may withhold certain testimonial or documentary evidence from a legal proceeding, including the right to prevent another from disclosing such information.[83] However, English law clearly distinguishes between a claim that a document is covered by a legal privilege against disclosure and the argument that it is subject to a duty of confidence.[84] Legal professional privilege is a rule of substantive law and not merely a procedural rule of evidence. This, in turn, confirms that the right can be asserted in response to any request for disclosure.[85]

Different arbitration institutional rules, take different approaches, though, in relation to the question of privilege. Whilst the American Arbitration Association Rules, provide in article 20(6) that: "... the tribunal shall take into account applicable principles of legal privilege, such as those involving the confidentiality of communications between a lawyer and a client.", the International Chamber of

---

[81]Briner and von Schlabrendorff (2001, p. 108).

[82]Hodges (2007, p. 163).

[83]Gallaher (2003, p. 45).

[84]In *Shearson Lehman Hutton Inc. v Maclaine Watson & Co* [1998] 1 WLR 946, even though the document's confidentiality was not at issue, there was no realistic prospect that the documents would be privileged from production. In *Prudential Assurance Co v Fountain Page Ltd* [1991] 1 WLR 756, it was stated, at 765, that a distinction existed, in that a legal privilege provides a permissive right, while a duty of confidence refers to a legal obligation. Collins (1995, p. 330).

[85]Heaps and Taylor (2006, p. 110).

Commerce, the London Court of International Arbitration, the International Centre for Settlement of Investment Disputes and the United Nations Commission on International Trade Law, have institutional arbitration rules that remain silent on the matter and leave the question to be decided on an *ad hoc* basis, in accordance with the circumstances of each case.[86] However, the English Arbitration Act 1996, gives the parties the ultimate authority to determine questions of procedure and evidence. Section 34(1) provides that: "It shall be for the tribunal to decide all procedural and evidential matters, subject to the right of the parties to agree any matter." The Act sets out a non-exhaustive list of examples of such procedural matters, including "whether and if so which documents should be disclosed between and produced by the parties" and also "whether to apply strict rules of evidence". However, under the English Arbitration Act 1996, the general duty of the tribunal is to adopt procedures suitable to the particular circumstances of the case and there is no guidance as to what principles should be applied, where there is a conflict of evidentiary laws.

Thus, different expectations of preservation of privilege may arise. This creates confusion and affects the element of confidentiality. A good example of the above is the widely used English phenomenon of "without prejudice" privilege which generally comprises written or oral communications made for the purpose of a genuine attempt to compromise a dispute between the parties.[87] These communications are, generally, not admitted in evidence because of public policy considerations which dictate that negotiations to settle a dispute should not be used against a party in subsequent proceedings. In *Cutts v Head*[88] it was stated that parties should not be discouraged to resort to arbitration by the knowledge that anything said may be used to their prejudice in the course of the proceedings.

The "without prejudice" privilege can only be waived with the consent of both parties, and only documents which are involved in a *genuine* attempt to settle the dispute will be afforded the protection.[89] However, none of the main international arbitration rules provide any specific guidelines on the admissibility of "without prejudice" documents in an arbitration and thus the international tribunals have to consider the rules that should be applied in each case and decide on a case by case basis.

In addition, there are few reported decisions on the question of "without prejudice" evidence.

The tribunal, in ICC Case No. 6653 1993[90] considered how it would treat such evidence and concluded that it was a well-established rule that negotiations to settle the dispute by the parties are confidential. In an unreported arbitral case[91] where the

[86]Gallaher (2003, p. 45).

[87]Hollander and Adam (2000, p. 170).

[88]*Cutts v Head* [1982] Ch.290.

[89]Gallaher (2003, p. 48).

[90]Arnaldez et al. (1997, p. 513).

[91]Arnaldez et al. (1997, p. 516).

respondent sought to rely on the content of various meetings that had been held "without prejudice", the arbitral panel ruled on the basis that the parties, by entering into settlement negotiations, had implicitly agreed that all communications relating to them could not be introduced as evidence.

Within Europe, different rules apply with regards to the production of documents and privilege. In Spain, all communication between lawyers are confidential and cannot be produced in court without the prior consent of the parties involved.[92] In Germany, parties are not required to disclose information, even if the information is relevant to the proceedings. The German Federal Court of Justice has stated that none of the parties need provide the procedural weapons for the other party's case.[93] Moreover, "fishing expeditions" are not allowed under the German legal system.[94] Exceptional cases where parties are required to disclose information, exist in the sense that Courts can draw a negative inference from a party's refusal to disclose information.[95] Thus, under German law, there is only limited need to protect a party by granting privilege.[96]

At European Community level, the ECJ in *Australia Mining and Smelting Europe Limited v Commission of the European Communities*[97] held that communications between external non-EU qualified lawyers and their EU-based client were not privileged.[98] In *AkzoNobel Chemicals v Commission of European Communities*[99] it was reaffirmed that in-house legal counsel cannot claim legal professional privilege protection and it was also stated that only communications emanating from independent lawyers qualified to practice in a member state within the EU can be privileged.[100] Some guidance is also available for European practitioners in the Code of Conduct for Lawyers in the EU, which provides as follows:

---

[92]See art. 22.3 Barcelona Law Society Bylaws; Gallaher (2003, p. 48).

[93]Federal Court of Justice, Bundesgerichtshof (BGH), Federal Court Reporter (BGHZ), no 93, pp. 191, 205.

[94]Under the so-called doctrine of "Verbot des Ausforschungsbeweises".

[95]However, if the party can show reasonable grounds for its refusal, Courts will not draw a negative inference from the refusal.

[96]Rützel and Christ (2006, pp. 141, 143, 147).

[97]*Australia Mining and Smelting Europe Limited v Commission of the European Communities* 1982 ECR 1575 (ECJ).

[98]Heaps and Taylor (2006, p. 120).

[99]*AkzoNobel Chemicals v Commission of European Communities*, Joint Cases T-125/03 and T-253/03, European Court of First Instance of 17 Sept. 2007.

[100]Allowing the advice of internal counsel to be used against a company, goes squarely against the very philosophy of privilege, as corporate counsel are useful, precisely because they help companies navigate legal risks. The same applies for non-EU qualified counsel. Advice from the best lawyer, may not be protected if it is not also from the right lawyer. The very purpose of privilege, should be to allow clients to confer openly about issues with the best person for the job both, in-house and external counsel, and should not be limited by the formality of Bar membership on which the court in *AkzoNobel Chemicals v Commission of European Communities*, Joint Cases T-125/03 and T-253/03, European Court of First Instance of 17 Sept. 2008, focused.

Article 5.3. Correspondence Between Lawyers

5.3.1. If a lawyer sending a communication to a lawyer in another member-state wishes it to remain confidential or without prejudice, he should clearly express this intention when communicating the document.

5.3.2. If the recipient of the communication is unable to ensure its status as confidential or without prejudice he should return it to the sender without revealing its contents to others.[101]

Although such guidelines do not bind parties to an arbitration, an arbitral panel or lawyers outside the EU, they nevertheless offer practical advice to lawyers, wishing to avoid any confusion with regard to the future admissibility of documents.[102]

An international tribunal, when faced with the question of legal privilege and "without prejudice" evidence, will have to balance a number of factors. They must decide whether it is better to refuse admission of such communications, or not. In reaching their decision, they should always consider the parties decisions, and the factors that made them choose to arbitrate. Given the obscure authority on how an international arbitral tribunal should address a claim for privilege, and the varied rules of evidence from country to country, there is no minimum international standard that can be applied, and the tribunal must, in each case, balance the need for the information against the privilege claimed.[103]

4.1.4 The Legal Nature of Confidentiality in Arbitration

The notion of confidentiality in arbitration proceedings has aroused many debates and has brought forward the need to compare its treatment in various jurisdictions. The untangling of the mystery of the legal nature of arbitration has often been debated in court rooms, whereby barristers or judges have been called on to express views on its legal nature, not least, due to the fact that in many legal jurisdictions the obligation to abide by the duty to protect confidentiality is not expressly statutorily granted for.[104]

English courts have defined the notion of the legal nature of confidentiality, in three respects, i.e. firstly, in terms of it being considered as a contractual obligation,

[101]Council of the Bar and Law Societies of the European Union Code of Conduct, Nov. 28, 1998; See Gallaher (2003, p. 48).

[102]Gallaher (2003, p. 48).

[103]Gallaher (2003, p. 49).

[104]For example, in England the Departmental Advisory Committee on Arbitration Law stated on their Report on the Arbitration Bill, paras 14–15, that the task of regulating confidentiality proved "controversial and difficult", in the light of the "myriad of exceptions and qualifications that had to follow", and, thus, it was decided that confidentiality would not be expressly regulated for within the Arbitration Act 1996, but, instead, it would be left to the courts to address the matter, in an *ad hoc* and *in concreto* basis; Thoma (2008, pp. 299–300).

secondly, in terms of it being considered as a legal duty, and, thirdly, in terms of it being considered from a spectrum perspective.[105]

Confidentiality as a contractual obligation has been analysed as an implied term of the agreement for arbitration. However, fairly recent case law such as *Associated Electric and Gas Insurance Services (AEGIS) v European Reinsurance Company of Zurich*[106] which dealt with the matter of express confidentiality clauses in an arbitration agreement has demonstrated that the previously well preserved guarantee of confidentiality which was entailed in an express confidentiality clause was not absolute, in that it could be reversed depending on the interpretation of the clause by courts at times.[107] Although in *Associated Electric and Gas Insurance Services (AEGIS) v European Reinsurance Company of Zurich*[108] Lord Hobhouse of Woodborough had acknowledged the common and legitimate concern of parties involved to an arbitration with regards to documentation exchanged or generated during the arbitration he nevertheless went on to express the opinion that the legitimate use of an earlier award in a later also private arbitration between the same two parties, would not raise the mischief against which the confidentiality agreement is directed.[109] He considered that precluding a winning party from referring to a previously pronounced award, against the same opposing party in the context of a subsequent and closely connected arbitration between them would amount to non-enforcement of the award. Thus, it can be argued that, in this respect *Associated Electric and Gas Insurance Services (AEGIS) v European Reinsurance Company of Zurich*[110] judicially established the rule that clauses can be interpreted so as to override a requirement for confidentiality, even if this contradicts their literal terms.[111]

In spite of the fact that the position under English law is that courts cannot override or change terms, as these have been set by parties,[112] or set them aside by implied terms,[113] because the existence of an express term, *per se*, automatically excludes the possibility of implying any term dealing with the same matter as an express term,[114] and, in spite of the fact that interpretation aims to combine the true and ordinary meaning of the words, as this is deduced from the objective

---

[105]Thoma (2008, p. 300).

[106]*Associated Electric and Gas Insurance Services (AEGIS) v European Reinsurance Company of Zurich* [2003] 1 All E.R. (Comm.) 253, paras. [1]–[22].

[107]Thoma (2008, p. 302).

[108]*Associated Electric and Gas Insurance Services (AEGIS) v European Reinsurance Company of Zurich* [2003] 1 All E.R. (Comm.) 253.

[109]*Associated Electric and Gas Insurance Services (AEGIS) v European Reinsurance Company of Zurich* [2003] 1 All E.R. (Comm.) 253, para. [8].

[110]*Associated Electric and Gas Insurance Services (AEGIS) v European Reinsurance Company of Zurich* [2003] 1 All E.R. (Comm.) 253.

[111]Thoma (2008, p. 302).

[112]*Jacobs v Bratavia & General Plantations Trust Ltd.* [1924] 1 Ch. 287, 297 (Ch).

[113]*Lynch v Thorne* [1956] 1 WLR 303, 306 (CA).

[114]*Aspdin v Austin* (1844) 5 QB 671, 683 (QB).

assessment of the contextual meaning of the contract, which denotes the intentions of the parties together with the judicial precedent; nevertheless, and to a certain extent, the courts have shown an eagerness to abandon the originally adopted tactic of literal interpretation,[115] together with a willingness to adopt other criteria in their interpretation, such as the commercial purpose of the transactions,[116] or, the adoption of the literal interpretation and intention of the parties criteria, only in cases where the purpose of the parties can shed light on the meaning of the words used by them.[117] In line with these approaches and new criteria, in *Associated Electric and Gas Insurance Services (AEGIS) v European Reinsurance Company of Zurich*,[118] apart from engaging in a literal reading of the clause, the court also emphasised the policy considerations, pertaining (a) to the importance of the implied obligation binding the parties to comply with the arbitral award, as well as, (b) to the fact that compliance with the arbitral award should not be inconsistent with confidentiality, whether express or implied. Thus, it was thought that in deterring parties from using an arbitral award in the context of a future dispute between them, on the basis of a strict interpretation of a confidentiality term, would defeat the purpose of arbitration.

Conversely, and in spite of the argument as to the adhering to commercial reasonableness, it is highly possible that, if the parties had expressly stipulated that no reference to a prior arbitral award would be possible in future disputes between them, the court, in *Associated Electric and Gas Insurance Services (AEGIS) v European Reinsurance Company of Zurich*,[119] would have adopted the strictly literal approach and interpretation of the confidentiality clause, and would have probably reached a different ruling.

Put otherwise, in such a case, there would be not much ground to support the argument that such a literal interpretation would run counter to the purpose of arbitration, as the clause would have been explicitly detailed and clear, in relation to future disputes between the parties involved. This would have, therefore, meant that the court would have had to enforce the contractually agreed term, in spite of any potential different judicial assessment of how a bargain could have better been made.[120]

---

[115] *Lovell & Christmas Ltd v Wall* (1911) 104 LT 85, 93 (CA).

[116] This is the approach adopted by Lord Steyn, in various cases, such as in *Lord Napier & Ettrick v R F Kershlaw Ltd* [1999] 1 WLR 756, 763 (HL); Thoma (2008, p. 302).

[117] This is the approach adopted by Lord Hoffmann, in *Investors Compensation Scheme Ltd v West Bromwich Building Society* [1998] 1 WLR 896, 912–913 (Lord Hoffmann, HL); Thoma (2008, p. 302).

[118] *Associated Electric and Gas Insurance Services (AEGIS) v European Reinsurance Company of Zurich* [2003] 1 All E.R. (Comm.) 253.

[119] *Associated Electric and Gas Insurance Services (AEGIS) v European Reinsurance Company of Zurich* [2003] 1 All E.R. (Comm.) 253.

[120] As per Lord Mustill, in *Charter Reinsurance Co Ltd v Fagan* [1997] AC 313, 315 (HL); Thoma (2008, pp. 300–304).

It follows, that where confidentiality is expressly provided in the arbitration agreement, its preservation is not guaranteed unless the term is so detailed as to exclude other than a strictly literal interpretation.

As stated earlier above, confidentiality as a contractual obligation has traditionally been identified and judicially recognised as an implied contractual term. The term is implied, either in fact, by operation of law, or by custom of usage of a market, trade, or locality. An implied term in fact derives from the need to give business efficacy to the arbitration agreement and parties are assumed to have agreed to such an implied term in order to make their agreement workable.[121]

There are, however, good arguments for encouraging express terms providing for the protection of the duty to observe confidentiality in arbitration agreements, given that implied terms of confidentiality are construed in the light of particular circumstances and the presumed intentions of the parties, at the time of their original agreement, and therefore may not safeguard the preservation of the duty of confidentiality.

In the case of confidentiality as a term implied by custom, although in *Hassneh Insurance Co of Israel v Steuart J Mew*,[122] the view that confidentiality was an implied term was supported, by Colman J., on the basis of a universal customary practice, it is arguable, whether this is correct. Customs or usages, are binding only when they are not contrary to law and only when they are consistent with the express terms of the contract. They bind the parties irrespective of whether they are aware of their existence, which is something that may be inconsistent with confidentiality, or because they are characterised by certainty which, as per past and current judicial trends, cannot be attributed to confidentiality. For all these reasons, it seems logical to exclude the customary implication of a duty to confidentiality.

As far as the treatment of confidentiality as a term implied by law is concerned, this was recognised in *Ali Shipping Co Ltd v Shipyard Trogir*,[123] in which the argument that confidentiality is a term implied in fact, on the ground of business efficacy was rejected and in which the necessity to treat confidentiality as a term implied by law was reaffirmed,[124] thus, making it an inherent element of arbitration and establishing that the duty arose directly from the arbitration agreement.[125]

As far as the treatment of confidentiality from a spectral perspective is concerned, in *Department of Economic Policy and Development of the City of*

[121]*The Moorcock* (1889) 14 PD 64, 68, 70 (CA); *Shirlaw v Southern Foundries* [1939] 2 KB 206 (CA); *Hassneh Insurance Co of Israel v Steuart J Mew*, [1993] 2 Lloyd's Rep 243 (Com.Ct.); *Insurance Co v Lloyds Syndicate* [1995] 1 Lloyd's Rep 272 (Com.Ct); Thoma (2008, pp. 305–306).

[122]*Hassneh Insurance Co of Israel v Steuart J Mew*, [1993] 2 Lloyd's Rep 243 (Com.Ct.).

[123]*Ali Shipping Co Ltd v Shipyard Trogir* [1998] 2 All ER 136 (CA).

[124]Following *Dolling-Baker v Merrett* [1991] 2 All ER 890 (CA). See also *Scally v Southern Health and Social Services Board (British Medical Association, third party)* [1991] 4 All ER 563, 571 (HL); Thoma (2008, p. 309).

[125]Thoma (2008, p. 309).

Moscow v Bankers Trust Co,[126] confidentiality was observed from a general perspective, and, although arbitral proceedings unlike court proceedings were indisputably considered as confidential,[127] it was established that in cases where parties resort to courts, to challenge arbitral awards, in doing so, they exercise a right given to them and established by law, which further entails the possible revealing of information, but which should not be perceived as a breach of their right to the preservation of confidentiality. In other words, by challenging arbitral awards in the courts, parties run the risk of disclosure of information concerning the arbitration, without losing the right to confidentiality in general. Confidentiality should only be perceived as a nexus to other legal relationships, or as an institutional element of arbitration, where the supervisory and supportive, role of the courts is vital and fundamental.[128]

4.2 The Legal Framework of Arbitration and the Position in Relation to Confidentiality in the Various Jurisdictions

4.2.1 England

In England, arbitration is statutorily regulated by the Arbitration Act 1996. The Arbitration Act 1996 implements the 1958 New York Convention, subject to the reservation that it applies only to awards made in the territory of another contracting party, insofar as it requires that contracting states recognise agreements in writing under which the parties undertake to submit disputes to arbitration (Article II(1) and (2)). The Arbitration Act 1996 came into force with effect from 31 January 1997 and applies to arbitration proceedings commenced as of 31 January 1997.[129]

The Arbitration Act 1996 is in large part based on the United Nations Commission on International Trade Law Model Law on International Commercial Arbitration of 1985 ("UNCITRAL Model Law"). However, the UNCITRAL Model Law, is intended to apply only to international commercial arbitration (Article 1(1) of the UNCITRAL Model Law), whereas, the Arbitration Act 1996, applies, equally, to all forms of arbitration and is not limited to international commercial arbitration. In this respect, the Arbitration Act 1996, does not adopt the UNCITRAL Model Law in its entirety. Moreover, in addition to applying to all forms of arbitration, the Arbitration Act 1996 differs from the UNCITRAL Model Law, in the following key ways. Under the Arbitration Act 1996:

---

[126]*Department of Economic Policy and Development of the City of Moscow v Bankers Trust Co* [2004] EWCA (Civ) 314.

[127]Thoma (2008, p. 312).

[128]Thoma (2008, pp. 312–313).

[129]Global Legal Group (2006, Chap. 21 – USA).

- The document containing the parties' arbitration agreement need not be signed.
- An English court is only able to stay its own proceedings and cannot refer a matter to arbitration.
- The default provisions for the appointment of arbitrators provide for the appointment of a sole arbitrator, as opposed to three arbitrators.
- A party retains the power to treat its party-nominated arbitrator as the sole arbitrator in the event that the other party fails to make an appointment (where the parties' agreement provides, that each party is required to appoint an arbitrator).
- There is no time limit on a party to oppose the appointment of an arbitrator.
- Parties must expressly opt out of most of the provisions of the English Arbitration Act 1996 which confer default powers on the arbitrators in relation to procedure.
- There are no strict rules for the exchange of pleadings.[130]

When listing the advantages and disadvantages of arbitration, as compared to litigation, it is usual to include "confidentiality" on the plus side for arbitration. In its Report on the Arbitration Bill in February 1996,[131] the Departmental Advisory Committee ("DAC"), stated that privacy and confidentiality are the features upon which parties, choosing to arbitrate in England, place great importance. However the Arbitration Act 1996 makes no reference to the obligation of confidentiality and this omission reflects nothing more than the difficulty of reaching a statutory formulation, in the light of "the myriad exceptions" and the qualifications as it that would have had to contain. The process that led the DAC to conclude, that confidentiality should not be regulated expressly, and that the courts should be left to continue to work out the implications of the duty to observe confidentiality on a *case-by-case basis*[132] is justified as follows:

Section 1 of the Arbitration Act 1996 lays down the general principles, upon which the Act is based.[133] It is made clear that in case of any ambiguity in the Act, the three stated principles are to have an overriding effect. The Act does not seek to define arbitration as such, but, rather, defines its most important features. Principle (a) is significant, as it forms part of the general duty of the arbitrators in their handling of the arbitration (section 33(1)(b)). Principle (b) encompasses two different limbs, i.e. that parties should be held to their agreement, and that they should be free to agree how their disputes are to be resolved. Principle (c) reflects a general

---

[130]Global Legal Group (2007, Chap. 18 – England and Wales).

[131]§§ 10–17.

[132]Robb (2004).

[133]Section 1 of the English Arbitration Act 1996 states:
General Principles
1. The provisions of this Part are founded on the following principles, and shall be construed accordingly– (a) the object of arbitration is to obtain the fair resolution of disputes by an impartial tribunal without unnecessary delay or expense; (b) the parties should be free to agree how their disputes are resolved, subject only to such safeguards as are necessary in the public interest (c) in matters governed by this Part the court should not intervene except as provided by this Part.

desire to minimise judicial intervention, in the running of arbitrations, where the parties or the arbitrators can resolve issues for themselves, in the interests of speed, finality and reduced costs, and replicates the principle underlying article 5 of the Model Law.

When section 1 of the Arbitration Act 1996 was being formulated, it was decided that an additional principle, on confidentiality should be not inserted. Lord Roskill had suggested on the Second Reading of the Bill, that a fourth general principle should be inserted, namely that arbitrations, documents used in them, and any resulting awards, are confidential. This matter had been considered by the DAC, in its 1996 Report, and its proposed solution was an amendment to what is now section 81(2) of the English Arbitration Act 1996, creating an express saving for the common law rules on confidentiality and privacy. This approach was not ultimately adopted, and confidentiality is not expressly mentioned in section 1 of the Arbitration Act 1996.[134]

4.2.2 USA

In its historical evolution the American law of arbitration stands in an intermediary position between its French and English counterparts. In keeping with the patterns developed in those systems, a sense of commercial realism and lobbying efforts brought about landmark legislation that eventually undermined the judicial hostility toward arbitration, undoing the perception that it amounted to a contractual usurpation of judicial jurisdictional authority.[135]

Arbitration in the USA is regulated by the Federal Arbitration Act of 1925 and the various related state laws. The Federal Arbitration Act 1925 is the landmark legislation that put an end to the era where the US courts were willing to entertain suits brought in violation of arbitration agreements. According to the celebrated language of section 2 of the Federal Arbitration Act 1925, arbitration agreements are "valid, irrevocable and enforceable". The intention of the federal legislation manifestly was to promote arbitration as a viable alternative to the court judicial resolution of disputes.[136] The Federal Arbitration Act 1925, codified at 9 U.S.C. § 1 *et seq.*, applies to arbitration agreements, evidencing any nexus to interstate commerce or admiralty. Chapter 1 of the Federal Arbitration Act 1925, specifically covers domestic USA arbitrations. Arbitrations, outside the purview of the Federal

---

[134]Merkin (2000, pp. 17–18).

[135]While the attitude of the American legal system, initially paralleled the English reluctance to embrace arbitration wholeheartedly, contemporary American statutory and case law, on arbitration, are in keeping with the unequivocal French acceptance of arbitral adjudication; Carbonneau (1989, pp. 105–106).

[136]Carbonneau (1989, pp. 105–106).

Arbitration Act 1925, however, are governed by state arbitration law.[137] The Federal Arbitration Act's Chaps. 2 and 3 govern international arbitration. Chapter 2 reflects the USA's accession to the 1958 New York Convention on the Recognition and Enforcement of Foreign Arbitral Awards ("New York Convention"), and, Chap. 3 reflects the USA's ratification of the Inter-American Convention on International Commercial Arbitration.[138]

Arbitration, as regulated by federal and state laws, is an adjudicatory process, i.e. a process in which a neutral third party, renders a final and binding decision upon a dispute that has been submitted to the arbitrator by disputing parties. Although its adjudicatory nature makes it similar to state court litigation, nevertheless, it is less formal, because formal rules of evidence and civil procedure, generally do not apply in Federal Arbitration Act. Arbitrations are also generally considered a "private" process so that confidentiality applies.

However, when considering the confidentiality of arbitration communications, a distinction needs to be drawn, between disclosures to third persons in the general public,[139] and disclosures to institutions, in the context of formal legal proceedings, which, unlike disclosures to third persons, involve public interests, such as the public's interest in accessing the information pursuant to governmental fact-finding, or, adjudication, or, policy development and legal regulation.

The Federal Arbitration Act 1925, and the related state laws, provide a basic structure for arbitrations conducted under them, but generally do not address issues of arbitration confidentiality. At the federal level, there are no real federal court rules, on confidentiality in arbitration. Likewise, at state level, there is equally minimal protection, for confidentiality in arbitration in the states. Fewer than half of the states, address the issue in either statutes or court rules, and of the states with statutes which protect confidentiality in arbitration, in relation to discovery and admissibility, only four states – Arkansas, California, Missouri, and Texas – have statutes that apply to arbitrations generally, regardless of any subject matter.

---

[137]Which state's law applies, to a given arbitration, is usually determined by the parties' arbitration agreement. However, the Federal Arbitration Act 1925 provides the substantive law that must be applied by all courts – state and federal – to any arbitration agreement, within the reach of the Federal Arbitration Act 1925. Thus, even if jurisdictional considerations require an arbitration matter to be heard in state court, the state court must apply the Federal Arbitration Act 1925, wherever applicable. In such cases, the court may concurrently apply state law if it is consistent with the Federal Arbitration Act 1925; otherwise, state law is preempted. Even if the Federal Arbitration Act 1925 is applicable, parties may agree to have certain aspects of a state's arbitration law apply – but only where the state law offers more protection than the Federal Arbitration Act 1925. A state court may also apply state procedural law to arbitrations governed by the Federal Arbitration Act 1925, and parties are entitled to elect state procedural rules; Global Legal Group (2006, Chap. 21 – USA).

[138]Global Legal Group (2006, Chap. 21 – USA).

[139]In the private realm, the law historically has permitted parties to regulate them through the law of contract; Reuben (2006, pp. 1259–1265).

Similarly, court rules are sparse in protecting confidentiality in arbitration. Thus, by and large, the issue is left to the common law.[140]

However, parties may agree to confidentiality in arbitration proceedings; indeed, this is a leading impetus for arbitration, because US court litigation is presumptively a matter of public record. Absent a confidentiality agreement and an order by the arbitration panel, any information disclosed in an arbitration will be subject to production.[141] Unless the parties request otherwise, arbitral institutions will maintain confidentiality of proceedings.[142] Without a confidentiality agreement, information disclosed, in arbitration, may be produced in a subsequent proceeding without notable restriction. Moreover, even if arbitration is protected, by confidentiality, information, disclosed, may subsequently be produced, in a court proceeding, if the court finds no compelling reason to protect the information and the information is necessary to the litigation. In short, if the parties do not agree to confidentiality, or confidentiality, is not imposed by the panel, then, the arbitration proceeding is not so protected.[143]

Another initiative, in the area of arbitration law in the USA, has been the enactment of the Uniform Arbitration Act 2000. In early August 2000, at its annual conference held in St. Augustine, Florida, the National Conference of Commissioners on Uniform State Laws, approved and recommended for enactment in all the states of the Uniform Arbitration Act 2000.[144] The Uniform Arbitration Act 2000 was the revision of a previous initiative. The Act was originally adopted in 1955, and had not been revised since 1956. The work of modernising and revising the legislation, initiated by the National Conference of Commissioners on Uniform State Laws Drafting Committee, was spurred by the rapid pace and the, sometimes, dramatic character of developments in the field of arbitration, i.e. from the realization that the increased scope of application for the arbitral process and the greater sophistication of arbitral doctrine demanded a new and more adapted uniform legislative framework.

As adopted, the Uniform Arbitration Act 2000 contains a number of provisions that incorporate the principles and concepts that have emerged from and have been developed in the contemporary case law on arbitration. In the final analysis, however, it is not a perfect statute, ready-made for incorporation into existing statutory law, because it is poorly drafted and many of its provisions are inelegantly rendered, and because there also exist inadequacies of language, which, in turn, give rise to problematic ambiguities and general perplexity, about the rule propounded.

---

[140] Reuben (2006, pp. 1259–1265).

[141] *Cont'ship Containerlines, Ltd. v. PPG Industries, Inc.*, No. 00-CIV-0194, WL 1948807 (S.D.N.Y. Apr. 23, 2003); Global Legal Group (2006, Chap. 21 – USA).

[142] Global Legal Group (2006, Chap. 21 – USA).

[143] Global Legal Group (2007, Chap. 57 – USA, § 11).

[144] The vote was nearly unanimous – Alabama abstained and the Michigan and Rhode Island state delegations were absent; See Editorial (2000, pp. 326, 333).

In addition the drafting committee appears to have addressed a number of controversial developments in the law, simply by taking a side on the question.[145]

4.2.3 France

Arbitration has not always been looked upon favourably, in France, and attitudes towards it have always been somewhat ambivalent in the past. A passage from Seneca pertinently illustrates the misunderstandings which have surrounded it and have caused it to be regarded with some suspicion,[146] where it states:

> Every matter, which may give rise to legal proceedings, must be set out, in legal form, in order to preclude absolute freedom of appraisal; in this way, a good cause will be presented in a better manner if it is put before a judge, than if it were submitted to an arbitrator, since a judge is confined to a prescribed formula which lays down limits which he must not infringe; whereas an arbitrator, will find that he has absolute freedom of conscience and is not subject to any binding restriction; thus, he may omit, or add, certain matters and make his award, not in accordance with the law and strict justice, but, based upon sentiment, kindliness or compassion.[147]

Even after the Middle Ages and the period of absolute monarchy, arbitration was regarded by French Courts with some reluctance.[148] During the French revolution it was naively thought that this trend would be reversed, given that the Constitutional Assembly perceived it as the usual and natural way to resolve disputes, and render justice, and attributed to national courts a subsidiary role. In effect, the Law of

---

[145]More specifically, in relation to confidentiality in arbitration, its section 14 states that: "Parties engage in arbitration, with a view to resolving their disputes privately. In order to maintain the confidentiality of arbitration, arbitrators and agents of arbitral institutions, cannot be compelled to testify about, or produce documents concerning the arbitration, by a court of law or an administrative or other tribunal. Moreover, information that such parties may voluntarily communicate, is not admissible in such proceedings. Post-award disclosures of, otherwise confidential, information regarding the arbitration, can result in the assessment of civil liability against an arbitrator or an arbitral institution. Arbitral immunity is not applicable in these circumstances. Such disclosures, also constitute a breach, of the ethical standards that apply to arbitrators and arbitral institutions. Other participants, in the arbitration, are encouraged to maintain the confidentiality of the proceedings. Wherever possible, contracts or arbitral rulings should provide for the assessment of penalties, for the violation of arbitral confidentiality by these other parties. The rule of arbitral confidentiality, does not apply to actions for the payment of fees and other costs, brought by an arbitrator or an arbitral institution against a party to the arbitral proceedings. In an action for the vacatur of an award, a record of the arbitral proceedings can only be constituted, if the party opposing the award establishes *prima facie* a serious basis for possible *vacatur*. Otherwise, the rule of confidentiality applies, to any information pertaining to the arbitration. Attempts to undermine the rule of confidentiality, by bringing actions which violate its requirements, shall result in the award of attorney's fees and court costs"; See Editorial (2000, pp. 326, 333).

[146]Devolve et al. (2003, p. 3).

[147]Prechac (2003, p. 3).

[148]Hilaire (2003, p. 187); Devolve et al. (2003, p. 3).

16–20 August 1790 prohibited any hindrance, to arbitration, in whatever manner or form. However, within a short time, the process of arbitration begun to be abused, and manifest injustice was done, with the result that the Napoleonic "Code de Procedure Civile" of 1806, articles 1003–1028, provided strict regulations about it such as that notice had to be given to the Department of the Public Prosecutor prior to submitting disputes to arbitration.[149] The Cour de Cassation increased these restrictions and by its judgment of 10 July 1843[150] held that clauses under which parties agreed to submit disputes to arbitration which might arise in the future were null and void as distinct from disputes existing at the time of the agreement as well as because it was felt that it was dangerous for parties to agree in advance to waive the protection of sound justice which, in its opinion, only the state courts could guarantee.

As a result of this hostility, arbitration did not develop properly in France, until the early twentieth century, when, after the end of the First World War, and as a result also of pressure from the business community, interest in it begun to grow. It then began to be realised, that businessmen needed greater speed and flexibility, for the settlement of their disputes than that provided by national courts. However, contrary to this background, the French Law, of 31 December 1925, validated only arbitration clauses relating to future disputes, and only those concerning commercial transactions. This situation did not change much for many years,[151] as arbitration continued to be largely regulated in a whole title of the old Code of Civil Procedure.

The provisions of the old Code of Civil Procedure, though largely utilised, became outdated, as international arbitrations developed and a need for a reform that would clarify and modernize French arbitration law became apparent at the end of the 1970s.[152] The reform was effected by two Decrees, i.e. the Decree of 14 May 1980, on domestic arbitrations, and the Decree of 12 May 1981 on international arbitrations, both of which are today embodied in the New French Code of Civil Procedure. These two texts, are profoundly different from what previously existed, as they may have consolidated the existing case law. However, certain provisions such as those relating to the duration of the arbitrator's mission, the power of commercial tribunals to intervene to arbitration, the resources and the powers of the courts of appeal, are audaciously new and innovative.[153]

Arbitration agreements, are governed by provisions, contained both in the French Civil Code, i.e. in article 2059 *et seq.* and in the New French Civil Procedural Code, which dedicates a whole chapter to arbitration, i.e. articles article 1442 *et seq.*, including a specific section for international arbitration. The demarcation, between

---

[149]Devolve et al. (2003, p. 4).

[150]Cass. Civ. 10 July 1843, S.1843.1. p. 561 and D. 1843.1. p. 343, republished in Revue de l' Arbitrage 1992, 399; Devolve et al. (2003, p. 4).

[151]Devolve et al. (2003, pp. 4–7).

[152]Devolve et al. (2003, p. 7).

[153]Devolvé (1982, pp. 57–58).

domestic and international arbitrations, is made in article 1492, of the New French Code of Civil Procedure, which states that arbitration is international, when it involves the interests of international trade.[154]

There is no formal prohibition on referring to information disclosed, in a previous arbitration, in subsequent court proceedings. A party deciding to do so may, however, incur liability, either for breach of confidentiality, or, more generally, for wrongful use of confidential information that would be characterised as a tort – notably in connection with unfair competition. A party wishing to prevent this use may also institute summary proceedings, before French courts, seeking an order precluding such use, notably on the ground of the urgency of the situation, and/or the imminent damage that the use of the information would generate. The parties may also provide for exceptions to confidentiality. Public policy rules, may also limit the scope of confidentiality, notably in the event of listed companies.[155]

Although no specific provisions of the law deal with the issue of the confidentiality of the arbitration proceedings, it is, nevertheless, widely accepted that, the agreement to arbitrate carries an implicit agreement to confidentiality, and courts have always considered confidentiality as part of the very nature of arbitral proceedings.[156] Moreover arbitrators are required not to divulge confidential information, disclosed during the proceedings, and must keep confidential all matters relating to the arbitration or to the award. Any disclosure of such information, may give rise to liability, under French criminal law, at least theoretically, for breach of professional secrecy.[157] In spite of the fact that French courts have traditionally, also, recognised the inherent confidentiality of arbitration,[158] however, recent judicial commentary may prompt further discussion, of the extent of the obligation in practice.[159]

4.2.4 Germany

Arbitration has a long tradition in Germany. As in many other legal systems, the state court systems developed from *ad hoc* tribunals, based on consent. Arbitral tribunals based on an agreement between the parties, were widely considered to be a useful supplement, in particular in commercial matters.[160]

---

[154] Devolvé (1982, p. 58).

[155] Global Legal Group (2007, Chap. 26 – France, § 11).

[156] This has been discussed in Courts in the case of *Bleustein et autres v. Société True North & Société FCB International*, Rev. Arb. no. 1, 189 (2003) Paris Commercial Court.

[157] Global Legal Group (2007, Chap. 26 – France).

[158] *Aita v Ojjeh* (1986) Revue de'l Arbitrage 583, confirmed in *Bleustein et autres v. Société True North & Société FCB International* (2003) Revue de'l Arbitrage 189.

[159] *Société Nafimco v. Société Foster Wheeler Trading Company AG*, Paris Court of Appeal (1e Ch. C), 22 January 2004.

[160] Böckstiegel et al. (2008, p. 4).

The first codification of arbitration law on a federal level in Germany, is contained in the 10th Book of the ZPO[161] and it adopted a very favourable approach to arbitration as the law was to a large extent already based on the same principles, which today underlying the UNCITRAL Model Law, i.e. party autonomy and limited court intervention.

However, shortly after the adoption of the UNCITRAL Model Law, efforts to modernise German arbitration law began, as it was widely felt that the provisions of the old law were incomplete, and sometimes outdated, and, that, in spite of their arbitration friendliness, they considerably diminished the attractiveness of Germany, as a place for international arbitrations. These provisions made impossible the existence and establishment of a certainty of German arbitration law from the text of the statute, as well as due to the fact that some of the default provisions, contained in the law, were no longer in line with arbitration practice.

Thus, of the major aims, of the proposed revision, was to make German arbitration more user friendly and bring it in line with international practice. Indeed, the 41 sections of the new German Arbitration Law, contained in the 10th Book of the ZPO, (§§ 1025–1066 ZPO), are, to a large extent, a *verbatim* adoption of the UNCITRAL Model Law. The use of the law is made easier by the detailed accompanying explanatory note, which describes the rationale underlying each article.[162]

The core of the German Arbitration Law, is integrated in the 10th Book of the ZPO. It is also supplemented by a few arbitration specific provisions, contained in other statutes, relating primarily to the non-arbitrability of certain disputes. Furthermore, some of the other provisions of the ZPO, may become applicable in arbitration-related court proceedings, in support or in supervision of the arbitration. These purely national sources are supplemented by the provisions in international instruments, such as the New York Convention on the Recognition and Enforcement of Foreign Arbitral Awards of 1958,[163] or in other bilateral treaties, to which Germany is a party and which often provide for dispute resolution by arbitration. The new German Arbitration Law applies to all arbitrations having their place of arbitration in Germany. The ZPO, in § 1025(2), also, lists a number of provisions,

---

[161] *Zivilprozessordnung* or "*ZPO*", i.e. Code of Civil Procedure.

[162] Bill of the Arbitration Law Reform Act, BT-Drs. 13/5274; Böckstiegel et al. (2008, pp. 4–5).

[163] Article II(1) and (2), of the New York Convention, require that contracting states recognise agreements, in writing, under which the parties undertake to submit disputes to arbitration. This obligation, is also implemented in Germany by the 10th book of the ZOP, which *inter alia* governs the enforcement and recognition of arbitration agreements. In international matters, reliance on more favourable foreign national laws may be permitted; Böckstiegel et al. (2008, pp. 8–9); The Federal Supreme Court, has confirmed that the most favoured treatment mandated by Article VII, of the New York Convention, requires national courts deciding on the enforcement of foreign arbitral awards, to consider the law governing the arbitration agreement, if this law contains more permissive form requirements than Article II of the New York Convention on the Recognition and Enforcement of Foreign Arbitral Awards of 1958 (*Federal Supreme Court*, Decision dated 21 September 2005, Schieds VZ 2005, pp. 306–308); Global Legal Group (2006, Chap. 25 – Germany).

which apply, where the place of arbitration is not in Germany, or, has not yet been determined.[164]

Arbitration proceedings, in Germany, are not public, and participation is confined to the parties and the arbitrators. Arbitrators, are subject to a duty of confidentiality,[165] and may not disclose the award, or details thereof, without the agreement of the parties. Arbitrators are also expected not to disclose the identity of the parties to an arbitration.

Since the basis for the duty of confidentiality is the parties' agreement, or the institutional arbitral rules which the parties have incorporated by reference into their agreement, it may be inferred that the issue of disclosure or not, of information of arbitral proceedings in a subsequent arbitration or of consolidation of arbitral proceedings, depends on the precise content of the contractual confidentiality obligations.[166]

The question, whether the parties themselves must treat the arbitration confidentially, is still disputed amongst German commentators. At the centre of the discussion, appears to be the interpretation of the arbitration agreement. Some argue that, in the absence of an express confidentiality term in the arbitration agreement, there is no general duty of confidentiality in arbitration proceedings sited in Germany, whilst other scholars argue, that the arbitration agreement, *per se*, can be interpreted as implying a duty of confidentiality.[167] Neither the German Arbitration Law, nor the UNCITRAL Model Law, contain a provision on the confidentiality of arbitral proceedings. However, it is widely recognised that, parties, arbitrators and arbitral institutions, are under an obligation to maintain the confidentiality of arbitral proceedings. Section 43(1) of the German Institute for Arbitration (Deutsche Institut für Schiedsgerichtsbarkeit, "DIS"[168]) Rules, states that the duty of confidentiality rests on all participants of the proceedings, such as the parties, their legal representatives, the persons assisting the parties, or the arbitral tribunal, in the proceedings, such as the DIS's Secretariat staff, which is involved in administering the proceedings but the same duty does not extend to witnesses and experts.

Thus, confidentiality includes the duty to refrain from passing information to anyone not involved in the proceedings. However, confidentiality does not prevent the participant from complying with statutory duties of information, where such duties take precedence, or, where the parties have agreed to exclude confidentiality.[169] However, if a third party request to produce information, in spite of being against the parties wishes, is based on a court order, the production of the requested

[164]Böckstiegel et al. (2008, pp. 8–9); Lachmann (2002, pp. 40–45); Global Legal Group (2007, Chap. 25 – Germany, § 11).

[165]Lachmann (2002, p. 42).

[166]Raeschke-Kessler et al. (1995, p. 163); Global Legal Group (2007, Chap. 25 – Germany, § 11).

[167]Lachmann (2002, p. 44); Global Legal Group (2007, Chap. 25 – Germany).

[168]Deutsche Institution für Schiedsgerichtsbarkeit ("DIS").

[169]Böckstiegel et al. (2008, p. 803).

document or information will have to be done[170] because under German law the obligation on DIS to maintain the confidentiality of the proceedings does not create a privilege to deny access to the information.

In the absence of an express duty of confidentiality, the parties may be free to use the information disclosed, in arbitral proceedings, for other purposes. Even if the parties are obliged to treat the information disclosed, in the arbitral proceedings, as confidential, further exceptions, to the parties' duty of confidentiality, relate to the protection of the legitimate interests of the parties. For example, a party to arbitral proceedings, can rely on information disclosed in these proceedings in subsequent proceedings against its insurer, if the latter has to indemnify the party, for the damages which the party is ordered, by the arbitral award, to pay.[171]

Thus, the extent of protection of confidentiality of proceedings, depends on the parties agreement as there are no particular rules in the ZPO in this regard. Even where the parties do not provide for express exceptions to their confidentiality obligations, arbitral proceedings, sited in Germany, are not protected by confidentiality, even if the legitimate interests of the parties so require. Also, the confidentiality of arbitration can be limited, as a result of regulatory, administrative and penal proceedings and requirements.[172]

4.3 The Case Law on Confidentiality in the Various Jurisdictions

4.3.1 General

The principle that arbitrations are private and confidential, as between the parties, would seem to be self evident. After all, is this not one of the most important of the perceived advantages of arbitration, and one of the main reasons why business people, around the world, have made arbitration the forum of choice for the resolution of international commercial disputes? However, although often an explicit or implicit presumption of confidentiality exists, between the parties to an international commercial arbitration, at the same time, there is a disconnection, between that presumption and the frequent realities of disclosure and publicity imposed by arbitrators, arbitral tribunal or the parties themselves.[173]

Our discussion will be divided into three parts, and will strive to discuss comparatively – to the extent that the availability of case law in all the various jurisdictions permits us to do so – firstly, the issue of confidentiality in arbitration

[170]Böckstiegel et al. (2008, p. 804).

[171]Raeschke-Kessler et al. (1995, p. 163); Global Legal Group (2007, Chap. 25 – Germany, § 11).

[172]Raeschke-Kessler et al. (1995, p. 163); Global Legal Group (2007, Chap. 25 – Germany, § 11).

[173]Brown (2001, p. 975).

proceedings, in relation to the arbitral proceedings themselves, i.e. confidentiality in relation to the existence of the proceedings, as well as in relation to the course of the proceedings and their possible consolidation; secondly, the issue of confidentiality, in relation to discovery (disclosure) of documents and other evidence used during the arbitral process; and, thirdly, the issue of confidentiality in relation to the arbitral award.

4.3.2 Confidentiality in Arbitration Proceedings in Relation to the Proceedings Themselves

4.3.2.1 England

Where two or more arbitral tribunals may need to be set up, there is always the attendant risk of inconsistent findings. Initiatives, by parties and arbitrators, to overcome this difficulty have led to litigation. Where separate disputes have common features, the practice in English law was to consolidate proceedings and, it was, therefore, possible for arbitrators to order that separate arbitrations be heard together, notwithstanding that privacy has long been recognised as an important feature of arbitration.[174] However, English courts have not always been consistent, in their rulings, with regards to the consolidation of arbitration proceedings. The strong English principle of confidentiality, presently, stands in the way of practical solutions.[175]

Subject to the parties agreeing otherwise, the arbitration held, pursuant to an agreement to submit to arbitration, is private, in the sense that it is not open to the public. The arbitrator will exclude strangers from the hearing, unless the parties consent to their attendance by a stranger. Perhaps, because the principle is uncontroversial, there is little authority on the point.

In 1984, Leggat J. qualified this long established tradition by holding in *Oxford Shipping Co v Nippon Yesen Kaisha [The "Eastern Saga"]*,[176] that concurrent hearings could be conducted, without infringing the concept of privacy of arbitration. It is, however, worth noting, that the Arbitration Act 1996 is silent on the issue of who may attend an arbitration hearing, and, it may be thought that, arbitrators have a discretion, subject, only, to their overriding duty in section 33(1)(a) of the 1996 Act to secure a fair hearing.[177]

---

[174]Collins (1995, p. 327).

[175]Shackleton (1999, pp. 125–126).

[176]*Oxford Shipping Co v Nippon Yesen Kaisha [The "Eastern Saga"]* [1984] 2 Lloyd's Rep. 373 (QB).

[177]Robb (2004).

The decision, in *Oxford Shipping Co v Nippon Yesen Kaisha [The "Eastern Saga"]*,[178] was, in a sense, unexpected, as the opposite view seemed attractive and sensible. But it came as a forceful reminder, that arbitration is a private process, and, that, at least in England, the implied right to privacy, a fundamental part of every arbitration agreement, was a substantive right which the court could readily uphold.

The ruling in *Oxford Shipping Co v Nippon Yesen Kaisha [The "Eastern Saga"]*,[179] has meant, in practice, that if arbitrators consider a concurrent hearing as appropriate, the parties can often agree to a common panel, whereas, if the parties are unable or unwilling to do so, it is unlikely that an order, for such concurrent hearing, will be made.[180]

In the case of *Sacor Maritima v. Repsol*,[181] disputes arising out of a primary and a subsequent charter were referred to two separate arbitrations, when cargo was found to be contaminated, as a result of not cleaning the tanks prior to their loading under the terms of the sub-charter. The owners, reimbursed the buyers of the cargo, and, commenced an arbitration against the charterers, under the primary charter. The charterers were found liable in this arbitration. The charterers commenced an arbitration against the sub-charterers, claiming indemnity for the amount they had paid to the owners – in accordance with the first arbitration ruling – and argued that the finding, in it, that the omissions of the surveyor evidencing their liability towards the owner, should be binding in the second arbitration.[182] A question arose as to the binding effect of findings of fact – in one arbitration – on parties to separate but related proceedings. The court queried on both the legitimacy of comparing the two awards, and observed, that, it was inherent in the nature of arbitration practice that any arbitration be regarded as a private matter, as regards both the issues which it raises and the evidence which is called in it. It held that although the two tribunals arrived at inconsistent findings, they did so in separate disputes, between different parties, and on the basis of different evidence. The court distinguished, attempts, to import into an arbitration prior determinations of liability, from attempts, to import mere findings of fact or causation under the arbitral mechanisms of another contract, in which one of the parties to a later arbitration did not participate.[183] It held, that the facts and conclusions, in the present case, were

---

178 *Oxford Shipping Co v Nippon Yesen Kaisha [The "Eastern Saga"]* [1984] 2 Lloyd's Rep. 373 (QB).

179 *Oxford Shipping Co v Nippon Yesen Kaisha [The "Eastern Saga"]* [1984] 2 Lloyd's Rep. 373 (QB).

180 Collins (1995, p. 327).

181 *Sacor Maritima SA v. Repsol Petroleo SA* [1998] 1 Lloyd's Rep. 518 (QBD (Comm)).

182 However, the Court distinguished the earlier case of *Lincoln National Life Insurance Co v. Sun Life Assurance Co of Canada* [2004] EWHC 343; [2004] 1 Lloyd's Rep. 737, CA; [2004] EWCA 1660, where the context in the two arbitrations involved was entirely the same.

183 Shackleton (1999, pp. 117–136).

sought to be transported, in a totally different context, in the second arbitration, and that there was no justification for consolidation of the proceedings.

To avoid inconsistent findings, a party, to more, than one, arbitrations, will, sometimes, appoint the same arbitrator, in each proceeding. English courts have considered the conduct of a common arbitrator, appointed in related proceedings in *Aquator Shipping Ltd v Kleimar NV (The Capricorn)*,[184] where sub-charterers (Scanports) met a claim for demurrage from the time charterers (Kleimar), with a cross-claim for damages in respect of omissions by the master alleged to have caused delay (the "sub-charter arbitration"). In a separate arbitration, Kleimar claimed against the owners (Aquator), any demurrage they might fail to recover from the sub-charterers (the "head charter arbitration"). In each arbitration, a three-member tribunal was set up. Kleimar appointed the same arbitrator, in both proceedings. In the head charter arbitration, Kleimar naturally used against Aquator all arguments advanced by Scanports, in the sub-charter arbitration, while, at the same time, relying on Aquator's position against Scanports. However, the parties did not agree to concurrent proceedings, pursuant to para. (c)(i) of Schedule 1 to the LMAA Terms. Evidence, used in one proceeding, was not made available to the other. The common arbitrator, advised the parties that he would prepare draft reasons for each award, because he had participated in both proceedings. Accordingly, the two awards were, in part, supported by identical reasons. Kleimar's claim, for demurrage, against Scanports, failed, because of Scanports' counter-claim. Kleimar's claim, against Aquator, succeeded. Aquator, appealed, on the basis that the arbitrators in the head charter arbitration had based, their award, and the quantum of damages, on evidence, submitted in the sub-charter arbitration, to which Aquator did not have access, and upon which, Aquator, was unable to adduce evidence.

The Court of Appeal, noted the necessary insulation and related confidential nature of the sub-charter arbitration, and, found that Aquator was entitled to assume that a common arbitrator would treat parallel proceedings separately. In the absence of an agreement to consolidate proceedings, the arbitrators' use of common reasons was, procedurally, defective. However, the Court of Appeal upheld the award, since no injustice occurred, and, it was highly improbable that, the arbitrators would have arrived at a different conclusion, in the absence of irregularity.[185]

The question of confidentiality, in relation to consolidated proceedings, was also clearly posed in *Ali Shipping Co. v Shipyard Trogir*.[186] Six companies, all owned and managed by Ali, entered into six separate contracts with Trogir which was to build one ship for each company. When Trogir failed to complete one of the hulls, Ali rescinded the corresponding contract and claimed damages in arbitration. Trogir, justified its failure to complete, by the fact that two of the other special purpose companies had not paid instalments, owing in respect of other ships under construction. Trogir, also sought to pierce the corporate veil, and treat all six

---

[184] *Aquator Shipping Ltd v Kleimar NV (The Capricorn)* [1998] 2 Lloyds Rep 379.

[185] Shackleton (1999, pp. 125–126).

[186] *Ali Shipping Co. v Shipyard Trogir* [1998] 1 Lloyd's Rep. 643.

contracts as a single transaction, under which it could set off damages, arising from the failure to complete one ship against unpaid instalments owing on the others. Considering, that the creation of six special purpose companies had been deliberate, the arbitrator awarded damages against Trogir. In separate arbitral proceedings, concerning three of the remaining ships, Trogir sought to introduce materials, generated in the first arbitration, notably the arbitrator's award, Ali's written submissions, and oral evidence, given by Ali's witness. Ali applied for an injunction, to prevent use of these documents.

At first instance, the Court found that, no duty of confidence blocked communication of the documents. There were no third party strangers, nor any evidence, that the single purpose companies had different personnel, and no distinction had been made between the parties, in relation to the documentation exchanged during pre-contractual negotiations. Although each buyer was a separate legal entity, the negotiations had been conducted by the same individuals. The Court of Appeal, disagreed with this highly practical approach. It held that as a matter of law, a duty of confidence prevented Trogir, from using documents from the first arbitration, and identified the third party strangers as the subsequent decision makers. Parties to an arbitration clause had an interest to withhold such documents, from the arbitrators, and this interest was found to have merited protection in the absence of circumstances to support a finding of fraud or abuse of process.

The Court of Appeal's decision, in *Ali Shipping Co. v Shipyard Trogir*,[187] stands in sharp contrast, to the general trend of recent English decisions, against technical legalism. It takes the doctrine of arbitral confidentiality, far beyond its original purpose, which was simply to close proceedings to the public. The decision is, however, consistent with the greater emphasis English judges place on contractual, as opposed to judicial, aspects of arbitration. Under section 34, of the Arbitration Act, arbitrators are allowed, and indeed, are encouraged, to play an active and inquisitorial role to ascertain the facts. The courts, should not interfere with arbitrators, who take their judicial role seriously, especially where the parties are foreign to England and arbitrate under laws which do not know so broad a principle of confidentiality, or so strict an observance of the corporate veil.

Having said that, English judicial orthodoxy, regarding confidentiality, must not obscure the wide-spread use of arbitral awards, in practice, and the increasing role of decisions rendered by arbitral tribunals, as a source of law. International arbitral tribunals, and counsel to parties before these tribunals, routinely refer to the arbitral awards of other tribunals. English courts, themselves, have also done so, recently.[188] Following *Ali Shipping Co. v Shipyard Trogir*,[189] in *Laker Airways Inc. v FLS Aerospace Ltd*,[190] Rix J. referred to an LCIA arbitration award, relating

[187]*Ali Shipping Co. v Shipyard Trogir* [1998] 1 Lloyd's Rep. 643.

[188]The Court of Appeal indicated that it was legitimate to hear evidence of the practice of arbitrators under institutional rules where the application of those rules was in dispute.

[189]*Ali Shipping Co. v Shipyard Trogir* [1998] 1 Lloyd's Rep. 643.

[190]*Laker Airways Inc. v FLS Aerospace Ltd* [1999] 2 Lloyd's Rep. 45.

to challenges of arbitrators.[191] In *Owners, Master and Crew of the Tug "Hamtun" v Owners of the Ship "St. John"*,[192] the Admiralty Court was shown a selection of Lloyd's Open Form salvage arbitration awards, to assist it in determining the quantum.[193]

More recently, the Privy Council case of *Associated Electric & Gas Insurance Services Ltd. (AEGIS) v. European Reinsurance Company of Zurich (Bermuda)*,[194] involved two successive arbitrations, between the same parties, (AEGIS and European Re), arising out of two separate disputes, under an automatic, facultative reinsurance agreement. Both disputes, involved the obligation of European Re to indemnify AEGIS. The reinsurance agreement required arbitration of disputes, before a three-member arbitration panel. The arbitrations were held in Bermuda, before differently constituted panels of arbitrators. In the first arbitration, the parties had entered into a confidentiality agreement, which was included in agreed procedural directions issued by the arbitral panel. The agreement, set out a general duty of confidentiality:

> The parties, their lawyers, and the Court of Arbitration agree, as a general principle, to maintain the privacy and confidentiality of the arbitration. In particular, they agree that the contents of the briefs or other documents, prepared and filed in the course of this proceeding, as well as the contents of the underlying claim documents, testimony, affidavits, any transcripts, and the arbitration result, will not be disclosed, at any time, to any individual or entity, in whole or in part, which is not a party to the arbitration between Aegis and European Re.

In the second arbitration, European Re sought to introduce the award from the first arbitration. Its purpose, was to establish an estoppel defence, arguing that the findings, in the earlier proceedings, were binding, on the parties and the arbitrators, in the second proceeding. AEGIS obtained an *ex parte* injunction, from a trial court in Bermuda, restraining European Re from introducing the first award, based on the confidentiality agreement. The Bermuda Court of Appeal, allowed European Re's appeal and then vacated the injunction. AEGIS appealed to the Privy Council, arguing, in support of the injunction, that to disclose the award, in the first arbitration, to the panel, in the second arbitration, would breach the principle of privacy, associated with arbitration, and, more specifically, the express confidentiality agreement, reached in the first arbitration. It also argued that, the estoppel defence of European Re, in the second arbitration, was so lacking in merit that it was an abuse of process to raise it.

The Privy Council, recognised the need to preserve confidentiality and the lawyer-client privilege, but, in its analysis, appeared to place more importance,

---

[191] *Laker Airways Inc. v FLS Aerospace Ltd* [1999] 2 Lloyd's Rep. 45 at 51–52.

[192] *Owners, Master and Crew of the Tug "Hamtun" v Owners of the Ship "St. John"*, March 11, 1999, Admiralty Court.

[193] Shackleton (1999, pp. 125–126).

[194] *Associated Electric & Gas Ins. Serv. Ltd. v. European Reinsurance Co. of Zurich (Bermuda)* [2003] UK PC 11 (Jan. 29, 2003) (AEGIS).

on the essential purposes of arbitration, to determine disputes between the parties, declare the rights and obligations of the parties, and bind them to that declaration, rather than, on the principle of confidentiality. The Privy Council, expressed reservations about the desirability or merit of adopting a duty of confidentiality, as an implied term of arbitration and then formulating exceptions, to which, such a duty, would be subject. It also stated, that, although commercial arbitrations are essentially private proceedings and, unlike litigation in the courts, do not place anything in the public domain, nevertheless, when it comes to the award, the same logic cannot be applied, since it might be necessary to refer to an award for an accounting or enforcement.

The AEGIS case, demonstrates that general principles of confidentiality are difficult to discern, and confidentiality agreements will be evaluated, having regard, to the circumstances in which they are made and to the basic principles and purposes of arbitration. However, it is doubtful, whether any legislated solution would be effective to resolve the issue of confidentiality, in all circumstances.[195]

It is concluded, that arbitral tribunals have no power to consolidate proceedings, if parties have not expressly opted for it, except in cases where earlier awards of a competent court could be used, to bind subsequent arbitrations. There are no set rules to determine such a usage or not, therefore general principles of law should be applied to determine the issue.[196]

4.3.2.2 USA

Conversely to the position, established by the majority of the case law in England, the predominant position, under American law, which was formulated by case law such as *Compania Espanola de Petroleos SA v Nereus Shipping SA*,[197] was that consolidation would be permitted and even encouraged in proper cases. In particular, American decisions, such as *Volt Info. Sciences v Board of Trustees*,[198] whereby a construction contract, between appellant and appellee, contained an agreement to arbitrate all disputes arising out of the contract, and, where the trial court, denied appellant's motion to compel arbitration, establish this trend.

However, in cases, such as *Government of UK v Boeing Co*,[199] the Second Circuit has held, that the aspect of the decision in *Compania Espanola de Petroleos SA v Nereus Shipping SA*[200] decision, is no good law and that, like in England,

[195]Thompson and Finn (2007, pp. 75–78).

[196]Uff and Noussia (2009, pp. 1428–1449).

[197]*Compania Espanola de Petroleos SA v Nereus Shipping SA*, 527 F2d 966 (2d Cir. 1975).

[198]*Volt Info. Sciences v Board of Trustees* (489 US 468 (1989)).

[199]*Government of UK v Boeing Co*, 998 F2d 68 (2d. 1993).

[200]*Compania Espanola de Petroleos SA v Nereus Shipping SA*, 527 F2d 966 (2d Cir. 1975).

consolidation cannot be ordered, in the absence of an agreement by the parties to arbitration.[201]

In *Weyerhaeuser Company v Western Seas Shipping Co*,[202] Weyerhaeuser appealed the district court's denial, of its petition to compel the consolidation of two maritime arbitrations into a single arbitration before five arbitrators. Weyerhaeuser, asserted that this Court had the power to compel consolidation, under the United States Arbitration Act, 9 U.S.C., sections 1–14, and under Fed.R.Civ.P. 81(a)(3) and 42(a).

The principal authority, relied upon by Weyerhaeuser for this proposition, was *Compania Espanola de Petroleos, S.A. v. Nereus Shipping, S.A.*[203] *Compania Espanola de Petroleos, S.A. v. Nereus Shipping, S.A.*,[204] involved an appeal from a district court order consolidating two arbitration proceedings – one between the owner of a ship and the ship's charterer and one between the owner and the charterer's guarantor. The Second Circuit, affirmed the district court order, relying on two grounds. First, the court held that all three parties had consented to consolidation. All three, had signed an addendum to the original charter party, to the effect that the guarantor would undertake all the charterer's duties in the event of the charterer's default. The court held that, since the original charter party imposed a duty to arbitrate, the addendum amounted to implicit consent to joint arbitration, in the event of a dispute. Second, the Second Circuit stated that, the liberal purposes of the Federal Arbitration Act clearly require that this act be interpreted so as to permit and even to encourage the consolidation of arbitration proceedings, in proper cases.

The 9th Circuit, insofar as *Compania Espanola de Petroleos, S.A. v Nereus Shipping, S.A.*[205] rested on the consent of the parties, distinguished the latter case from *Weyerhaeuser Company v Western Seas Shipping Co*,[206] stated that it was clear that the parties in *Weyerhaeuser Company v Western Seas Shipping Co*[207] did not consent to joint arbitration, and, insofar as *Compania Espanola de Petroleos, S.A. v Nereus Shipping, S.A.*[208] held that federal courts may order consolidation in the absence of consent, declined to follow it.

In *Baesler v Cont'tal Grain Co*,[209] the 8th Circuit stated that consolidation of arbitral proceedings, absent a consent, is impossible, and agreed with the majority view that the Federal Arbitration Act precludes federal courts from ordering consolidation of arbitration proceedings. It was also stated, that the Supreme Court has explicitly rejected the assertion that the overriding goal of the Act is to

---

[201] *Government of UK v Boeing Co*, 998 F2d 68 (2d. 1993); See Collins (1995, pp. 324–326).

[202] *Weyerhaeuser Company v Western Seas Shipping Co* 743 F.2d 635 (9th Circ. 1984).

[203] *Compania Espanola de Petroleos, S.A. v. Nereus Shipping, S.A.*, 527 F.2d 966 (2d Cir.1975).

[204] *Compania Espanola de Petroleos, S.A. v. Nereus Shipping, S.A.*, 527 F.2d 966 (2d Cir.1975).

[205] *Compania Espanola de Petroleos, S.A. v. Nereus Shipping, S.A.*, 527 F.2d 966 (2d Cir.1975).

[206] *Weyerhaeuser Company v Western Seas Shipping Co*, 743 F.2d 635 (9th Circ. 1984).

[207] *Weyerhaeuser Company v Western Seas Shipping Co*, 743 F.2d 635 (9th Circ. 1984).

[208] *Compania Espanola de Petroleos, S.A. v. Nereus Shipping, S.A.*, 527 F.2d 966 (2d Cir.1975).

[209] *Baesler v Cont'tal Grain Co*, 900 F2d. 1193 (8th Cir. 1990).

promote the expeditious resolution of claims and has recognized the passage of the Act as being motivated, first and foremost, by a congressional desire to enforce agreements into which parties had entered. In accordance with this purpose, the court read the Federal Arbitration Act 1925, as requiring federal courts to enforce arbitration agreements, as they are written, and, accordingly, it also held that absent a provision in an arbitration agreement authorizing consolidation, a district court, is without power to consolidate arbitration proceedings.

In *Protective Life Ins. Corp. v Lincoln Nat'l Life Ins. Corp. v. Lincoln Nat'l Life Ins. Corp.*,[210] Lincoln National Life Insurance Company, appealed the district court's grant of summary judgment and its order consolidating the arbitration of Lincoln's dispute with appellee Protective Life Insurance Company and the arbitration of claims between Protective and a third party, Munich American Reassurance Company. On the issue, whether a district court may consolidate arbitration proceedings, if the parties have not provided for consolidation in their arbitration agreements, the 11th Circuit ruled that it may not.

In *Government of the United Kingdom of Great Britain v Boeing Co*, ("Boeing")[211] the 2nd Circuit reversed the district courts' order for consolidation of arbitration proceedings, arising from separate agreements to arbitrate, absent the parties' agreement to allow such consolidation and stated that the courts need to enforce arbitration contracts, in accordance with the arbitration agreement terms.

In *American Centennial Ins Co v National Casualty Co*,[212] the 6th Circuit concluded that, in the absence of a provision for consolidation, it was without authority to circumvent the mandate of the Act that district courts are to direct parties "to proceed to arbitration in accordance with the terms of the agreement".[213]

Compania Espanola de Petroleos, S.A. v Nereus Shipping, S.A., ("Nereus")[214] is said to be the case that empowered federal courts to consolidate separate arbitral proceedings, even absent an agreement by the parties. The 4th and 1st Circuit, in cases like *Maxum Founds v Salus Corp.*[215]and *New England Energy Inc. v Keystone Shipping Co*,[216] are said to have followed the *Nereus Shipping*[217] ruling. However, as we note, *Boeing*[218] overruled *Nereus*[219] and since then, in general, the majority of the Circuits prohibit non consented consolidation, in effort to support confidentiality in arbitration and, at the same time, to promote the principle of party autonomy.

[210]*Protective Life Ins. Corp. v. Lincoln Nat'l Life Ins. Corp. v. Lincoln Nat'l Life Ins. Corp.*, 873 F.2d 281 (11th Cir. 1989).

[211]*Government of the United Kingdom of Great Britain v Boeing Co*, 998 F2d. 68 (2d Cir. 1993).

[212]*American Centennial Ins Co v National Casualty Co*, 951 F2d 107, (6th Cir. 1991).

[213]9 U.S.C. § 4, 761 F.Supp. 472.

[214]*Compania Espanola de Petroleos, S.A. v. Nereus Shipping, S.A.*, 527 F.2d 966 (2d Cir.1975).

[215]*Maxum Founds v Salus Corp.* 817 F2d. 1086 (4th Cir. 1987).

[216]*New England Energy Inc. v Keystone Shipping Co*, 855 F2d I, 4 (1st Cir. 1989).

[217]*Compania Espanola de Petroleos, S.A. v. Nereus Shipping, S.A.*, 527 F.2d 966 (2d Cir.1975).

[218]*Government of the United Kingdom of Great Britain v Boeing Co*, 998 F2d. 68 (2d Cir. 1993).

[219]*Compania Espanola de Petroleos, S.A. v. Nereus Shipping, S.A.*, 527 F.2d 966 (2d Cir.1975).

4.3.2.3 France

In France the doctrine of confidentiality in arbitration has always retained a strong and dominant position. However, late case law, such as *Nafimco v Foster Wheeler Trading Company AG*,[220] exemplifies the change of attitude of the French judiciary.

In *Nafimco v Foster Wheeler Trading Company AG*,[221] it was stated, that the party claiming breach of a confidentiality agreement, need prove, the existence of such a duty to observe confidentiality in arbitration, under French law, as well as that the parties, may, have not chosen to renounce such an obligation.

4.3.2.4 Germany

In Germany, as stated above, arbitration proceedings are not public. Although it is clear that, the arbitrators themselves are subject to a duty of confidentiality[222] and may not disclose the award or details thereof without the agreement of the parties, there is a debated conflict of academic opinions on the matter of the obligation of the parties themselves to treat the arbitration confidential. Thus, the academic scholar community is divided, in that, on the one hand, it is supported that absent an express confidentiality clause there is no general duty of confidentiality in arbitration proceedings; whereas, on the other hand, it is supported that the arbitration agreement, *per se*, can be interpreted as implying a duty of confidentiality.[223] Moreover, although, neither the German Arbitration Law, nor the UNCITRAL Model Law, contain any provision, on the confidentiality of arbitral proceedings, it is, nevertheless, widely recognised that all parties, involved in an arbitration process, are under an implied obligation to maintain the confidentiality of arbitral proceedings.

In relation to the arbitration proceedings *per se*, representative case law has shown, that the obligation to preserve confidentiality is maintained, only so far as the proceedings themselves are concerned and so long as they last and that it does not extend beyond them.

In a decision of the OLG Karlsruhe Court of 27.11.2007,[224] it was stated that although the parties had committed themselves to secrecy and preservation of confidentiality, nevertheless an offense of this obligation, in relation to a claim of the parties for damages after the conclusion of the contract, was not to be justified as such, firstly because the parties had committed themselves to the observation of confidentiality, only in relation to "operational information", which did not include the current disclosure of information in relation to the claim for damages; and, secondly, because, in any case, the said obligation to preserve confidentiality had,

[220] *Nafimco v Foster Wheeler Trading Company AG*, Cour d'Appel de Paris, 22.01.2004.

[221] *Nafimco v Foster Wheeler Trading Company AG*, Cour d'Appel de Paris, 22.01.2004.

[222] Lachmann (2002, p. 42).

[223] Lachmann (2002, p. 44); Contrast with Raeschke-Kessler et al. (1995, p. 141); Global Legal Group (2007, Chap. 25 – Germany).

[224] OLG Karlsruhe, Beschl. v.27.11.07 – Case 8 U 164/06.

as per clause 9 of the contract, become void after the conclusion of the latter, insofar, as it regarded the supply of a thermal select plant, and upon the end of the contract.

The court, in adjudicating, has supported the scholarly view which states that, absent an express confidentiality clause, there is no general duty of confidentiality in arbitration proceedings. Thus, confidentiality was not agreed to extend to the time point of the arbitration proceedings, as there was no express stipulation over it, On the contrary, there was a stipulation in the contract, with regards to the exact extent and scope of the duty to observe confidentiality, as well as with regards to the time point of its termination, i.e. the time of the conclusion of the said contract.

4.3.2.5 Tentative Observations

There is much to be said, for allowing consolidated arbitration proceedings or ordering concurrent hearings, when the circumstances of the case allow so. Formulating a proposition, regarding confidentiality, that would be applicable, in all cases, is difficult, and courts should be wise, not to attempt such a task. Perhaps, a rule disallowing the use of arbitral material, without the consent of parties or without the court's permission, provides a workable solution.

Thus, it is respectfully suggested that, the English approach which differentiates between the award and reasons, on the one hand, and the raw materials used in the arbitration, on the other hand, achieves the right balance, between the conflicting interests of the three parties involved, as it permits the use of the former for a cause of action against or defending a claim, brought by a third party, without the need of an application to the court, whilst prohibiting the use of the material, in question, for purposes unconnected with the arbitration. It is also suggested that, unless, and until, the court determines, on an application made to it, that the ends of justice require the confidentiality of the documents be overridden, in the case before it.[225]

4.3.3 Confidentiality in Arbitration Proceedings in Relation to Discovery (Disclosure) of Documents and Other Evidence During the Arbitral Process

4.3.3.1 England

In English civil litigation, there is a long-standing tradition of restraining parties from making any use of documents disclosed during the process of discovery, now called disclosure, for any purpose other than use in the proceedings, in which the documents were disclosed.[226]

---

[225]Collins (1995, pp. 335–336).

[226]Uff and Noussia (2009, pp. 1428–1449).

In *Alterskye v Scott*[227] Jenkins L.J. referred to: "...the implied undertaking, under which a party obtaining discovery is, not to use documents for any collateral or ulterior purpose." This dictum was very broadly construed in later cases so that, for example in *Distillers Co (Biochemicals) Ltd v Times Newspapers Ltd*,[228] it was held that there was an absolute prohibition upon using such documents, in any, subsequent, or parallel, litigation, not involving the same parties.[229]

The existence of the duty of confidentiality, in relation to documents disclosed on discovery in arbitral proceedings, was judicially established in *Dolling-Baker v Merrett*.[230] Clearly, the efficacy of a private arbitration will be damaged, even defeated, if proceedings in the arbitration are made public by the disclosure of documents relating to the arbitration. It was on this basis, that the Court of Appeal, in *Dolling-Baker v Merrett*[231] restrained a party to an arbitration from disclosing on discovery in a subsequent action documents, relating to the arbitration.[232]

In *Dolling-Baker v Merrett*,[233] the plaintiff claimed against the defendants money due, under a policy of reinsurance under which the first defendant was one of the insurers and the second defendants were the placing brokers. On the plaintiff's application, the judge ordered that the first defendant, make a list of all documents relating to a similar policy disclosed in an arbitration, where the defendants were in the same position as insurer and placing broker. The first defendant, applied for an injunction, restraining, the second defendants, from disclosing the documents. The application was refused, but, on appeal, the Court of Appeal held that the documents, ordered to be discovered, were not relevant to the issues in the action, and that producing the documents, was not necessary for disposing fairly of the case. The Court stated, obiter, that there existed an implied

[227] *Alterskye v Scott* [1948] 1 All E.R. 469, 470.

[228] *Distillers Co (Biochemicals) Ltd v Times Newspapers Ltd* [1974] 3 W.L.R. 728.

[229] In *Distillers Co. (Biochemicals) Ltd. v Times Newspapers Ltd* [1974] 3 W.L.R. 728, those who disclosed documents on discovery, were entitled to the court's protection, against any use of the documents, otherwise than in the action in which they were disclosed, and, such protection, was held to extend to prevent the use of the documents by any person into whose hands they came, unless that use was directly connected with the action in which they were produced. It was, further, held that, it was in the public interest that documents, disclosed on discovery, should not be permitted to be put to an improper use. The position is, now, governed by CPR r. 31.22, which provides that a party, to whom a document has been disclosed, may use the document, only for the purpose of the proceedings in which it is disclosed, except, where: (a) the document has been read to or by the court, or referred to, at a hearing which has been held in public; (b) the court gives permission; or (c) the party who disclosed the document and the person to whom the document belongs agree. However, the court may make an order, restricting or prohibiting the use of a document which has been disclosed, even where the document has been read to, or by, the court, or referred to, at a hearing which has been held in public. In view of this history, it is not, therefore, surprising to find that similar principles to those set out by Jenkins L.J. were applied to documents disclosed in arbitral proceedings; Uff and Noussia (2009, pp. 1428–1449).

[230] *Dolling-Baker v Merrett* [1991] 2 All E.R. 890.

[231] *Dolling-Baker v Merrett* [1991] 2 All ER 891.

[232] Robb (2004).

[233] *Dolling-Baker v Merrett* [1991] 2 All ER 891.

confidentiality element, within the very nature of an arbitration agreement. The Court, did not define the extent of the obligation to preserve confidentiality, but, implied that the implied duty to observe confidentiality, covers all documents and materials used in the arbitration proceeding, and, in the award rendered, and that it may be subject to certain exceptions, in cases where disclosure and inspection is necessary for the fair disposal of the action.[234] Parker LJ, emphasised that the obligation arose out of the nature of arbitration itself, and that the fact that a document is used in an arbitration does not confer on it any confidentiality or privilege, which can be relied upon in subsequent proceedings, but, in considering a question as to production of documents or discovery by list or affidavit, the court must nevertheless have regard to the obligation. However, Parker LJ concluded that, if the court is satisfied that, despite the implied obligation, discovery and inspection are necessary for the fair disposal of the action, nevertheless, discovery, and inspection, must take place, though other means of achieving a similar result should be taken into account.[235]

Following *Dolling-Baker v Merrett*,[236] the decisions in *Hassneh Insurance Co. of Israel v Mew*,[237] *Insurance Co v Lloyd's Syndicate*[238] and in *Ali Shipping Corporation v Shipyard Trogir*,[239] reaffirmed the existence of an implied duty of confidentiality, but recognised that it was subject to exceptions.

In *Insurance Co. v Lloyd's Syndicate*,[240] it was stated that, although anyone acquiring confidential information arising from the arbitration would also be subject under English law to the same self-duties of confidentiality as the party to the arbitration, nevertheless those duties were not self-evident, and that English judicial authorities,[241] have demonstrated, that the nature and the extent of the duty of confidentiality in arbitration, are by no means fully chartered but subject to certain limitations and exceptions.

Hassneh Insurance Co of Israel v Stuart J Mew,[242] anticipated the policy, adopted by CPR r. 31.22, that any disclosed documents may not be used, except in the proceedings in which they are disclosed, subject to exceptions. In this case, the defendant was reinsured by the plaintiffs, under various reinsurance contracts, between 1979 and 1984. When disputes arose, the defendant commenced an arbitration claiming to recover under the policies. An interim award was rendered,

---

[234]Brown (2001, p. 977); Uff and Noussia (2009, pp. 1428–1449).

[235]Robb (2004).

[236]*Dolling-Baker v Merrett* [1991] 2 All E.R. 890.

[237]*Hassneh Insurance Co. of Israel v Mew* [1993] 2 Lloyd's Rep. 243.

[238]*Insurance Co v Lloyd's Syndicate* [1995] 1 Lloyd's Rep. 272.

[239]*Ali Shipping Corporation v Shipyard Trogir* [1998] 1 Lloyd's Rep. 643.

[240]*Insurance Company v Lloyd's Syndicate*, and in *Hyundai Engineering v Active Building & Civil Construction (Pte) Limited (in liquidation)*, unreported, Judgment of 9 March 1994.

[241]Such as *The Eastern Saga* [1998] 2 Lloyd's Rep 373, *Dolling-Baker v Merrett* [1990] 1 WLR 1205 and *Hassneh Insurance Co. of Israel v Mew* [1993] 2 Lloyd's Rep. 243.

[242]*Hassneh Insurance Co of Israel v Stuart J Mew* [1993] 2 Lloyd's Rep 243.

and the reassured wished to proceed against the placing broker, for negligence and breach of duty as placing broker. The reassured wanted to disclose to the broker the interim award and the reasoning, and also, to have other documents in the arbitration disclosed for possible future use. The plaintiffs agreed for the award and for the reasoning, insofar as it concerned the placing broker, to be disclosed, but they objected to the disclosure of the whole of the reasons or any other documents. The defendant, asked for leave to disclose, and, contended that, the duty of confidence was lifted, in cases where disclosure to a third party was reasonable and necessary for a party's own interest. Colman J., held that there was good reason for leave to disclose, in the following cases: firstly, if it was reasonably necessary to do so, for the establishment by the defendant of his causes of action against the placing broker; secondly, if the documents, such as pleadings, witness statements, disclosed documents in the arbitration and transcripts, were subject to a duty of confidentiality, as these documents were merely the materials which were used to give rise to the award, which defined the rights and obligations of the parties to the arbitration. Accordingly, it was held that the qualification to the duty of confidentiality, based on the reasonable necessity for the protection of an arbitrating party's rights against a third party, could not be expected to apply to them, but, on the contrary, it would be the final determination of rights, expressed in the award, which was pertinent as against third parties and not the raw materials for that determination.[243] Hence, in *Hassneh Insurance Co. of Israel v Mew*,[244] the court went a step further, in recognising that exceptions to confidentiality may exist, in order to facilitate subsequent proceedings.[245]

Before moving on to discuss the case of *Ali Shipping Corporation v Shipyard Trogir*,[246] in relation to confidentiality in arbitration proceedings in terms of discovery of documents and other evidence during the arbitral process, it is essential that we discuss two decisions of courts, from the Australian and the Swedish jurisdictions, both of which legal systems are not covered in terms of the present monograph, i.e. the decision of the High Court of Australia, in *Esso Australia Resources Ltd v Plowman*,[247] and the decision, of the Swedish Supreme Court, in *Bulgarian Foreign Trade Bank Ltd. v A.L. Trade Finance Inc.*,[248] because their illustration will not only contrast but also further enhance our current discussion.

The opinion, of the High Court of Australia, in *Esso/BHP v Plowman*,[249] crashed like a giant wave, a veritable indeed Australian tsunami, on the shores of other

---

[243] Robb (2004).

[244] *Hassneh Insurance Co. of Israel v Mew* [1993] 2 Lloyd's Rep. 243.

[245] Uff and Noussia (2009, pp. 1428–1449).

[246] *Ali Shipping Corporation v Shipyard Trogir* [1998] 2 All ER 136.

[247] *Esso Australia Resources Ltd v Plowman (Minister for Energy and Minerals)* (1995) 128 A.L. R. 391.

[248] *Bulgarian Foreign Trade Bank Ltd. v. A.L. Trade Finance Inc.*, Judgment of October 27, 2000, Swedish Supreme Court.

[249] *Esso/BHP v Plowman* (1995) 128 A.L.R. 391, High Court of Australia.

jurisdictions wordwide, because, in ruling that, distinct from privacy, confidentiality was not an essential attribute of the arbitral process, it caused an uproar in the world of international commercial arbitration.

The case, involved a dispute between the company, namely Esso, and the Australian Minister for Energy and Minerals. Esso, had commenced arbitration proceedings against two Australian public utility companies. The Australian Minister for Energy and Minerals, contended that, emanating from his public duty, to supervise public utilities and the chargeable rates for oil supplies, was also his right to inspect documents produced for the arbitration. Esso argued, that the documents were confidential, but the Ministry did not contend with this opinion.

The High Court of Australia, ruled that the documents were not covered by the veil of confidentiality. In ruling so, the High Court of Australia, largely agreed with the ruling on appeal, which had been issued by the Supreme Court of Victoria, and, which stated, that contrary to the long supported view by English courts, a duty of confidence, did not emanate from an implied right of privacy. Thus, the High Court of Australia, found that confidentiality, is not part of the inherent nature of the arbitration contract, and of the relationship thereby established, and that, even in cases where the duty to confidentiality exists, it is nevertheless subject to exceptions, such as the "public interest exception" which was present in the case before it.[250]

The rationale, for the approach of the High Court in *Esso/BHP v Plowman*[251], was, essentially, that confidentiality is unachievable, because no obligation of confidentiality attaches to witnesses, and, secondly, because there are various ways in which an award may come before a court, involving disclosure to the court by a party to the arbitration and publication of the court proceedings. In other words, it would seem futile to try to impose an obligation of confidence, which, in reality, cannot be enforced.

However, such a simplistic recitation of the decision in *Esso/BHP v Plowman*,[252] is to misstate the position. The consequence of the Australian approach, is not that no confidentiality attaches to anything produced in the course of arbitration. The High Court, was clear that documents produced by a party compulsorily, pursuant to a direction of the arbitrator, would attract the same confidentiality that would attach to them, if they were litigating their dispute, subject only to the legitimate interest of the public, in obtaining information about the affairs of public authorities.[253]

The decision of the High Court in Australia in *Esso Australia Resources Ltd v. Plowman*,[254] reversed prior practices, according to which confidentiality was

---

[250]Brown (2001, pp. 978–980).

[251]*Esso/BHP v Plowman* (1995) 128 A.L.R. 391, High Court of Australia.

[252]*Esso/BHP v Plowman* (1995) 128 A.L.R. 391, High Court of Australia.

[253]*Esso Australia Resources Ltd v Plowman* (1995) 183 CLR 10, 33 per Mason CJ, 47 per Toohey J.

[254]*Esso Australia Resources Ltd and others v. The Honourable Sidney James Plowman and others (1995)* 183 C.L.R. 10.

generally preserved, either because of an implied duty or due to the parties' express agreement. It caused a tremor, in the international arbitration world, by holding that there was no implied or imposed duty of confidentiality in arbitration.[255]

Following *Esso/BHP v Plowman*,[256] other, more recent, case law, denotes that the trend, established by the High Court of Australia, in *Esso/BHP v Plowman*,[257] does not necessarily form the rule, but more the exception, of the Australian attitude, towards confidentiality in arbitration.[258]

The Swedish Arbitration Act 1999, provides no rules with regard to confidentiality, for parties and arbitrators, and neither do the ICC Rules, or the SCC Rules. Notably, the Arbitration Institute of the Stockholm Chamber of Commerce, does not itself disclose any information regarding proceedings being under their supervision. Yet, the general perception in Sweden, as well as other jurisdictions, is, nevertheless, that some kind of obligation of confidentiality exists. Especially, since confidentiality is one of the common arguments, for using arbitration, as opposed to general and public court proceedings, in the first place.

---

[255] Uff and Noussia (2009, pp. 1428–1449).

[256] *Esso/BHP v Plowman* (1995) 128 A.L.R. 391, High Court of Australia.

[257] *Esso/BHP v Plowman* (1995) 128 A.L.R. 391, High Court of Australia.

[258] In *Transfeld Philippines Inc & Ors v Pacific Hydro Ltd & Ors [2006] VSC 175*, the Supreme Court of Victoria was asked, *inter alia*, to order preliminary discovery of certain documents which, it was alleged by Transfield, might show that there had been judicial or governmental impropriety in proceedings which had been conducted in the Philippines. The question before Hollingworth J., was whether, certain documents, which had been obtained during the course of the first arbitral proceedings, could form part of the evidence to support Transfield's application for preliminary discovery. Transfield, stated that it should be excused, from any implied undertaking not to use the documents, other than for the purposes of the arbitration. This, leads us to ask the following: can a party be excused, from an implied undertaking, not to use the documents for ulterior purposes and, what power, if any, did the Supreme Court of Victoria have to release a party from the undertaking? In order to be released from an undertaking, special circumstances are required, and it must be demonstrated that the release would not cause injustice to the party who produced the document. The discretion, to relieve a party from the undertaking, is one to be exercised sparingly, even where there might be special circumstances. *Prima facie*, it was arguable, that, the Victorian Supreme Court would have the power to release Transfield, from the undertakings, given in relation to the subpoenaed documents, at least. However, the arbitration agreement, required that the arbitration be conducted in Singapore, on ICC Terms. It was, therefore, subject to Singaporean procedural law. The matter had ended up before the Victorian Supreme Court, because, for the parties' convenience, some of the arbitral hearings had been held in Melbourne. Most significantly, the parties had agreed that there would be no right to make any application for interlocutory orders to the Court, in relation to arbitration proceedings. Hollingworth J., was therefore content, to dismiss Transfield's application to be released, from the undertaking, on the basis that it was brought in breach of the arbitration agreement. It was thought, also, that what had to be prevented was any steps, that would render the judicial proceedings inefficacious. It is not clear, how, releasing one party from an obligation, to keep certain documents confidential, could render the Court process inefficacious. The court, thought that the application, in the case involved, simply did not fall within this rationale, and was, thus, reluctant to recognise the existence of a judicial inherent jurisdiction, to release a party, such as Transfield, from the implied undertaking given in separate arbitral proceedings; Derrington (2007, pp. 188–190).

In *Bulgarian Foreign Trade Bank Ltd. v A.L. Trade Finance Inc*,[259] the Supreme Court ruled that a party, in arbitration proceedings governed by Swedish law, is not bound by confidentiality, unless the parties have entered into a specific agreement to that effect. The dispute occurred after a debt had been transferred to a company from an Austrian creditor. The agreement, in question, was entered into between the Austrian creditor and a Bulgarian Bank. The Bulgarian Bank, never consented to the transfer of the debt. Based on the lack of consent, the Bulgarian Bank refused to pay the outstanding and transferred debt. The company initiated arbitration proceedings, as provided in the agreement, which also stipulated that the ECE-rules were to apply to the proceedings, and the proceedings were to be held in Stockholm, and that Austrian law was to apply. A decision of the tribunal, was subsequently sent to Mealey's by a representative of the company. The chairman of the tribunal was informed of the disclosure, while the arbitration proceedings continued. Later on, the chairman of the tribunal, attended a dinner party, where, he disclosed information about the decision, to a Justice of the Supreme Court, who was working on a case which also involved the transfer of rights in an agreement to a third party. The Supreme Court Judge, later, used the decision, and, in the subsequent judgement, reference was made to the published article in Mealey's. In the arbitration proceedings, the Bulgarian Bank claimed revocation of the arbitration agreement, and disqualification of the Chairman of the Tribunal. The Bulgarian Bank, claimed that the disclosure of the decision, by the company and by the Chairman, rendered the arbitration agreement null and void. The Tribunal, dismissed this claim and later issued its award.

The Svea Court of Appeals, held that the ECE-rules, article 29, applied to oral proceedings before a tribunal, but not to written documents, or to awards, or decisions given by a tribunal. Given the nature of the information that had been disclosed, through the publication of the decision, the Svea Court of Appeal held, that it did not constitute a material breach of the parties' mutual duty of loyalty, argued by the Bulgarian Bank, which would have given the Bulgarian Bank the right to revoke the agreement.

On appeal, the Supreme Court tested only the issue of whether the company's disclosure had given the Bulgarian Bank the right to revoke the agreement, rendering the award invalid. Firstly, the Supreme Court established that a judgment, in favour of the Bulgarian Bank, would only be possible, if the company had been bound by an obligation in the agreement to adhere to confidentiality. It was established, that there was no such explicit obligation, in this respect, in the agreement, and that Swedish law did not provide a basis for any general and legally sanctioned undertaking, to this effect. It was further established, that the ECE-rules only applied to oral proceedings before a tribunal, and not to the dispute as a whole. The Supreme Court, also emphasised that, in an arbitration dispute, the nature of the information dealt with, varies to a great extent, and, therefore, that a disclosure by

[259] *Bulgarian Foreign Trade Bank Ltd. v A.L. Trade Finance Inc.*, Judgment of October 27, 2000, Swedish Supreme Court.

a party may lead to different considerations, depending on the nature of the information in question.

The Supreme Court, therefore, concluded that a disclosure may constitute a breach under the specific rules of the Swedish Trade Secrets Act, i.e. disclosure of specific information being kept secret by an entrepreneur. It also went on, and stressed that the private character of arbitration proceedings implies that third parties do not have the right, to attend hearings, or, obtain submissions, or petitions of the parties. However, it remarked, that, notably, this did not hinder disclosure of information about the arbitration proceedings. Thus, the Supreme Court seems to have given great weight, to the fact that the Swedish Arbitration Act of 1999 did not contain any rules on confidentiality.

The Supreme Court, also embarked on a comparative search for a common foreign legal position on this subject. For example, it was noted that the general opinion under the laws of England, obliged the parties to adhere to confidentiality. Specific reference was also made to the Australian case of *Esso Australia Resources Ltd v Plowman*,[260] where the High Court ruled in favour of the opposite position.

In conclusion, the Supreme Court found no international consensus, that could enlighten the position of the Swedish law, on the subject. The Supreme Court unanimously ruled that a party, in arbitration proceedings, governed by Swedish law, could not be bound by confidentiality, absent a specific agreement to this effect. The company's disclosure, in Mealey's, therefore, did not constitute a material breach of the agreement, giving the Bulgarian Bank the right to revoke it.[261]

The Swedish Supreme Court, by holding, in *Trade Finance Inc v Bulgarian Foreign Trade Bank Ltd*,[262] that there is no implied duty of confidentiality in private arbitrations, that the disclosure of the outcome of an arbitration proceeding, is not forbidden, and that Swedish law does not make arbitration proceedings secret, unless the parties contract for secrecy, received widespread attention, because of the dramatic circumstances and ramifications that the ruling imposed. Accordingly, there are only two ways to ensure the confidentiality of arbitration proceedings under Swedish law, i.e. expressly contract for it, or, to adopt arbitration rules, that expressly provide for it.[263]

Thus, it is accepted that, the myth, about the duty of confidentiality in arbitration, fatally wounded in 1995 by the Australian High Court, has now been laid to rest, at least in Sweden.

The Swedish Supreme Court, has accepted that arbitral proceedings will generally be conducted in private, and the parties are expected to treat the information surrounding the arbitration with the appropriate discretion. However, unless the

---

[260] *Esso Australia Resources Ltd v Plowman (Minister for Energy and Minerals)* (1995) 128 A.L. R. 391.

[261] The award was deemed valid, and the appeal was dismissed; See *Comment on Arbitration and Confidentiality*, Transnational Dispute Management, Volume I, Issue 02 – May 2004.

[262] *Trade Finance Inc v Bulgarian Foreign Trade Bank Ltd* Case No Y 1092-98, SVEA Court of Appeal.

[263] Sarles (2002, pp. 13–14).

parties have expressly provided that this information is to remain confidential, there is no implied legal duty of confidentiality. This position, is to be contrasted, with that of the English courts.

In practice, the conclusion, to be drawn from the Supreme Court's decision is that parties must draft their arbitration clauses, with more care, if they wish to retain confidentiality in relation to the arbitration and the information which is disclosed during the arbitral proceedings. Ideally, they should expressly state that the proceedings and all documentation are to be confidential; alternatively, they might opt for institutional rules, which include such a duty of confidentiality, and this is a matter which the arbitral institutions should bring to the attention of the parties.

It should be noted that a contract, containing a general confidentiality clause which makes no particular reference to arbitration, may not be sufficient for these purposes. What is needed, is a clause which states expressly, not only that the arbitral proceedings will be private, but, also, that all documents, evidence, the award and possibly the very existence of the arbitration, shall be treated as confidential. Any disclosure will, only, be made, if required by law or by a competent regulatory body. To avoid such a drastic consequence, as repudiation of the arbitration agreement, the clause would also need to address the sanctions to follow, in case of breach. However, parties will not always include such an elaborate arbitration clause, in their contracts. At that time, parties are often not particularly inclined to go into details about the seemingly unlikely event that they will end up in dispute.

The parties might agree on procedural issues, such as confidentiality when the dispute has arisen, but the more realistic solution will be for the arbitral institutions to continue to develop and promote confidentiality rules, which will apply to the arbitrations conducted, under their respective auspices. At least, as regards institutional arbitrations, this would take things in arbitration back to the point they had been we were before 1995, i.e. prior to the decisions in *Bulgarian Foreign Trade Bank Ltd. v A.L. Trade Finance Inc.*[264] and in *Esso Australia Resources Ltd v Plowman*,[265] and would establish and define confidentiality, as a fundamental principle of (institutional) international commercial arbitration.[266]

Having discussed *Esso Australia Resources Ltd v Plowman*[267] and *Trade Finance Inc v Bulgarian Foreign Trade Bank Ltd*,[268] we turn on to consider the case of *Ali Shipping Corporation v Shipyard Trogir*,[269] in relation to confidentiality

[264] *Bulgarian Foreign Trade Bank Ltd. v. A.L. Trade Finance Inc.*, Judgment of October 27, 2000, Swedish Supreme Court.

[265] *Esso Australia Resources Ltd v Plowman (Minister for Energy and Minerals)* (1995) 128 A.L. R. 391.

[266] Bagner (2001, pp. 247–249).

[267] *Esso Australia Resources Ltd v Plowman (Minister for Energy and Minerals)* (1995) 128 A.L. R. 391.

[268] *Trade Finance Inc v Bulgarian Foreign Trade Bank Ltd* Case No Y 1092-98, SVEA Court of Appeal.

[269] *Ali Shipping Corporation v Shipyard Trogir* [1998] 2 All ER 136.

in arbitration proceedings, in terms of discovery of documents and other evidence during the arbitral process.

In *Ali Shipping Corporation v Shipyard Trogir*,[270] the Court of Appeal applied the reasoning of the Court of Appeal in *Dolling-Baker v Merrett*.[271] Following a dispute, between the claimants and the defendants, arising out of a shipbuilding contract, an arbitration award was made in favour of the claimants. Subsequently, a further dispute arose, between the defendants and three other companies in the same corporate group as the claimant. That dispute also went to arbitration. The defendants, wished to rely in the second arbitration on certain materials, generated in the course of the first arbitration, in support of the plea of issue estoppel. The claimant applied and obtained an *ex parte* injunction, restraining the defendants from doing so, on the basis that use of the material would amount to a breach of the defendant's implied obligation of confidentiality in respect of the first arbitration.[272]

The court, had to establish, whether the injunction should be lifted. The ultimate outcome, became even more significant, due to the following facts: first, Ali Shipping, Lavender Shipping, Leeward Shipping and Leman Navigation, were all ship-owning companies 100% owned by the same parent company, i.e. Greenwich Holdings, which was itself owned by a single individual; second, Ali Shipping and its three sister companies, Lavender Shipping, Leeward Shipping and Leman Navigation, all shared the same lawyers; third, all four ship-building contracts, in dispute, had been negotiated by the same people; fourth, all four sister companies had the same personnel; fifth, Shipyard Trogir wanted to disclose Ali Shipping's documents to Ali's own sister companies and not to strangers.[273]

It was held, that the implied term upon which confidentiality rested was implied, as a matter of law, and not as a matter of fact, and, accordingly, arose in the same way in every arbitration and not by reason of the presumed intentions of the parties.[274]

The Court of Appeal, held that the material from the previous arbitration could not be disclosed, as there existed a duty of confidentiality, and noted that confidentiality attaches as a matter of law and does not depend on the private nature of the material in question, nor on custom, usage or business efficacy. The court acknowledged that the boundaries, of the obligations of confidence, which thereby arise, have yet to be delineated, and that the manner to achieve this best would be to formulate exceptions of broad application, to be applied in individual cases, rather than seek to reconsider and adapt the general rule on each occasion, in light of the particular circumstances and presumed intention of the parties at the time of their original agreement.[275] The Court of Appeal, also, stated that the exceptions,

---

[270]*Ali Shipping Corporation v Shipyard Trogir* [1998] 2 All ER 136.

[271]*Dolling-Baker v Merrett* [1990] 1 W.L.R. 1205; (1990) 134 S.J. 806, CA.

[272]Sheppard (1998, p. N53).

[273]Brown (2001, pp. 978–980).

[274]Sheppard (1998, p. N53).

[275]Brown (2001, pp. 980–985).

applied, to the general rule of non-disclosure of pleadings, witness statements and notes of evidence, in an arbitration; and, that a party, unless it has the consent of the other party, to the arbitration, can only disclose other documents relating to an arbitration, either with the leave, or order of the court.[276]

There are several things, that we can learn, from the case of *Ali Shipping Corporation v Shipyard Trogir*.[277] First, it cannot be assumed that there is an accepted international practice with regard to the nature and scope of confidentiality in international arbitration.[278] Second, a corollary of this, is the necessity of legislatures and major arbitral bodies to deal with the question of confidentiality in international commercial arbitration.[279] Thirdly, implying the obligation of confidentiality, as a matter of law, may have the advantage of not requiring the detailed investigation of surrounding circumstances, inherent in implying a term, as a matter of business efficacy; but, that, doing so, leaves several questions unanswered, as to the nature of the contracts which will not be found to be of the relevant type for the implication of confidentiality, or as to the extent of the scope of the excepting circumstances.

Moreover, the Court of Appeal, considered that, in spite of it being possibly convenient, it was not reasonably necessary to admit the evidence in this case, and, that, such a test, was apt for argument.

However, because subsection 34(1) of the English Arbitration Act 1996 states, that it is for the tribunal to decide all evidential matters, it is uncertain, what effect any argument, over the admissibility of such evidence, will have upon the tribunal's perception of the case, where the evidence is persuasive but not reasonably necessary.[280]

Also, in relation to the admissibility of evidence and its supply, as evidence of breach of confidentiality, it is uncertain what the court would have decided, if the case did not concern an arbitrating party's rights, in relation to a third party, but, instead, was a case where a third party, which had obtained reasonably necessary evidence from an arbitration to which it was not a party.[281]

Thus, in *Ali Shipping v Shipyard Trogir*,[282] the English courts formulated a decision which gave teeth to confidentiality protection in international arbitration. Rather than rethinking, in the light of the *Esso Australia Resources Ltd v Plowman (Minister for Energy and Minerals)*[283] decision, their view on confidentiality as an

---

[276]Sheppard (1998, p. N53).

[277]*Ali Shipping Corporation v Shipyard Trogir* [1998] 2 All ER 136.

[278]We can see from the courts, of major common law countries, that there is stark contrast between different judicial approaches.

[279]Secomb (2000, p. 94).

[280]Sheppard (1998, p. N53).

[281]Sheppard (1998, p. N53).

[282]*Ali Shipping v Shipyard Trogir* [1998] 1 Lloyd's Rep 643.

[283]*Esso Australia Resources Ltd v Plowman (Minister for Energy and Minerals)* (1995) 128 A.L. R. 391.

implied-in-law obligation, the English courts, dug in their heels and fortified their position. It is arguable, however, whether the English courts, in *Ali Shipping v Shipyard Trogir*,[284] went too far, in allowing Ali Shipping to use confidentiality as a "strategy" in its dispute resolution battle, simply because there are also various implications to be considered, not only in considering exceptions to a confidentiality rule, but, also, in defining the latter in very wide terms.[285]

Glidepath BV and Others v Thompson and Others,[286] concerned an application by a non-party for copies of documents of a court record and the stay of court proceedings, pursuant to s. 9 of the English Arbitration Act 1996, and the applicant was not a party to the arbitration agreement.

More specifically, the applicant wished to have access to the particulars of claim, notices of application, for the freezing injunction, as well as the respective orders. He also, sought access to all other applications, made before the respective proceedings, which had been stayed, and to any witness statements, that had been filed with the court, as he claimed that the documents would assist him in his claim in an employment tribunal. The defendants, resisted the application. They argued that, all the classes of documents, covered by the application, were confidential to the parties to the arbitration; and, that the claimants had wrongly resorted to the courts, instead of referring the disputes to arbitration, and, that, accordingly, as regards a non-party, the court should protect the confidentiality of the arbitral procedure by declining to permit any of the documents to be disclosed. The applicant argued, that the court should not decline to permit access on the grounds of confidentiality. The confidentiality, which would otherwise attach to the documents had they been engendered in the course of an arbitration, had to yield to the public interest in access to them, in so far as they had been engendered prior to the stay of proceedings.

The issue that arose was, whether the court documents were subject to rules of confidentiality, which attach to arbitral proceedings, pursuant to CPR 5.4(5). It was held that, the permission of the court to a stranger to an arbitration and to proceedings, in which a section 9 of the English Arbitration Act 1996 stay had been applied for, to inspect either an application notice, under section 9 of the English Arbitration Act 1996, and any evidence on the court file or arbitration claim forms for ancillary relief, under section 44 of the English Arbitration Act 1996, and evidence appended on the court file, should not be granted, unless all the parties to the arbitration consented, or there was an overriding interest of justice. Further, it was stated, that, in case where the application under section 9 of the English Arbitration Act 1996 was preceded by an application for a freezing injunction, the exercise of the court's discretion upon an application by a stranger to the arbitration agreement or the proceedings to inspect those applications or the evidence supporting them on the court file, should similarly be exercised by reference to the principles of confidentiality attaching to arbitral proceedings.

---

[284] *Ali Shipping v Shipyard Trogir* [1998] 1 Lloyd's Rep 643.

[285] Brown (2001, pp. 980–985).

[286] *Glidepath BV and Others v Thompson and Others* [2005] 2 Lloyd's Rep. 549.

The court, also, stated that, on the facts of the present case, the applicant had failed to establish that, access to the documents, in question, was reasonably necessary to protect or establish the legal rights which he sought to enforce in the proceedings, before the employment tribunal, or, otherwise, in the interests of justice. Accordingly, the applicant had failed to bring himself within either of those threshold exceptions[287] to the confidentiality rule.

It was also stated that, following *Ali Shipping Corporation v Shipyard Trogir*,[288] arbitration proceedings, and materials produced in the course of them, are treated as confidential to the parties, and the arbitrator subject to certain exceptions, such as, disclosure by leave, or order of the court, which may be given when and to the extent that it is reasonably necessary to protect or establish the legal rights of a party to the arbitration by a third party, or, otherwise, in the interests of justice, and that there exists no authority for the proposition that a third party could, outside the ambit of disclosure by a party to an arbitration, obtain an order from the court, for access to materials, in an arbitration to which he is not a party, so as to deploy them, as evidence, in other proceedings in which he would be a party.

Most recently, in *Emmott v Michael Wilson & Partners Ltd*[289] the issue, for the court to decide, was whether, a party to an arbitration, could disclose documents, generated in that arbitration, in foreign litigation.

The Claimant company (MWP), was incorporated in the British Virgin Islands and provided legal services in Kazakhstan. MWP, alleged that, Mr John Emmott, one of its employed lawyers, was trying to divert business from it in breach of contract and of trust, and commenced arbitration in England, pursuant to an arbitration clause in Mr Emmott's employment agreement. It also initiated simultaneous court proceedings, arising out of similar facts, against other respondents, closely associated with Mr Emmott, in New South Wales and the British Virgin Islands. MWP, initially made allegations of conspiracy and fraud in the London arbitration, but, later, withdrew them. In contrast, the NSW proceedings, did not initially include claims of conspiracy and fraud, but, MWP later amended its claim to include them. Mr Emmot, alleged that MWP's case, in the arbitration, was materially inconsistent with its case in the BVI and NSW proceedings, and that there was therefore a danger of the courts, in those proceedings, being misled. He applied to the court, in England, to be allowed to disclose certain documents, from the London arbitration, in the BVI and New South Wales proceedings.

Collins L.J., stated, in *Emmott v Michael Wilson & Partners Ltd*,[290] that, by applying *Ali Shipping Corp v Shipyard Trogir*,[291] which Flaux J. had accepted at first instance, the material was in principle confidential, but, that the confidentiality was subject to two possible exceptions, i.e. firstly where disclosure was reasonably

[287]*Ali Shipping Corporation v Shipyard Trogir* (CA) [1998] 1 Lloyd's Rep 643.

[288]*Ali Shipping Corporation v Shipyard Trogir* (CA) [1998] 1 Lloyd's Rep 643.

[289]*Emmott v Michael Wilson & Partners Ltd* [2008] EWCA Civ 184.

[290]*Emmott v Michael Wilson & Partners Ltd* [2008] EWCA Civ 184.

[291]*Ali Shipping Corp v Shipyard Trogir* [1999] 1 W.L.R. 314.

necessary for the protection of the legitimate interests of an arbitrating party, including reasonably necessary for the establishment or protection of an arbitrating party's legal rights vis-à-vis a third party, in order to found a cause of action against a third party, or to defend a claim or counterclaim brought by the third party;[292] secondly, that, in the present case, there was no principled reason for the application of that exception, in relation to the proceedings in New South Wales and the Bahamas Virgin Islands, because Mr Emmott did not need the amended points of claim, or his own defence, to establish or protect his legal rights vis-à-vis a third party, in order to found a cause of action against that third party, or, to defend a claim or counterclaim brought by that third party,[293] as he was not a party to the proceedings in those jurisdictions, nor had, by definition, a claim been brought against him by a third party; and, thirdly, that, even if he were a party, it would be MWP, and not a third party, which was bringing the claim, in the case of an exception being emanated by public interest.[294]

The interests of justice required that the English court, so far as possible, should ensure that parties to London arbitrations should not seek to use the cloak of confidentiality, with a view to misleading or potentially misleading foreign courts, *a fortiori*, where the cases, which were being presented in the foreign courts, were essentially raising either the same or similar allegations, and were proceeding in parallel. In the case, the original points of claim in the London arbitration had been disclosed in New South Wales, but, the amended points of claim had not been disclosed. The order to disclose the documents was made, by Flaux J., in order to ensure that the British Virgin Islands court was not misled, at the time of the application, to appoint a receiver, over Temujin, into supposing that these allegations, of fraud and conspiracy, were still being pursued in London. However, Collins L.J., expressed the view[295] that, it was premature to authorise disclosure in the Bahamas proceedings, because all that had taken place in the Bahamas was a challenge to the jurisdiction by MWP, which failed at first instance, and an appeal was to be heard by the Bahamas Court of Appeal.

Furthermore, he stated that, the uncontroversial starting point in English law was that arbitration is a private process,[296] and cited *Russell v Russell*,[297] where Sir George Jessel M.R., had stated that:[298] "... as a rule, persons enter into [arbitration agreements], with the express view, of keeping their quarrels from the public eyes, and of avoiding that discussion in public, which must be a painful one, and which might be an injury even to the successful party to the litigation, and most surely would be to the unsuccessful...". He went on, to state that this same principle had

[292] *Hassneh Insurance Co of Israel v Mew* [1993] 2 Lloyd's Rep. 243.

[293] *Michael Wilson and Partners Ltd v Emmott* [2008] EWCA Civ 184 at 487.

[294] *London & Leeds Estates v Paribas (No.2)* [1995] 1 E.G.L.R. 102.

[295] *Michael Wilson and Partners Ltd v Emmott* [2008] EWCA Civ 184, § 30.

[296] *Michael Wilson and Partners Ltd v Emmott* [2008] EWCA Civ 184, 484.

[297] *Russell v Russell* (1880) 14 Ch D 471.

[298] *Russell v Russell* (1880) 14 Ch D 471 at 474.

underlined the decision in *The Eastern Saga*,[299] where it was expressed that it is implicit, in the concept of private arbitration, that strangers would be excluded from the hearing and conduct of the arbitration, and where Leggatt J. had stated[300] that "...the concept of private arbitrations, derive[d] simply from the fact that the parties ha[d] agreed to submit to arbitration particular disputes, arising between them and only between them.... and that it [was] implicit in this that strangers would be excluded from the hearing and conduct of the arbitration..." and, in addition, he noted that the DAC, in its Report on the Arbitration Bill 1996,[301] had stated (a) that privacy and confidentiality in arbitration, was not to be included, in the, then, forthcoming, legislative instrument, namely the Arbitration Act 1996, and that there was no doubt that the users of commercial arbitration in England place much importance on privacy and confidentiality which are considered essential features of English arbitration, i.e. important advantages of it, if compared with litigation, for commercial people;[302] (b) that confidentiality was considered as implicitly existing within the parties' choice to arbitrate in England;[303] (c) that it would be difficult to conceive of any greater threat to the success of English arbitration, than the removal of the general principles of confidentiality and privacy;[304] (d) that the privacy of arbitration is also underlined, by CPR r.62.10(3)(b) and by various institutional rules;[305] (e) that confidentiality, is expressly or implicitly protected by institutional rules;[306] (f) that the parties' wish, for confidentiality and privacy, outweighed the public interest in a public hearing;[307] and, (g) that any exceptions, to confidentiality, although undisputed, had to be resolved by the English courts, on an individual and pragmatic, case-by-case, basis.

---

299 *The Eastern Saga* [1984] 2 Lloyd's Rep. 373.

300 *The Eastern Saga* [1984] 2 Lloyd's Rep. 373, 379.

301 Mustill and Boyd (1989, Appendix 1).

302 See *Hassneh Insurance Co of Israel v Mew* [1993] 2 Lloyd's Rep. 243 at 246–247; *Department of Economic Policy and Development of the City of Moscow v Bankers Trust Co* [2004] EWCA Civ 314; [2005] Q.B. 207 at [2] and [30].

303 See *Esso Australia Resources Ltd v Plowman (Minister for Energy and Minerals)* (1995) 128 A. L.R. 391 at 398, per Mason C.J.

304 See §§ 10, 12, *Report on the Arbitration Bill 1996*, Departmental Advisory Committee, reprinted in Mustill and Boyd (1989, Appendix 1).

305 Thus, the privacy of the hearings is provided for, in art. 19(4) of the Rules of London Court of International Arbitration (LCIA); art. 21(3) of the rules of the Court of Arbitration of the International Chamber of Commerce (ICC); art. 53(c) of the arbitration rules of the World Intellectual Property Organisation (WIPO); and art. 25(4) of the UNCITRAL Rules. The confidentiality of the award is provided for by art. 30(1) of the LCIA Rules and also by the principle of non-publication of the award in art. 30(3); by art. 28(2) of the ICC Rules; by art. 75 of the WIPO Rules; and by art. 32(5) of the UNCITRAL Rules.

306 Article 30(1), 43(1) of the LCIA Rules, Art. 52, 73 of the WIPO Rules, § 31 of the UNCITRAL Notes on Organizing Arbitral Proceedings; See Redfern and Hunter (2004, Appendix D).

307 *Department of Economic Policy and Development of the City of Moscow v Bankers Trust Co* [2004] EWCA Civ 314.

He also pointed out that, even if a court decides that the "public interest" may outweigh the confidentiality of arbitration documents,[308] it does not necessarily follow that a party may voluntarily disclose documents to third parties, on the ground that it is in "the public interest", and that it does not follow, from the fact that a court refers to the possibility of an exception for the order of the court or leave of the court, in a case where it has the power to make the order or give leave,[309] that the court has a general and unlimited jurisdiction, to consider whether an exception to confidentiality exists and applies.

Finally, he summed up by stating[310] that, although exceptions, due to public interest, may occur,[311] nevertheless, the bulk of case law, of the last twenty years, has established that there is an obligation, implied by law and arising out of the nature of arbitration, on both parties, not to disclose or use, for any other purpose, any documents prepared for and used in the arbitration; or disclosed or produced in the course of the arbitration; or transcripts or notes of the evidence in the arbitration or the award; and not to disclose, in any other way, what evidence has been given by any witness in the arbitration. Further, that this obligation is not limited to commercially confidential information, in the traditional sense, but, in reality, is a substantive rule of arbitration law, reached through the device of an implied term, and that the limits of that obligation have been, so far, depicted via the judicial authorities, in the following cases: first, where there is consent, express or implied; second, where there is an order, or leave of the court, although courts have no general discretion to lift the obligation of confidentiality; third, where it is reasonably necessary, for the protection of the legitimate interests of an arbitrating party; and, fourth, where the interests of justice or public interest require disclosure.

With regards to the case of *Emmott v Michael Wilson & Partners Ltd*,[312] he stated that the judge, at first instance, was right, in the current unusual case circumstances, to authorise the disclosure of the amended points of claim, the skeleton argument, and the defence, in New South Wales and the British Virgin islands, on the basis of existing interests of justice required, which were justified as follows: i.e. firstly, because MWP had told the New South Wales court, in March 2007, that the underlying contentions in the New South Wales proceedings and the London arbitration were the same; secondly, because MWP had sought amendments in the New South Wales proceedings, in October 2007, in order to bring a "level of parity" to the proceedings in New South Wales, the British Virgin islands

308 *London & Leeds Estates v Paribas (No.2)* [1995] 1 E.G.L.R. 102.

309 *Dolling-Baker v Merrett* [1990] 1 W.L.R. 1205; (1990) 134 S.J. 806, CA; *Glidepath BV v Thompson* [2005] EWHC 818 (Comm); [2005] 2 Lloyd's Rep. 549; [2005] 1 C.L.C. 1090, QBD.

310 *Michael Wilson and Partners Ltd v Emmott* [2008] EWCA Civ 184 at 495.

311 *Department of Economic Policy and Development of the City of Moscow v Bankers Trust Co* [2004] EWCA Civ 314; [2005] Q.B. 207; *West Tankers Inc v Ras Riunione Adriatica di Sicurta* [2007] UKHL 4; [2007] 1 Lloyd's Rep. 391; *Lesotho Highlands Development Authority v Impregilo SpA* [2005] UKHL 43; [2006] 1 A.C. 221; *Westacre Investments Ltd v Jugo-Import-SPDR Holding Co Ltd* [2000] Q.B. 288.

312 *Emmott v Michael Wilson & Partners Ltd* [2008] EWCA Civ 184.

and the London arbitration; thirdly, because notwithstanding that claims of fraud, against Mr Emmott, had been dropped in the London arbitration, he was still said, in the New South Wales proceedings, to have been guilty of fraud; fourthly, because, without being informed of the London arbitration, there was a danger that the New South Wales court would be misled. Not least, he stated that the concentration, in the appeal in front of him, and the judgment, which was to follow, with regards to the limits of confidentiality in arbitration, should not obscure the fact that the overwhelming majority of arbitrations in England are conducted in private and with complete confidentiality.

This is a well-reasoned, and pragmatic decision of the Court of Appeal, bringing further clarity to the development of the law on confidentiality and privacy in English arbitrations.[313]

It seems indisputable, that English case law has helped judicially establish the duty to observe confidentiality in arbitration. Once it is accepted, that, unless the parties agree otherwise, strangers are to be excluded from arbitration, it would follow that the parties are under a duty, not to disclose to strangers what has occurred in the process of the arbitration.

To sum up, we conclude the following: the exceptions to the duty to observe confidentiality were initially established in *Dolling-Baker v Merrett*,[314] were, then, re-embraced, by English law, in *Hassneh Insurance Co of Israel v Mew*[315]and in *Ali Shipping Corp v Shipyard Trogir*,[316] and, finally, were extended in *Associated Electrics and Gas Insurance Ltd (Aegis) v. European Reinsurance Co of Zurich*[317] and in *John Foster Emmott v Michael Wilson & Partners Ltd.*[318]

The existence of an implied duty of confidentiality, in arbitration, makes it essential that confidentiality be provided for expressly. Its preservation is, in certain situations, crucial for business reasons. Nevertheless, even where this is the case, public interest, justice or other considerations, may require for it to be overruled.

As shown, in *John Foster Emmott v Michael Wilson & Partners Ltd*,[319] confidentiality should not be an obstacle, when parties wish to use an earlier award in later proceedings, in view of enhancing the court's powers to define the issues accurately. Thus, parties wanting to guarantee the preservation of confidentiality, should include detailed confidentiality clauses in the arbitral agreements. Courts, should also assist in the above respect, by refusing to enforce confidentiality agreements, only where the circumstances make it absolutely necessary.[320]

---

[313]Friel (2008, p. N48).

[314]*Dolling-Baker v Merrett* [1991] 2 All ER 890.

[315]*Hassneh Insurance Co of Israel v Mew* [1993] 2 Lloyd's Rep. 243 (QB).

[316]*Ali Shipping Corp v. Shipyard Trogir* [1998] 1 Lloyd's Rep. 643.

[317]*Associated Electrics and Gas Insurance Ltd (Aegis) v. European Reinsurance Co of Zurich* [2003] UKPC 11; [2003] 1 All E.R. (Comm) 253.

[318]*John Foster Emmott v Michael Wilson & Partners Ltd* [2008] EWCA Civ 184.

[319]*John Foster Emmott v Michael Wilson & Partners Ltd* [2008] EWCA Civ 184.

[320]Noussia (2009, pp. 1–37).

The decision in *John Foster Emmott v Michael Wilson & Partners Ltd*,[321] confirms England as an arbitration-friendly jurisdiction, which respects the desire of the parties for confidentiality, while recognising that there will be occasional legitimate circumstances which require confidentiality to be relaxed.

Nevertheless, it is submitted that whilst confidentiality is protected, it is not elevated above all other considerations. Thus, parties drafting arbitration clauses, who are concerned to ensure a confidential arbitration process, should consider: (1) whether the law of the location of the arbitration is a strong defender of confidentiality in arbitration, and, (2) if an arbitral institution has been chosen, which exact confidentiality provisions, if any, are contained in those rules. If there remain concerns, about the level of confidentiality afforded by the chosen process, it will be prudent to include specific wording in the arbitration clause, to ensure confidentiality.[322]

4.3.3.2 USA

In the USA, the Federal Arbitration Act 1925 provides,[323] that arbitral tribunals may subpoena persons and documents. The ability to obtain pre-arbitral discovery, pursuant to the Federal Arbitration Act 1925, was demonstrated in *Amgen Inc v Kidney Center of Delaware County Ltd*[324] where the court, observing the powers to compel discovery, codified in 9 USC § 7, ordered a third party to produce documents and appear in a pre-arbitration disposition. While *Amgen Inc v Kidney Center of Delaware County Ltd*[325] arose in a domestic context, the court, in it, demonstrated its willingness to facilitate discovery in arbitral proceedings, outside the courts jurisdiction.

USA law, also, allows, in 28 USC § 1872, district courts to assist foreign and international tribunals in obtaining evidence. The Uniform Arbitration Act, which is codified in the statutes of the majority of the states, also provides for arbitral tribunals, to subpoena documents and witnesses. Not least, the Federal Rule of Civil Procedure 26(c)(7), assists parties to protect confidential information, where recourse to courts is possible and parties have agreed to the discovery pursuant to the Federal Rules of Civil procedure or state rules.[326] Upon showing of a good cause, the courts may order a protective order or take any other appropriate action to protect confidential information. However, arbitrators are not always willing to

---

[321] *John Foster Emmott v Michael Wilson & Partners Ltd* [2008] EWCA Civ 184.

[322] Herbert Smith Newsletter, Confidentiality in Arbitration: An Update, Herbert Smith Newsletter No 71, July 2008.

[323] 9 USC § 7.

[324] *Amgen Inc v Kidney Center of Delaware County Ltd* 879 F.Supp. 878 (N.D.III 1995).

[325] *Amgen Inc v Kidney Center of Delaware County Ltd* 879 F.Supp. 878 (N.D.III 1995).

[326] *Britain v Stroh Brewery Co.*, 136 FRD 408 (MDNC 1991).

engage the parties in extensive discovery, in an effort to ensure the protection of the parties needs or because they may be unsure of their power to do so.[327]

The extent to which US courts will exclude arbitral documents, from a subsequent action, is unclear.

In *Samuels v Mitchell*,[328] the court found that documents, provided not for legal or expert witnesses purpose, were protected by the work product doctrine. In *International Ins. Co. v Peabody Intern. Corp.*,[329] the court also found that documents, from a prior arbitration, were protected by the work product doctrine. In the case of *United States v Panhandle Eastern Corp.*[330] the court refused to exclude documents, from the prior arbitration, on the ground of confidentiality, where there was no express party or tribunal intention to keep the documents confidential.[331]

More specifically, the Federal District Court of Delaware, found, in *United States v Panhandle Eastern Corporation*,[332] that, absent an explicit agreement by parties or institutional rules on point, arbitration proceedings are not necessarily confidential. In this case, the United States government sought the production of documents, related to a previous arbitral proceeding, which had been held in Geneva, under ICC rules. The court, ruled that, because the arbitration agreement and applicable arbitration rules did not provide for the confidentiality of the proceedings, the government could access the documents. Fundamentally, the court failed to recognise any general principle of confidentiality, in international arbitration, and, this entails that, under this holding, any duty of confidentiality can be implied-in-fact. The import of this holding, at least in the USA, was to underscore the necessity of broad confidentiality clauses in arbitration agreements. However, even the presence of a, seemingly all-encompassing, confidentiality provision does not necessarily protect the parties.[333] The court, specifically rejected the arguments, that internal arbitration rules require confidentiality, or, that a "general understanding" of confidentiality by the parties could justify a protective order. The court, also rejected general assertions of economic harm, that might be caused by disclosure as inadequate to establish good cause. The court's rejection of these arguments is significant, because they are the types of arguments, that are likely to be raised in future cases on arbitration confidentiality, and the court's reflexive repudiation of them suggests that other courts may be similarly unreceptive.

---

[327]*Re Complaint of Koala Shipping & Trading Inc.*, 587 F.Supp. 140 (SDNY 1984); See Baldwin (1996, pp. 475–480).

[328]*Samuels v Mitchell*, 155 FRD 195 (ND Cal 1994).

[329]*International Ins. Co. v Peabody Intern. Corp.* No 87-C464, 1988 US Dist. LEXIS 5109 /ND III June 1, 1988).

[330]*United States v Panhandle Eastern Corp.* 118 FRD 346 (D.Del. 1988).

[331]Baldwin (1996, pp. 485–486).

[332]*United States v Panhandle Eastern Corporation*, 118 F.R.D. 346 (D.Del. 1998).

[333]Brown (2001, p. 976).

The decision in *United States v Panhandle Eastern Corporation*[334] has been followed in principle, if not in name, by other Federal District Courts that have considered the issue, in unreported decisions.

In *Cont'ship Containerlines, Ltd. v PPG Industries, Inc.*,[335] the district court compelled the discovery of arbitration communications, from an international commercial arbitration held in London. The court rejected the argument that confidentiality is somehow implied at law, as a part of the agreement to arbitrate. This holding, departs from English decisions holding that the duty of confidentiality is implied, at law, from the agreement to arbitrate, as a necessary predicate for the operation of the arbitration process.[336] In its ruling, the *Cont'ship Containerlines, Ltd. v PPG Industries, Inc.*[337] court, also noted the lack of external constraints, on the disclosure of arbitration communications by the parties, such as a contractual confidentiality agreement between the parties, or the rule of an arbitral body prohibiting such disclosures.

It is unclear what effect such facts, if established, might have had on the court's decision. The decision in *United States v Panhandle Eastern Corp.*,[338] suggests that internal arbitration rules, most likely, would not have been persuasive, since the court, in *United States v Panhandle Eastern Corp.*,[339] rejected that argument, much in the manner of the private arbitration equivalent of local court rules. As a result, if it had been decided, under *United States v Panhandle Eastern Corp.*,[340] the outcome in *Cont'ship Containerlines, Ltd. v PPG Industries, Inc.*[341] would likely have been the same, i.e. the arbitration communications evidence would have been discovered and admitted into evidence.

Neither *United States v Panhandle Eastern Corp.*,[342] nor *Cont'ship Containerlines, Ltd. v PPG Industries, Inc.*,[343] dealt with situations in which the parties had executed a confidentiality agreement. However, in *Lawrence E. Jaffee Pension Plan v Household International, Inc.*,[344] the parties had an explicit confidentiality provision, in the arbitration agreement, and the court still compelled the production

---

[334] *United States v Panhandle Eastern Corporation*, 118 F.R.D. 346 (D.Del. 1998).

[335] *Cont'ship Containerlines, Ltd. v. PPG Industries, Inc.*, No. 00 Civ. 0194 RCCH BP, 2003 WL 1948807 (S.D.N.Y. Apr. 23, 2003).

[336] Reuben (2006, pp. 1266–1267).

[337] *Cont'ship Containerlines, Ltd. v. PPG Industries, Inc.*, No. 00 Civ. 0194 RCCH BP, 2003 WL 1948807 (S.D.N.Y. Apr. 23, 2003).

[338] *United States v Panhandle Eastern Corp.* 118 FRD 346 (D.Del. 1988).

[339] *United States v Panhandle Eastern Corp.* 118 FRD 346 (D.Del. 1988).

[340] *United States v Panhandle Eastern Corp.* 118 FRD 346 (D.Del. 1988).

[341] *Cont'ship Containerlines, Ltd. v. PPG Industries, Inc.*, No. 00 Civ. 0194 RCCH BP, 2003 WL 1948807 (S.D.N.Y. Apr. 23, 2003).

[342] *United States v Panhandle Eastern Corp.* 118 FRD 346 (D.Del. 1988).

[343] *Cont'ship Containerlines, Ltd. v. PPG Industries, Inc.*, No. 00 Civ. 0194 RCCH BP, 2003 WL 1948807 (S.D.N.Y. Apr. 23, 2003).

[344] *Lawrence E. Jaffee Pension Plan v. Household International, Inc.*, No. Civ. A. 04-N-1228 (CBS, 04-X-0057), 2004 WL 1821968 (D. Colo. Aug. 13, 2004).

of arbitration communications evidence. The court found, that the parties reached an agreement to treat as confidential all documents, disclosed by the parties in connection with the arbitration, and that the arbitrator accepted the agreement. However, the court said the defendant would still have to establish "good cause" for a protective order, under Federal Rule 26(c), to preclude discovery of the evidence, thus, preserving the crucial distinction, described above, between disclosures to the general public and disclosures in the context of formal legal proceedings. The court acknowledged some tension, between the parties' confidentiality agreement and the court's obligation to establish good cause to enter the protective order, but, ultimately, decided that the documents, sought to be protected, were already subject to disclosure pursuant to another discovery order, thus, avoiding a decision on the merits.[345]

Similarly, in *Urban Box Office Network v Interfase Managers*,[346] the Southern District of New York, looked beyond the confidentiality provision, in an arbitration clause, in upholding the discovery of documents produced at an arbitration, and in rejecting arguments, in a later case, that were shielded by the attorney-client privilege and by a confidentiality provision in the arbitration clause. The court, found that there was a valid confidentiality agreement in the arbitration clause. However, it also found that, the confidentiality agreement did not trump the party's waiver of the attorney-client privilege, with respect to certain documents, when it disclosed them at the prior arbitration. Again, the demonstrated expectations of the parties were significant to the court. The court, noted that the parties took no affirmative steps, to invoke the confidentiality provisions of the arbitration clause, such as stamping the documents confidential. The court, permitted the discovery of the arbitration communications evidence.

In *Re Application of Leonard Bernstein et al v On-Line Software International Inc. et al*,[347] where, after an arbitration hearing was held before a panel, in connection with dispute between the individual applicants and computer firm, over computer software product, and, where, the individuals moved to confirm in an arbitration the award of damages to them, and, the Supreme Court of New York County granted the motion and entered judgment for the individual applicants. On appeal, by the computer firm, the appellate division of the Supreme Court, held that the arbitration panel had properly continued, to the damages phase of the proceedings, after the resignation of one of the arbitrators, and, that the order of the panel, which was prohibiting the parties to contact each other's witnesses, without their consent, was proper. The confidentiality order, which was issued by the arbitration panel, with respect to certain subpoenaed material, obtained from competitor in computer software industry, which restricted access to material to outside counsel

[345]Reuben (2006, p. 1268).

[346]*Urban Box Office Network v. Interfase Managers* No. 01 Civ. 8854 (LTS) (THK), 2004 WL 2375819 (S.D.N.Y. Oct. 21, 2004).

[347]*Re Application of Leonard Bernstein et al v On-Line Software International Inc. et al*, 232 A.D.2d 336, 648 N.Y.S.2d 602.

and parties' experts, was allowable, in order to protect trade secrets obtained, in the course of discovery.

In *Industrotech Constructors Inc. v Duke University and Turner Construction Company*,[348] one of the numerous prime contractors, who worked on the university medical center, brought an action against Duke University, for damages arising from various breaches of the respective construction contract. In connection with discovery, the contractor sought the production of the transcripts of the arbitration proceeding, involving Duke University and another prime contractor on the same job, the Superior Court of the Durham County, ordered the sought discovery, under certain protected restrictions. On appeal, from Duke University, the Court of Appeals held that, neither the contract nor confidentiality barred disclosure; that the Duke University had failed to meet its burden of establishing that the materials sought were prepared in anticipation of litigation; and, that, in any case, the sought transcripts were not protected from discovery, on grounds they were "peppered" with opinions, legal theories, and other work product of attorneys.

In *ITT Educational Services Inc. v Roberto Arce et al*,[349] a for-profit provider of technology-oriented postsecondary degree programs sought a declaratory judgment, that a confidentiality provision in its contract with former students, was enforceable; and, where, an injunction, preventing former students from revealing any aspect of arbitration of students' claims of fraudulent inducement, was also sought; the confidentiality clause, in the contract between the for-profit provider of postsecondary degree programs and its students, provided that "*[a]ll aspects of the arbitration proceeding, and any ruling, decision or award by the arbitrator, will be strictly confidential*", and permanently enjoined them from revealing the contents of the arbitration, including rulings, decisions and awards by the arbitrator. The students and clark appealed. The students, argued that the arbitrator's award constituted a finding of fraudulent inducement to contract, and that, therefore, the entire agreement, including the confidentiality provision, was void. ITT disputed that, the arbitral award constituted a finding of fraudulent inducement, but, that, even if it did, the confidentiality provision, was part of the arbitration clause, and was therefore severable under US Supreme Court precedent. The Court of Appeals, agreed that the Supreme Court had found arbitration provisions severable from the contracts, in which they are embedded, unless otherwise specified. It, then, proceeded to analyze the arbitration provisions. The Court, found that the confidentiality requirement was part of the arbitration provision, based on the facts that it appeared under the single heading "Resolution of disputes", and it was specifically enumerated, as an exception to traditional arbitration procedures. Further, precedent allowed such a requirement to be integrated into an arbitration clause. Therefore, the confidentiality clause was enforceable.

---

[348]*Industrotech Constructors Inc. v Duke University and Turner Construction Company* 1984 67 N.C.App. 741, 314 S.E.2d 272, 17 Ed. Law Rep. 269.

[349]*ITT Educational Services Inc. v Roberto Arce et al* 2008, 533 F.3d 342; WL 2553998 (C.A. 5, June 27, 2008).

At state level, the decision upholding admissibility, i.e. *A.T. v State Farm Mutual Automobile Insurance Co.*,[350] was a Colorado Appeals Court decision, which was analytically similar to the federal cases described above. In that case, the plaintiff, A.T., a self-employed chiropractor, claimed uninsured motorist benefits from State Farm, for injuries incurred in an automobile accident. The matter went to arbitration, where the plaintiff provided medical records, disclosing that she had been diagnosed with a psychological disorder. The plaintiff, later testified, as an expert medical witness, in unrelated litigation between one of her chiropractic patients and State Farm, and the insurance company introduced evidence, from the arbitration of her psychological disorder, during its cross-examination of her. She sued State Farm, for invasion of privacy and various harms, arising from their introduction of the psychological disorder evidence, which she claimed was confidential to the arbitration. The Court of Appeals, affirmed the trial court's decision, to admit the evidence in the later case. As the federal courts had discussed earlier, the appellate court looked to the expectations of the parties for guidance, granting that there was no confidentiality provision in the arbitration agreement, and that there were no internal arbitration rules, that would have established the confidentiality of the proceedings. Rather, it found that, the arbitration was conducted under the state's version of the Uniform Arbitration Act 2000, which permits arbitration awards to be filed, challenged, and enforced in courts, and, that the records, relating to the arbitration, are public records. Because the psychological disorder records were potentially public, and because the plaintiff made no effort to secure a protective order, to preserve them as confidential proactively, the court held that the records were public, discoverable, and admissible.[351]

By contrast, the decision rejecting admissibility was, by the Missouri Court of Appeals, in *Group Health Plan, Inc. v BJC Health Systems, Inc.*,[352] an action by a hospital network against the sponsor of a managed health care plan, for breach of contract. At the arbitration, the health plan sponsor sought to introduce a transcript, exhibits, and the arbitration award, from one of its prior arbitrations, which had been subject to, both, an express confidentiality provision, and a protective order. The hospital network, moved to quash in state court, arguing that the arbitration was confidential under the state's arbitration law, which clearly precluded the discovery and admissibility of the arbitration communications. The Court of Appeals, proceeded to rule that, the sought-after arbitration communications were not otherwise discoverable, under the Missouri statute, because the parties had sought and received a protective order, from the arbitrator, to secure their confidentiality. Citing judicial policy, favouring the use of arbitration, the court ruled that, the protective order should be viewed as an arbitration award, entitled to deference from the courts. Because the documents were covered by the protective order, they

---

[350] *A.T. v. State Farm Mutual Automobile Insurance Co.*, 989 P.2d 219 (Colo. Ct. App. 1999).

[351] Reuben (2006, pp. 1269–1270).

[352] *Group Health Plan, Inc. v BJC Health Systems, Inc.*, 30 S.W.3d 198 (Mo. Ct. App. 2000).

could not be otherwise discoverable, under the statute, and the arbitration documents were held not to be discoverable.[353]

The decision, in *Group Health Plan, Inc. v BJC Health Systems, Inc.*,[354] especially its emphasis on judicial policy favoring arbitration, provides some evidence that state courts may be willing to shield arbitration communications from discovery and admissibility, at least when there is clear statutory authority. However, such authority is rare.[355]

The common assumption, that the process of arbitration is a confidential means of adjudicating disputes, has been challenged by many court rulings and developments in arbitral practice. In spite of the existence of a general agreement, that arbitral proceedings are private, it is, nevertheless, difficult to find a legal basis and judicial support, for a legal duty to maintain the confidentiality of the arbitration, as there is lack of rules, or of any clearly developed law on the question.

Under US case law, arbitration documents are subject to discovery. There is no work product privilege, for documents produced for arbitration, and the courts do not give much, if any, deference to the confidentiality of arbitral proceedings.[356] Moreover, US courts have not recognized any implied duty of confidentiality, upon the arbitrating parties.[357] In assessing whether arbitration communications are discoverable and admissible, the courts appear mindful of the tension, between the judicial system's need for relevant evidence, and the parties' expectations of confidentiality. The judicial system's need, for relevant evidence generally has prevailed, especially when there is no confidentiality clause, in the agreement to arbitrate, or other clear evidence of the parties' expectation of confidentiality. Internal arbitration rules, may be a consideration in a court's determination, but have not been persuasive evidence of the parties' expectations. However, where there is evidence of party expectations, such as through the securing of a protective order, courts may be more willing to defer to the protective order, if it otherwise meets relevant standards.[358] Where, statutory law clearly precludes the discovery and admissibility of arbitration communications, such protective orders, are likely to be upheld.

This sketch of the terrain, only provides an initial impression, of what the emerging case law on this issue might look like. Many details, remain to be filled in, by future cases.[359]

---

[353]Reuben (2006, pp. 1270–1272).

[354]*Group Health Plan, Inc. v BJC Health Systems, Inc.*, 30 S.W.3d 198 (Mo. Ct. App. 2000).

[355]Kratky-Dore (2006, pp. 474–475).

[356]*Milone v General Motors Corp.* 446 NYS 2d 650 (App.Div. 1981); *Industrotech Constructors Inc. v Duke University*, 314 SE 2d 272 (N C Ct App. 1984), *United States v Panhandle Eastern Corp.* 118 FRD 346 (D Del 1988); *Gossard v ADIA Servs, Inc.*, 922 F. Supp. 558 (M D Fla. 1995).

[357]Carbonneau (2001, pp. 703–707).

[358]Such as, for example, the good cause requirement, contained in the Federal Rule of Civil Procedure 26(c).

[359]Reuben (2006, p. 1272).

4.3.3.3 France

In *Société True North et Société FCB Internationale v Bleustein et al*,[360] the French court of Appeal dealt again with the implied duty of confidentiality in French arbitration law.

One of the involved parties, revealed information related to the arbitration, following which, action the other party withdrew from the arbitration, on the basis of breach of the duty to observe confidentiality.

The court stated that arbitration being a private procedure, it follows that the former entails a confidentiality element, which is, only to be broken in case there is a legal obligation coercing a party to produce information. When a party, without any legal obligation to produce information related to the arbitral process, reveals such information, he has violated his obligations, under the arbitration agreement and has given the right to the other party to withdraw from the proceedings.

It was also stated that, parallel to the obligation imposed by the society for financial transparency, co-existed the obligation to preserve confidentiality in arbitration.

4.3.3.4 Germany

The duty of confidentiality being the parties' agreement, or the institutional arbitral rules the parties have incorporated by reference into their agreement, it is inferred that the issue of disclosure or not of information of arbitral proceedings, to subsequent ones, or of consolidation of arbitral proceedings, depends on the precise content of the contractual confidentiality obligations.

The ability of an arbitral tribunal, to obtain discovery, may be of natural concern to a party seeking to protect confidential information in international arbitration.[361] The German Civil Procedure Code, (ZPO), restricts the disclosure of documents.[362] ZPO §§ 420–444, and 142, allow only a limited production of documents. Although these rules do not apply to arbitral proceedings in Germany; nevertheless, the right of an arbitral tribunal to require production of documents, must be seen against this backdrop. The German arbitration law, does not specifically state, that the arbitral tribunal may order the parties to produce documents, but, merely, mentions, in ZPO § 1049(1), Sentence 2, that the arbitral tribunal can order the parties to produce documents to an expert. In addition, as per ZPO § 1048(3), the arbitral tribunal may continue the proceedings, if a party fails to produce documentary evidence.[363]

---

[360] *Societe True North et Societe FCB Internationale v Bleustein et al*, Cour d'Appel de Paris 1999, Rev Arb 2003, 189.

[361] Baldwin (1996, p. 470).

[362] § 1036 Zivilproceßordnung (ZPO).

[363] This provision only makes sense, if the arbitral tribunal has the right to order a party to produce documents.

Thus, it follows, from ZPO §§ 1049(1) and 1048(3), and from the principle, that the arbitral tribunal may establish the facts of the case, by all appropriate means, that it may order the parties to produce documents. The right of the arbitral tribunal is limited, to documents, which have been described with reasonable particularity, and are considered, by the arbitral tribunal, as relevant and material to the dispute.[364] If a third party, refuses to comply voluntarily, the arbitral tribunal may seek the assistance of state courts, in conducting discovery, as per ZPO § 1050,[365] if it feels that the document is absolutely necessary for the resolution of the dispute.[366] According to ZPO § 1025(2), the German provision of ZPO § 1050 applies, even if the arbitral tribunal has its seat abroad, or the seat has not been defined.[367]

In the absence of an express duty of confidentiality, the parties may be free to use the information disclosed in arbitral proceedings for other purposes. Even if the parties are obliged to treat the information disclosed in the arbitral proceeding as confidential, further exceptions, to the parties' duty of confidentiality, relate to the protection of the legitimate interests of the parties.

The extent of the protection afforded to the confidentiality of proceedings, depends on the parties agreement, as there are no particular rules in the ZPO in this regard. Even where the parties do not provide for express exceptions, to their confidentiality obligations, arbitral proceedings, sited in Germany, are not protected by confidentiality, where the legitimate interests of the parties so require. Also, the confidentiality of arbitration can be limited, as a result of regulatory, administrative and penal proceedings and requirements.[368]

The confidentiality of documents can be problematic for an arbitrator, in continental law countries, where the arbitration laws give arbitrators the power to modernise the arbitral proceedings, and, especially, the hearing of the evidence. Arbitrators, can arrange the adduction of documents, which in one arbitration proceedings are pertinent to the decision. Arbitrators, can also order the production of documents, which are in an arbitration pertinent to the decision. To achieve this, they have to resort to the help of the state courts, as they have no authority to enforce the parties to produce these documents. The onus of proof, for the relevance of a document to the arbitration proceedings, stays with the party which claims that

---

[364]These limitations follow, from the traditions of German civil procedure law and from the aim to avoid "fishing expeditions" in German arbitration proceedings. In addition, such limitations are in line with internationally accepted principles on document production, such as the "IBA Rules on Evidence"; Rützel et al. (2005, pp. 133–134).

[365]Possible measures, include testimony of a witness, or an expert, the administration of an oath, or orders for production of documents in the possession of third parties. Rützel et al. (2005, p. 136).

[366]Rützel et al. (2005, pp. 133–134).

[367]This is a novelty among arbitration laws, since pursuant to article 1(2) of the UNCITRAL Model Law, article 27 of the UNCITRAL Model Law, only provides for court assistance, at the seat of the arbitral tribunal. The liberal approach, of the German arbitration law, has hardly been noticed internationally, which is certainly due to the fact that a German Court is very limited, in its ability to enforce orders for production of documents; Rützel et al. (2005, p. 138).

[368]Raeschke-Kessler et al. (1995, p. 163); Global Legal Group (2007, Chap. 25 – Germany, § 11).

the document is relevant to the arbitration involved. Otherwise, when the party is in no position to prove so, the arbitral tribunal can claim so.

It is uncommon that parties resort to fishing expeditions, with regards to certain documents, and arbitral tribunals have the authority to deal with such matters. When a party declares that a document is important, for the arbitral proceedings, the onus of preserving the confidentiality of that document, lies with the opposing party.[369] Of the methods used, to avoid conflict, between discovery and confidentiality, are the claim that only the arbitral tribunal gains access to the documents to be preserved and to remain confidential; as well as the claim, in particular, that only the judge has the right to gain total access to such documents, and that the parties gain limited, and to the extent that it is absolutely needed, access to such documents.[370]

4.3.3.5 The Public Interest Exception

Confidentiality, of the arbitral process and of the documents, created or disclosed in the course of arbitration proceedings, has long been mentioned, as one of the advantages of arbitration, as well as one of the reasons for resorting to arbitration.[371] Case law, together with the players in international arbitration, show, that confidentiality is still an important facet of the arbitral process.[372] At the same time, courts have formulated exceptions to this principle, and its application is certainly not absolute.

One of the exceptions, of the duty to observe confidentiality, is the "public interest" exception. It seems that the logic behind enforcing confidentiality, between private parties, does not extend to situations in which one of the parties is a public actor, because these concern not only the parties alone, but, also, people, in general.

---

[369] Günther (2000, pp. 345–349); Berger (1992).

[370] Günther (2000, pp. 351–354); Laeuchli (2007, p. 84).

[371] Paulsson and Raeding (1995, p. 303); Neil (1996, p. 287); Misra and Jordans (2006, p. 39).

[372] *The Eastern Saga* [1984] 2 Lloyd's Rep. 373 (Q.B.); *Hassneh Ins. Co f Israel* v *Mew* [1993] 2 Lloyd's Rep. 243 (Q.B.); *Insurance Co.* v *Lloyd's Syndicate* [1995] 1 Lloyd's Rep. 272; *Dolling Baker* v *Merrett* [1990] 1 W.L.R. 1205 (C.A.); *Ali Shipping* v *Shipyard Trogir* [1998] 1 Lloyd's Rep. 643 (C.A.); *Aita* v *Ojjeh, Paris*, February 18, 1986; See, e.g., Boyd (1995, p. 273) where at § 6 he states: "It became apparent to me, very soon, after taking up my responsibilities at the ICC that the users of international commercial arbitration, i.e. the companies, governments and individuals who are parties in such cases, place the highest value upon confidentiality as a fundamental characteristic of international commercial arbitration. When enquiring, as to the features of international commercial arbitration which attracted parties to it, as opposed to litigation, confidentiality of the proceedings, and the fact that these proceedings, and the resulting award, would not enter into the public domain, was almost invariably mentioned. Indeed, it became quickly apparent to me, that should the ICC adopt a publication policy or any other policy, which would mitigate or diminish the strict insistence on confidentiality by the ICC, this would constitute a significant deterrent to the use of ICC arbitration."; Misra and Jordans (2006, pp. 39–40).

The state, can certainly have obligations to disclose information about its activities to its citizens.

In the continental countries, other legal regimes recognise confidentiality,[373] and others not.[374] In the common law world, English judicial decisions support the implied duty to observe confidentiality,[375] although exceptions to the principle are recognized. However, in other common law countries, such as Australia and the USA, such an implicit duty is not recognised.[376] Although, English case law deals with confidentiality of arbitral proceedings, nevertheless, the English Arbitration Act 1996, does not contain a provision on confidentiality.

Apart from the differences, between these legal systems, judges in the respective nations tend to make exceptions from the approaches of their countries. An example, is the case of *Aegis* v *European Re*,[377] a case concerning two arbitration proceedings, between the same two parties, where, in the Privy Council, it was stated that the confidentiality agreement was intended to prevent third parties from relying on material, generated during the arbitration against either of the two insurance companies; and, where it was also stated that the legitimate use, of an earlier award, in a later arbitration, between the same two parties, was, therefore, not a breach of the confidentiality agreement.

However, with respect to confidentiality in international commercial arbitrations, nothing should be taken for granted,[378] and, there is, in fact, no settled rule in either the common or civil law world. The status of the "public interest" exception, in itself, is quite complicated. On the one hand, European nations seem more reluctant, to admit the public interest exception to confidentiality, as this has been supported by the decision of the European Court of First Instance, in *Postbank NV* v *Commission of the European Communities*,[379] in which the court clearly mandated the taking of all necessary precautions, to protect any disclosure of confidential documents or information. In the common law world, on the other hand, the concept is nascent. Although courts, in Australia[380] and the United States,[381] have

[373]Such as France, e.g. *Aita v Ojjeh* (1986) Revue de' l Arbitrage 583.

[374]For example, the Swedish Supreme Court has ruled, that there is no real duty to observe confidentiality in *Bulgarian Foreign Trade Bank Ltd.* v *A.I. Trade Finance Ltd.*, Case No. T 1881-99 (Swedish Sup. Ct). However, in Sweden, as in Germany, the parties, to an arbitration agreement, are free to include a confidentiality clause in their agreement.

[375]*The Eastern Saga* [1984] 2 Lloyd's Rep. 373 (Q.B.); *Hassneh Ins. Co f Israel* v *Mew* [1993] 2 Lloyd's Rep. 243 (Q.B.); *Dolling Baker* v *Merrett* [1990] 1 W.L.R. 1205 (C.A.); *Ali Shipping* v *Shipyard Trogir* [1998] 1 Lloyd's Rep. 643 (C.A.).

[376]*Esso/BHP v Plowman* (1995) 128 A.L.R. 391; *US v Panhandle Eastern Corp.*, D. Delaware 1988, 118 F.R.D. 346.

[377]*Associated Electric and Gas Insurance Services Ltd. v European Reinsurance Co. of Zurich*, UKPC 11, [2003] 1; Rawlings and Seeger (2003, p. 483).

[378]Trackman (2002, pp. 1–18).

[379]*Postbank NV v Commission of the European Communities*, [1996] E.C.R. II-8, at 90.

[380]*Esso/BHP v Plowman* (1995) 128 A.L.R. 391.

[381]*US v Panhandle Eastern Corp.*, (D.Del.) 1988, 118 F.R.D. 346.

acknowledged the existence of the exception, it is highly unlikely that the English courts, which have not yet faced a case requiring its application, would embrace it, due to the fact that, under English law, it seems that the concept of privacy and confidentiality have not been separated. Thus, for English courts which believe, quite correctly, that arbitration proceedings are private, it would, indeed, be strenuous to admit a public interest exception.

However, in *Esso/BHP v Plowman*,[382] the High Court of Australia held that confidentiality is not an inherent part of arbitration in Australia, and even if it were considered to be, public actors might be under a positive duty to disclose information to the public, as there may be circumstances, in which third parties and the public have a legitimate interest in knowing what has transpired in an arbitration, and where, subsequently, this would give rise to a public interest exception. Although, *Esso/BHP v Plowman*[383] has been characterised as a rigid exception to confidentiality, the decision does impose checks and balances, as to the duty to observe the public interest exception, and lift the veil of confidentiality. Application of this "public interest exception" is not, however, limited to arbitration, in which a state entity is involved. It may be applied, even in cases involving non-state actors.[384]

Contrary to the opinion, supporting the observance of the "public interest" exception in arbitration, there are also several factors, which tend to limit the "public interest" exception and prompt for the observance of the duty to preserve confidentiality in arbitration. For once, public image dictates so. Also, it is considered a truism, in international commercial arbitration, that one of the reasons private companies incline to arbitration over litigation, is to safeguard such a public image. Although, on the one hand, the desire to keep a low profile, on disputes that may have the potential to tarnish a company's public image or reputation, may be an important factor, weighing in favour of confidentiality and against disclosure under the public interest exception; on the other hand, when that is weighed against a state's moral or legal obligation, to inform its citizens of the progress/final outcome of an arbitration, then, the private parties' desire, to keep a low profile on disputes, becomes of a lesser importance. Another important factor, that would tend to militate in favour of greater confidentiality, is the desire to protect intellectual property, belonging to the private party to an arbitration. Equally with the factors, which tend to limit the "public interest" exception and prompt for the observance of the duty to preserve confidentiality in arbitration, there are also factors, which tend to expand the "public interest" exception, and prompt for the lifting of the veil of confidentiality in international commercial arbitration.

The work that lies ahead, for courts and arbitral tribunals, falls into, first, refining the notion of what is of "legitimate public interest". As the majority judgment, in

[382]*Esso/BHP v Plowman* (1995) 128 A.L.R. 391.

[383]*Esso/BHP v Plowman* (1995) 128 A.L.R. 391.

[384]De Saint Marc Denoix (2003, p. 211); Misra and Jordans (2006, pp. 39–48).

the *Esso/BHP v Plowman*[385] case, shows, there is real potential for all information, arising from a mixed, but, otherwise, ordinary commercial arbitration, which, broadly speaking, addresses matters of public interest, to be deemed to be "in the public interest" and, thus, to be disclosed indiscriminately.[386]

4.3.3.6 Tentative Observations

In *Esso/BHP v Plowman*,[387] the High Court of Australia held that arbitration is private, but declined to find a duty of confidentiality, attached to documents and information obtained during the course of an arbitration. In contrast, the English Court of Appeal, in *Ali Shipping v Shipyard Trogir*,[388] held that an implied term of confidentiality, ought, properly, to be regarded as attaching as a matter of law.

The decisions in *Esso/BHP v Plowman*[389] and in *Ali Shipping v Shipyard Trogir*,[390] provide a stark illustration of different approaches, adopted in two common law jurisdictions. In the light of the notoriety, that followed the High Court of Australia's decision, in *Esso/BHP v Plowman*,[391] and the trenchant criticism that the case received, together with the previously widely held assumption that arbitration is confidential, it might be though that the High Court of Australia's decision was an aberration. However, to consider so, would be like going much too far.

In the USA, the authority of *US v Panhandle Eastern Corp.*,[392] which predates the one in *Esso/BHP v Plowman*,[393] suggests that arbitration is not confidential.[394]

In France, unless legally obliged to, parties revealing otherwise information, with regards to discovery of documents, or other evidence used in arbitration proceedings, are regarded as breaking the duty to observe confidentiality, which is inherent to arbitration.

In Germany, where there is a lack of any ZPO provision, providing for the duty to preserve confidentiality, the extent of the protection of confidentiality, depends on what the parties have agreed.

---

385 *Esso/BHP v Plowman* (1995) 128 A.L.R. 391, High Court of Australia.

386 Pongracic-Speier (2002).

387 *Esso/BHP v Plowman* (1995) 128 A.L.R. 391.

388 *Ali Shipping* v *Shipyard Trogir* [1998] 1 Lloyd's Rep. 643 (C.A.).

389 *Esso/BHP v Plowman* (1995) 128 A.L.R. 391.

390 *Ali Shipping* v *Shipyard Trogir* [1998] 1 Lloyd's Rep. 643 (C.A.).

391 *Esso/BHP v Plowman* (1995) 128 A.L.R. 391.

392 *US v Panhandle Eastern Corp.*, (D.Del.) 1988, 118 F.R.D. 346.

393 *Esso/BHP v Plowman* (1995) 128 A.L.R. 391.

394 Pryles (2008, pp. 528–529).

4.3.4 Confidentiality in Arbitration Proceedings in Relation to the Award

4.3.4.1 England

Another important aspect, is the extent to which an award is confidential. Generally, an arbitration award is final and binding, only upon the parties to the arbitration and those claiming under or through them. The parties, by submitting their dispute to arbitration, undertake to be bound by the award. In what circumstances, are the findings in an award binding upon arbitrators, in a subsequent arbitration between different parties?[395]

In *Department of Economic Policy & Development of the City of Moscow (DEPD) v Bankers Trust Co*,[396] Bankers Trust sought to challenge an arbitration award, in favour of DEPD, on the basis that the arbitrator had failed to act fairly and impartially. The judgment, which rejected the applications of Bankers Trust, was given in private, and, when the parties disagreed, whether this should be published, the court held that the sensitivity of the material of the award favoured the preservation of confidentiality.

It is clear also, from the judgment in *Department of Economic Policy & Development of the City of Moscow (DEPD) v Bankers Trust Co*,[397] that applications not involving points of law will be primarily heard in private, unless the court orders otherwise. This, in effect, gives a lot of discretion to the courts, as to whether or not a judgment should remain private, but, if the court orders a hearing in public, this may obstruct the aim of arbitration as a private dispute resolution mechanism. It is notable, also, that, in *Department of Economic Policy & Development of the City of Moscow (DEPD) v Bankers Trust Co*,[398] the Court of Appeal, held that, the jurisprudence of the European Court of Human Rights, under article 6 of the ECHR, permitted both private hearings, and, where appropriate, also private judgments. Second, it was necessary to consider the developments, in the procedure applicable to arbitration applications, or claims, which took place in 1997 and 2002. These showed, that there was a trend towards greater privacy in the hearing of arbitration applications. Third, it was necessary to distinguish, between the question, whether a hearing ought to be in private, and the question whether the judgment ought to be private. CPR 62.10, dealt in terms with a hearing. Whatever the starting point, or actual position during a hearing, it was, although clearly relevant, not determinative of the correct approach to publication of the resulting judgment. There was a clear

[395]Woolhouse (2004, p. 150).

[396]*Department of Economic Policy & Development of the City of Moscow (DEPD) v. Bankers Trust Co.* [2003] EWHC 1337; [2003] 1 W.L.R. 2885.

[397]*Department of Economic Policy & Development of the City of Moscow (DEPD) v. Bankers Trust Co.* [2003] EWHC 1337; [2003] 1 W.L.R. 2885.

[398]*Department of Economic Policy & Development of the City of Moscow (DEPD) v. Bankers Trust Co.* [2003] EWHC 1337; [2003] 1 W.L.R. 2885.

distinction, between the considerations governing a hearing and the resulting judgment and order. Further, even though the hearing may have been in private, the court should, when preparing and giving judgment, bear in mind that any judgment should be given in public, where this can be done without disclosing significant confidential information.

The public interest, in ensuring appropriate standards of fairness in the conduct of arbitrations, militates in favour of a public judgment, with regards to judgments given on applications under section 68. The desirability of public scrutiny, as a means by which confidence in the courts can be maintained, and the administration of justice made transparent, apply here also, as well as in other areas of court activity, under the principles of article 6. Arbitration, is an important feature of international, commercial and financial life, and, there is legitimate interest in its operation and practice. The desirability of a public judgment, is, particularly, present, in any case where a judgment involves points of law or practice, which may offer future guidance to lawyers or practitioners. It was no surprise, that there had been, since the introduction of CPR 62.10, a number of reported judgments on arbitration claims, where the starting point of the hearing was privacy. The factors, militating in favour of publicity, have to be weighed, together with the desirability of preserving the confidentiality of the original arbitration and its subject-matter. When weighing the factors, a judge has to consider, primarily, the interests of the parties, in the litigation before him, or in other pending or imminent proceedings. The concerns or fears of other parties should not be a dominant consideration. Nor, could there be any serious risk, of them being deterred from arbitrating in England, if the court weighed the relevant factors appropriately. If, in the absence of other good reason for publication, the court withholds publication, where a party before it would suffer some real prejudice from publication, or where the publication would disclose matters by the confidentiality of which one or both parties have set significant store, but, nevertheless, publishes its judgments in other cases, businessmen can be confident that their privacy and confidentiality in arbitration will, where appropriate, be preserved.

The limited, but necessary, interface between arbitration and the public court system, means, that more cannot be expected. There can be no question, of withholding publication of reasoned judgments, on a blanket basis, out of a generalised opinion, that their publication would upset the confidence of the business community in English arbitration. The Court of Appeal, did not consider that a party, inviting the court to protect evidently confidential material about a dispute, must necessarily prove detriment, beyond the undermining of its expectation that the subject-matter would be confidential. This, had to be balanced against Moscow's failure to provide any good reason for requiring publication either, since it can freely state the end result of the arbitration and the end result of the litigation. The Court of Appeal, did not consider, the fact that it was Bankers Trust which had made the application of section 68, to be a significant factor.[399]

[399]Robb (2004).

The judgment demonstrates, that the English courts will undertake a balancing exercise, between the public interest in the administration of justice being transparent, on the one hand, and the protection of genuinely confidential and sensitive information, on the other hand. Such an approach ought, in theory, to give appropriate protection to the interests of the particular parties, while permitting the law to develop, through the publication of judgments relating to arbitration matters, whenever possible. There are some jurisdictions in which publicity is difficult to avoid, when challenging arbitral awards, since the arbitral award will be physically annexed to the public court documents. However, parties, selecting England as the seat of their arbitration, can have some confidence that the underlying details of their dispute will remain confidential, even if the matter comes before the courts, where truly confidential or sensitive information is involved.[400]

The qualification to implied undertaking, namely that an award and reasons might be disclosed as of right, if it was reasonably necessary for one party to disclose them for the purpose of the establishment of that party's rights against a third party, either in order to found a defence, or as a basis for a cause of action,[401] was, further, considered in *Insurance Co v Lloyd's Syndicate*,[402] where the question, which arose, was, whether it was open to a reassured, as of right, to disclose to reinsurers, who constitute the following market, an arbitration award and the reasons made in an arbitration award between the reassured and the leading reinsurance underwriter.

It was held, granting the injunction, that there was nothing in the reinsurance contracts, by which the following market agreed to be bound by the leading underwriter's settlement, that there was an implied duty of confidence between Insurance and the Lloyd's Syndicate, in respect of the award;[403] that the mere fact that the arbitration award would be persuasive on the following market, did not bring the award within any of the exceptions entailed in *Hassneh Insurance Co of Israel v Mew*;[404] and it was only necessary to disclose the award, if the right in question could not be enforced or protected, unless the award and its reasons were disclosed to a stranger; that there was no justification for the implication of a wider qualification, in the sphere of the reinsurance market, as the award and its reasons were not necessary elements in the establishment of Lloyd's Syndicate's claim; that, where there was an implied negative covenant, as to confidentiality, it was not necessary to prove specific loss and damage, in order to obtain an injunction, unless enforcement would impose severe hardship on the Lloyd's Syndicate; and, lastly, that there was no non-conscionability, on the facts, sufficient to deprive Insurance of an injunction.

---

[400] Hill and Fletcher (2004, p. N50).

[401] *Hassneh Insurance Co of Israel v. Stuart J Mew* [1993] 2 Lloyd's Rep. 243.

[402] *Insurance Co v Lloyd's Syndicate* [1995] 1 Lloyd's Rep. 272.

[403] *Hassneh Insurance Co of Israel v. Stuart J Mew* [1993] 2 Lloyd's Rep. 243 applied.

[404] *Hassneh Insurance Co of Israel v. Stuart J Mew* [1993] 2 Lloyd's Rep. 243.

Unlike in *Hassneh Insurance Co of Israel v Mew*,[405] where the Court had taken the view that the disclosure of an award and reasons was allowed as "reasonably necessary",[406] in *Insurance Co v Lloyd's Syndicate*,[407] the Court took the view that "reasonably necessary", covered only the case where the right in question could not be enforced or protected, unless the award and reasons were disclosed to a stranger to the arbitration, and that the making of an award must be a necessary element, in the establishment of the party's legal rights against the stranger, as shown, also, in *Ali Shipping Corp. v Shipyard Trogir*,[408] where Ali Shipping obtained an injunction, to prevent Shipyard Trogir to rely on an award rendered between them, and where the court decided that Shipyard Trogir was unable to lift the confidentiality veil. The decision of the English Court of Appeal, in *Ali Shipping v Shipyard Trogir*,[409] signalled a revived moment toward a judicially enforceable duty of confidentiality. However, the question of confidentiality, in international arbitral proceedings, is far from settled,[410] the parties expectations, about the privacy and

[405]*Hassneh Insurance Co of Israel v Mew* [1993] 2 Lloyd's Rep 243.

[406]In *Hassnesh v Mew* [1993] 2 Lloyd's Rep 243, relying largely on *Dolling-Baker v Merrett* [1990] 1 WLR 1205, the court found, that arbitration proceedings are subject to an implied duty of confidentiality, and stated, that if privacy is an inherent attitude of the arbitral process, then confidentiality must be as well, simply because privacy is meaningless without its confidentiality corollary. In addition, an exception to the confidentiality rule was found, in *Hassnesh v Mew* [1993] 2 Lloyd's Rep 243, and, it was held that disclosure of an arbitral award was permissible, if it was also necessary in order to establish causes of action in a subsequent proceeding. With regards to the circumstances, under which an award can be disclosed in subsequent proceedings, Colman J., held as follows: (1) if it was reasonably necessary for the establishment or protection of an arbitrating party's legal rights, vis-a-vis a third party, that the award should be disclosed to that third party, in order to found a defence, or as the basis for a cause of action, then it followed that, to disclose it, including its reasons, would not be a breach of the duty of confidence; (2) if it was reasonably necessary, for the establishment by the defendant of his causes of actions against Heath that he should disclose or, in his pleadings, quote from the arbitration award, including the reasons, for such a quotation or disclosure, he should be entitled to do so, without editing either the award or the reasons and without having to apply to the Court for leave to do; (3) it was to be implied, as a matter of business efficacy in the agreement to arbitrate, that, if it was reasonably necessary, in order to run off the contracts, to have access to the award, including the reasons of it, that the defendant would be entitled to disclose that document to Heath; (4) the documents, created by or in the course of an arbitration, to which an objection of confidence attached, could not, in principle, have any different status from any other documents, which were the subject of a duty of confidence; there was nothing to justify the voluntary disclosure, to a third party, of such arbitration documents, other than the award, in anticipation of the commencement of proceedings by or against that third party; and, to disclose such documents, without the consent of the other arbitrating party, would be a breach of the obligation of confidence; in so far as the injunction currently applied, to the whole of the reasons, as well as the award, the order should, to that extent, be discharged; Robb (2004); Brown (2001, pp. 977–978).

[407]*Insurance Co v Lloyd's Syndicate* [1995] 1 Lloyd's Rep. 272.

[408]*Ali Shipping Corp. v Shipyard Trogir* [1991] 1 W.L.R. 314, C.A.

[409]*Ali Shipping v Shipyard Trogir* (1998) 1 Lloyd's Rep. 643.

[410]In *Ali Shipping v Shipyard Trogir* [1998] 2 All ER 136, the Court of Appeal identified the following further circumstances, in which disclosure of an award would be allowed: (1) "consent", i.e. where disclosure is made with the express or implied consent of the party who originally

confidentiality of their arbitral proceedings, are often disappointed, or, negated, by courts, and nothing should be taken for granted, with respect to confidentiality in international commercial arbitration.[411]

The ruling in *Ali Shipping Corp v Shipyard Trogir*,[412] was extended in *Associated Electrics and Gas Insurance Ltd (Aegis) v European Reinsurance Co of Zurich*,[413] where the Privy Council held that an award could be produced, in subsequent proceedings, as the documents to be used included material which

---

produced the material. Consent may, in exceptional circumstances, arise from the custom and practice of the relevant trade; (2) order of the court; (3) leave of the court. The practical scope of this exception i.e. the grounds on which such leave would be granted, would give rise to some difficulty. However, on the analogy of the implied obligation of secrecy between banker and customer, leave would be granted; (4) disclosure when, and to the extent to which, it is reasonably necessary for the protection of the legitimate interests of an arbitrating party. It went on to note that the concept of reasonable necessity, ought not to require the party seeking disclosure "to prove necessity, regardless of difficulty or expense". Instead, the court was to take a rounded view, "taking account of the nature and purposes of the proceedings, for which the material is required, the powers and procedures of the tribunal, in which the proceedings are being conducted, the issues to which the evidence or information sought is being directed, and the practicality and expense of obtaining such evidence or information elsewhere". However, it held that "it is not enough that an award or reasons might have a commercially persuasive impact"; (5) where, the interests of justice require so. This principle, was derived from the judgment of Mance J., in *London and Leeds Estates Ltd v Paribas Ltd (No 2)* [1995] 2 EG 134. Potter LJ, held that, this was not a wide ranging exception, but, rather a limited one, based upon the importance of a judicial decision being reached, upon the basis of truthful or accurate evidence of the witnesses concerned; Robb (2004); Brown (2001, pp. 970–971).

[411]In *Trade Finance Inc v Bulgarian Foreign Trade Bank Ltd* Case No Y 1092-98, SVEA Court of Appeal, the Swedish Court of Appeal, reversed a Stockholm City Court decision, that had sanctioned A.I. Trade Finance Inc., for publishing an arbitral award. Essentially, the court, rejected the principle that a duty of confidentiality is implied, in law, and formulated a new "duty of loyalty" doctrine, and, in doing so, distinguished between various elements of the arbitral proceedings. For example, it was noted that disclosure, of the fact of the arbitration, is much different, than disclosure of a party's trade secrets. The court stated, that the reason and effect of breach should be considered, in determining the sanctioning or not of a person breaching its duty of good faith and loyalty. In ruling so, the Swedish Court of Appeal, deviated from the English courts, in particular, from the line of approach in *Ali Shipping v Shipyard Trogir* [1998] 1 Lloyd's Rep 643, and has, as such, been sharply criticised, in not contributing to the development and forwarding of the evolution of the duty to confidentiality. However, there is also another view to be seen, in the ruling of the Swedish Court of Appeal, in *Trade Finance Inc v Bulgarian Foreign Trade Bank Ltd* Case No Y 1092-98, SVEA Court of Appeal, i.e. that the case, in spite of the ripples of worry that it has on the one hand created in the world of international commercial arbitration, has, on the other hand, undoubtedly, also taken a common sense approach to the confidentiality issue. In effect, in rejecting the bright-line rules of *Ali Shipping v Shipyard Trogir* [1998] 1 Lloyd's Rep 643., *Trade Finance Inc v Bulgarian Foreign Trade Bank Ltd* Case No Y 1092-98, SVEA Court of Appeal, may have prompted for less predictability for the parties; but, if followed, it may also be, that it will create increased efficiency, in international commercial arbitration, in that it may encourage wide publication of awards, and, thus, help create a precedent system; Brown (2001, pp. 986–987).

[412]*Ali Shipping Corporation v. Shipyard Trogir* [1998] 1 Lloyd's Rep. 643.

[413]*Associated Electrics and Gas Insurance Ltd (Aegis) v. European Reinsurance Co of Zurich* [2003] UKPC 11; [2003] 1 All E.R. (Comm) 253.

could be useful to the public; and, also, because it felt that the implied duty, that all documents relating to arbitration are confidential, could be disregarded here, in light of public interest considerations, and, finally, distinguished *Ali Shipping Corp v Shipyard Trogir*,[414] on the basis, that the parties in it were not the same.[415]

Furthermore, in *Lincoln National Life Insurance Co v Sun Life Assurance Co of Canada*,[416] where a party to the second of two arbitrations, on a reinsurance dispute, attempted to rely on the award of the first tribunal, to which they were not parties, in order to avoid certain reinsurance policies, on the grounds that the first award had held that one of the arbitration parties in the first arbitration, namely Cigna, had reinsured them, the High Court held, that a third party should be allowed to rely on an award, that they were not privy to, provided that was fair to do so and, also, provided that the administration of justice would not be brought into disrepute. The Court of Appeal, reversed this finding, and, stated that, considerations of general justice were only applicable to litigation, and that the nature of arbitration may induce different rulings, in arbitrations on closely related issues, and that parties should be able to profit from the confidentiality and non-binding character of earlier awards.[417]

Cases preceding the ruling in *Lincoln National Life Insurance Co v Sun Life Assurance Co of Canada*,[418] show that courts are reluctant, to allow the use of an earlier award on subsequent arbitration between different parties.

In *Sacor Maritima v. Repsol*,[419] disputes, arising out of the head charter and the sub-charter, were referred to two separate arbitrations. It was held, that there was no principle on which the sole arbitrator's findings of fact, or conclusion, or causation, on the evidence before him, in the arbitration under the head charter, could be

---

[414] *Ali Shipping Corp v Shipyard Trogir* [1998] 1 Lloyd's Rep. 643.

[415] In *Associated Electric & Gas Insurance Services Limited v European Reinsurance Company of Zurich* [2003] UKPC 11, the Privy Council cast some doubt on the decision of the Court of Appeal, in *Ali Shipping v Shipyard Trogir* (1998) 1 Lloyd's Rep. 643. Their Lordships, expressed reservations about the desirability or merit of adopting the approach of Potter LJ, in *Ali Shipping v Shipyard Trogir* (1998) 1 Lloyd's Rep. 643, where he characterised the duty of confidentiality, as an implied term, and set out the exceptions to which it would be subject. Their Lordships, considered that this approach ran the risk of failing to distinguish between different types of confidentiality, which attach to different types of documents or to documents which have been obtained in different ways, and elided privacy and confidentiality. Commercial arbitrations were essentially private proceedings, and, unlike litigation in public courts, did not place anything in the public domain. This may mean, that the implied restrictions, on the use of material, may have a greater impact than those applying in litigation. However, the same logic could not be applied to the award. An award may have to be referred to, for accounting purposes, or for the purpose of legal proceedings, or for the purposes of enforcing the rights, which the award confers. Generalisations and the formulation of detailed implied terms, were not appropriate; See Robb (2004).

[416] *Lincoln National Life Insurance Co v. Sun Life Assurance Co of Canada* First Instance [2004] EWHC 343; [2004] 1 Lloyd's Rep. 737, CA; [2004] EWCA 1660.

[417] Uff and Noussia (2009, pp. 1428–1449).

[418] *Lincoln National Life Insurance Co v. Sun Life Assurance Co of Canada* First Instance [2004] EWHC 343; [2004] 1 Lloyd's Rep. 737, CA; [2004] EWCA 1660.

[419] *Sacor Maritima SA v. Repsol Petroleo SA* [1998] 1 Lloyd's Rep. 518 (QBD (Comm)).

regarded as binding, in the context of a different arbitration, involving different evidence, between Sacor and Repsol. It was noted, that the two tribunals, despite their overlapping constitution, had arrived at inconsistent factual findings, but, that they did so in disputes between different parties, under different contracts and on different evidence. This was a risk inherent in separate arbitrations, where, in the absence of consent, there is no procedure, as there is in civil litigation, for consolidation of proceedings. In this case, what was sought was to take findings of fact and conclusions of causations, made in the first arbitration, and transpose them onto the second arbitration. On the question, whether Repsol incurred any liability to indemnify Sacor in respect of Sacor's unquestioned liability to Kosan, this was found to have been a matter for determination by the second tribunal. This was different from *Lincoln National Life Insurance Co v Sun Life Assurance Co of Canada*,[420] in which the issue in the Lincoln arbitration was precisely the same, as in the Cigna arbitration, namely, what was the scope of the Cigna reinsurance.

In *Nesté Chemicals SA v DK Line SA (The Sargasso)*,[421] Stargas chartered a vessel from Petredec, as disponent owner under a time charter. Nesté chartered the same vessel from Stargas, for the carriage of a cargo of propylene under a voyage charter. The cargo of propylene was contaminated, with the chemical carried by the vessel on her previous two voyages. Nesté claimed against Stargas, for breach of the voyage charter, in an arbitration, and was awarded damages against Stargas. Stargas, claimed an indemnity, from Petredec. Clarke J. held, that Stargas was entitled to recover damages, in the amount of the award together with interest and costs, unless Petredec pleaded and proved, that Stargas failed to take reasonable steps to mitigate their loss, or, that the award was such that no reasonable arbitrators could reach on the evidence, or, was in some other respect perverse. Here, a party to a previous award was relying on the award, against a stranger, rather than the other way round, as was the case in *Lincoln National Life Insurance Co v Sun Life Assurance Co of Canada*.[422]

The implications of the decision, in *Lincoln National Life Insurance Co v Sun Life Assurance Co of Canada*,[423] appear, *prima facie*, to be far reaching. The Lincoln arbitrators, had to give not only persuasive consideration to the Cigna award, but, they were held to be bound by it, on an issue which had not been necessary for the determination of the Cigna arbitration. Sun/Phoenix, argued that the Lincoln arbitrators were not bound by the reasoning of the Cigna arbitrators, nor

---

[420] *Lincoln National Life Insurance Co v. Sun Life Assurance Co of Canada* First Instance – [2004] EWHC 343; [2004] 1 Lloyd's Rep. 737, CA; [2004] EWCA 1660.

[421] *Nesté Chemicals SA v DK Line SA (The Sargasso)* [1994] 2 Lloyd's Rep. 6 [1994].

[422] *Lincoln National Life Insurance Co v. Sun Life Assurance Co of Canada* First Instance – [2004] EWHC 343; [2004] 1 Lloyd's Rep. 737, CA; [2004] EWCA 1660; Woolhouse (2004, pp. 150, 152, 153).

[423] *Lincoln National Life Insurance Co v. Sun Life Assurance Co of Canada* First Instance – [2004] EWHC 343; [2004] 1 Lloyd's Rep. 737, CA; [2004] EWCA 1660; Woolhouse (2004, pp. 150, 152, 153).

by findings of fact, which did not determine the ultimate position between Cigna and Sun/Phoenix.

If the question related to litigation, *res judicata* would only apply to the answers from the previous litigation, which are necessary to a decision and fundamental to it. However, the ultimate result, in *Lincoln National Life Insurance Co v Sun Life Assurance Co of Canada*,[424] it is submitted, was fair and just. Both Cigna and Lincoln contracts, included arbitration clauses. The Lincoln arbitration depended partly upon the scope of the Cigna reinsurance. The issue, whether losses under the Unicover reinsurance would have been recoverable under the Cigna reinsurance, decided the applicability of the net, retained lines clause of the Lincoln reinsurance, to losses under the Unicover whole account reinsurances.

The question of the scope of Cigna reinsurance, was finally decided between Cigna and Sun Life under the contractual machinery provided for dispute resolution. The findings should be equally binding, in a subsequent arbitration between different parties, whether the decision on the cope of Cigna reinsurance was made by a competent court, or by an arbitral tribunal. However, *Lincoln National Life Insurance Co v Sun Life Assurance Co of Canada*[425] is not an authority for the general proposition that an award, in an arbitration between A and B, is always binding, on the same issue, in a subsequent arbitration, between B and C.

The general principle, is still that an award has no effect, whatever, upon non-parties to the arbitration; it cannot confer rights, nor can it impose obligations, upon third parties, unless they have expressly agreed to be bound by the outcome of the arbitration. An award is final and binding, upon the parties and on "any persons claiming through or under them". This is similar to the principle applicable to decisions of court, *in personam*, which only operate as estoppel in favour of or against parties and those claiming through them, but not in favour of, or against third parties and strangers. The facts, of each case, will have to be examined and considerations of justice and fairness applied thereto. Thus, the arbitrators, in a subsequent arbitration, will have to examine, at the very least, the circumstances giving rise to the first arbitration, the issues referred to the first arbitration, the formal or otherwise nature of the first arbitration, the scope and extent of the arbitrators' enquiry and evidence in the first arbitration, the reasons in the award, as well as other factors that may apply to each case. Considerations of confidentiality will decide, whether the subsequent arbitrators have access to all the relevant materials in the first arbitration.[426]

---

[424] *Lincoln National Life Insurance Co v. Sun Life Assurance Co of Canada* First Instance – [2004] EWHC 343; [2004] 1 Lloyd's Rep. 737, CA; [2004] EWCA 1660; Woolhouse (2004, pp. 150, 152, 153).

[425] *Lincoln National Life Insurance Co v. Sun Life Assurance Co of Canada* First Instance – [2004] EWHC 343; [2004] 1 Lloyd's Rep. 737, CA; [2004] EWCA 1660; Woolhouse (2004, pp. 150, 152, 153).

[426] Woolhouse (2004, pp. 150–153).

Aegis v *European Re*,[427] concerned the construction of an express confidentiality agreement in one arbitration, and the question whether the later use of the award, from that arbitration, to support a plea of issue estoppel, in a subsequent arbitration, constituted a breach of that confidentiality agreement. Two disputes arose, under the same reinsurance agreement, between Associated Electric & Gas Insurance Services Ltd ("Aegis") and European Reinsurance Company of Zurich ("European Re"), which were referred to arbitration before two separate tribunals. Both disputes, concerned an alleged obligation of European Re to indemnify Aegis. In the first arbitration ("the Boyd arbitration"), the parties agreed, by means of an express procedural direction, that the arbitration would be confidential. An award was rendered, in favour of European Re, following which, European Re sought to rely on it in the second arbitration ("the Rowe arbitration"). Aegis submitted, *inter alia*, that this would be in breach of the confidentiality agreement and of the general principle of "privacy" of arbitrations. Aegis obtained an *ex parte* injunction, preventing disclosure of the award, which was later discharged by the Court of Appeal of Bermuda. Aegis appealed, to the Privy Council, to have the injunction reinstated. In the confidentiality agreement, in the Boyd arbitration, the parties had, *inter alia*, agreed that the arbitration result will not be disclosed at any time to any individual or entity, in whole or in part, which is not a party to the arbitration between AEGIS and European Re. In construing that wording, the Privy Council held that it could not conceivably impose an absolute ban on disclosure of the award, as this would clearly render the award incapable of being enforced in the courts. It went on to state that, the, otherwise, legitimate use of an earlier award, in a later, also private, arbitration, between the same two parties, would not raise the mischief against which the confidentiality agreement is directed; such as, the material generated during the arbitration, falling into hands of persons with interests adverse to either of the arbitrating parties. The Privy Council, further, held, that the essential purpose and foundation of arbitration, was the determination of the parties' rights, by the arbitrators, pursuant to the authority given to them, by the parties. It was an implied term, of the arbitration agreement, that the parties agreed to perform the award, i.e. to recognize and respect the rights it declared. The award, in the Boyd arbitration, had decided the rights of the parties, under the disputed article of the reinsurance agreement. Aegis was, therefore, prevented from disputing the arbitrators' decision in the Rowe arbitration. The confidentiality agreement, was intended to prevent third parties from relying on material, generated during the arbitration, against either of the two insurance companies. The legitimate use of an earlier award, in a later arbitration, between the same two parties, was, therefore, not a breach of the confidentiality agreement.

The decisive part, of the Privy Council's reasoning, related to the nature of the plea of issue estoppel. It held, that relying on an issue estoppel, in a subsequent arbitration, was one species of enforcement of the previous award. European Re,

[427] *Associated Electric and Gas Insurance Services Ltd v European Reinsurance Co. of Zurich* UKPC 11, (2003) 1 WLR 1041.

was effectively attempting to enforce the rights, conferred on it by the Boyd tribunal's determination of the given article of the reinsurance agreement against Aegis, which, in the Rowe arbitration, sought to dispute that European Re had those rights. In other words: for Aegis, to raise again the same dispute, in the Rowe Arbitration, amounted to a failure, by Aegis, to recognise and perform the earlier award, and, therefore did not infringe the stipulations of the confidentiality agreement properly construed.[428]

The Privy Council, did not embark on an examination of the extent and the nature of any implied duty of confidentiality in arbitration, as this was thought to be unnecessary, given the existence of an express confidentiality agreement in the Boyd arbitration, and the finding that the raising of the issue estoppel, by European Re, amounted to a method of enforcement. It expressly avoided, commenting on Lord Justice Potter's analysis of such implied duty, in *Ali Shipping Corporation v Shipyard Trogir,*[429] and, held that, there was no place, in the present case, to express more general statements, concerning the privacy of arbitration proceedings and the duty of one party to respect the confidentiality, as well as reservations, about the desirability or merit of adopting the approach encapsulated in *Ali Shipping Corporation v Shipyard Trogir,*[430] where the duty of confidentiality was, initially, characterised as an implied term, and, then, exceptions to it were formulated.

Whether the Privy Council's reluctance, to embrace any general principle of confidentiality in arbitration constitutes a judicial step backwards, or merely a pragmatic realisation, that the issue is of such complexity that it needs to be determined on a case-by-case basis, rather than by formulating principles of general application in the abstract, remains to be seen. Given that the Privy Council, could avail itself of an express confidentiality agreement, from the Boyd arbitration; the fact that it decided not to delve deeper, into a detailed analysis of any such principles of general application, is perhaps not surprising.

The Privy Council's decision, to uphold European Re's arguments and refuse the injunction, was eminently sensible in the circumstances of the case. The private and, in theory, confidential nature of arbitration, should not mean that parties can go on arbitrating the same point *ad infinitum*, until they get the result they prefer. This problem, is obviously even more acute, in the insurance and reinsurance industry, where there are often chains of contracts involving related, although different, parties.

However, their Lordships' focus, on the nature of the issue estoppel, as a form of enforcement of an earlier award, has not furthered the confidentiality debate. Other than in the context of a subsequent arbitration, between exactly the same parties and concerning an actual determination by the tribunal of the same clause, in the same contract, giving rise to enforceable rights; it is normal to wonder, when, and in what circumstances, an award can be publicised without the consent of both parties. It

---

[428]Rawlings and Seeger (2003, pp. 485–486).

[429]*Ali Shipping Corporation v. Shipyard Trogir* [1998] 1 Lloyd's Rep. 643.

[430]*Ali Shipping Corporation v. Shipyard Trogir* [1998] 1 Lloyd's Rep. 643.

seems that this, as well as further questions, concerning, if and to what extent, the supposed principle of confidentiality attaches, to the various stages and elements of an arbitration, remain unresolved, and, will continue to require detailed judicial examination, as and when they arise.

In the meantime, given the prevailing sense of confusion amongst practitioners, as to the precise nature and scope of any implied duty of confidentiality in arbitration, and as to the exceptions to any such duty, parties would be well advised not to take anything for granted, and to continue including express confidentiality provisions, in their arbitration agreement, or in procedural directions at the outset of the case.[431]

In an ideal world, interdependent disputes, like those in *Lincoln National Life Insurance Co v Sun Life Assurance Co of Canada*,[432] would be decided by a single tribunal in a consolidated arbitration. However, a tribunal has no power to consolidate proceedings, unless the parties agree to confer such a power. In most cases, the decision of an arbitral tribunal, would be binding, only on the parties to the arbitration and those claiming through them.

The exceptions, when an earlier award is held to be binding on a subsequent arbitration tribunal, appear to have been made in the following cases:(a) when the earlier award, under a contractual machinery for dispute resolution, determined the rights and obligations of the parties to a contract A and B, so that the award can be treated as part of the contract, and, thus, be proved in the same way, as any contract can be proved; and (b) where, the breach of a charter-party and subcharter, is proved to be the same, and the arbitrators have held the charterer, under a charter-party, liable to a sub-charterer, in a particular amount, then, the better view, as a matter of principle, is to say that the cause of the liability, so determined, was the breach of the charter-party.

By analogy, in cases involving re-sale of goods, similar principles should apply. If the earlier determination were in a judgment of a competent court, it would be binding on the subsequent arbitral tribunal in similar circumstances. However, a settlement of an earlier dispute, between A and B, unless incorporated into a consent award, might not necessarily have the same effect as an award or a judgment of a competent court. The subsequent tribunal, will have to consider whether the settlement was a reasonable one. Confidentiality of an arbitration award and of other materials generated in the arbitration, further complicate the matter, and, where, in a subsequent arbitration, a party is unable to obtain access, to all the relevant materials from the earlier arbitration, the tribunal might have to decide the issue afresh.

In conclusion, there are no hard and fast rules, for deciding when the earlier award would be binding, in a subsequent arbitration between different parties, and, indeed, it will be difficult to set out rules, which will be applicable to every

---

[431] Rawlings and Seeger (2003, pp. 488–489).

[432] *Lincoln National Life Insurance Co v. Sun Life Assurance Co of Canada* [2004] EWHC 343; [2004] 1 Lloyd's Rep. 737, CA; [2004] EWCA 1660.

conceivable set of facts. Broad considerations, of what is fair and just, should lead to the right answer in each case.[433]

4.3.4.2 USA

In the USA, the confidentiality of international arbitral awards, is not a presumption and does not exist as an implicit term of the parties' arbitration clause.

In *United States v Panhandle Eastern Corp.*,[434] the district court was faced with a US government request, for the production of documents related to a previous arbitral proceeding held under the ICC Rules. The court ruled that, because the arbitration agreement and applicable arbitration rules did not provide for the confidentiality of the proceedings, the government could access the documents. The decision should not be considered surprising, because the genesis of the court's reasoning appears in the domestic arbitration court cases.

A review, of domestic, arbitration-related, court decisions, reveals the standard on which the Panhandle court was relying.[435] For example, in *A.T. v State Farm Mutual Automobile Insurance*,[436] the appellate court had no difficulty in supporting the district court's determination, to apply the generally accepted lack of confidentiality, afforded to documents and awards without an express agreement. The court concluded that, because the arbitration statute provides for an arbitration award to be filed, enforced, and challenged in court, thus, an arbitration record may become an open public record. Therefore, because the plaintiff did not obtain a confidentiality, or protective order, or agreement, the record was available for use, by State Farm, in later, separate litigation. The State Farm court's reasoning, is not unique, within the domestic arbitration law of the United States.

In *Parilla v IAP Worldwide Services, VI, Inc.*,[437] it was determined that, the parties had agreed to protect as confidential the disputing parties names, and, thus, without subsequent agreement to the contrary, the names could not be released; and, in *Hutcherson v Sears Roebuck & Co.*,[438] it was reasoned that, because the parties had not selected rules that afforded protection to the arbitration award, the award was capable of being released.

Moreover, the US courts have found no difficulty in extending the general rule, which requires parties to expressly agree to confidentiality of documents and awards, to arbitration with an international nexus, such as the case was in the Panhandle court decision. Thus, although, clearly, a distinction should be made between international and domestic arbitration, in the area of confidentiality

[433]Woolhouse (2004, pp. 150–156).

[434]*United States v Panhandle Eastern Corp.* 118 F.R.D. 346 (D. Del. 1988).

[435]Raymond (2005, pp. 494–495).

[436]*A.T. v State Farm Mutual Automobile Insurance* 989 P.2d 219 (Colo. App., 1999).

[437]*Parilla v IAP Worldwide Services, VI, Inc.*, 368 F.3d 269, (3d. Cir. 2004).

[438]*Hutcherson v Sears Roebuck & Co.*, 793 N.E.2d 886, (Ill. App. 1st Dist. 2003).

afforded awards and documents, the distinction is not as clear. Therefore, the domestic decisions can be important to examine, if, for no other reason, than to, again, recognize that the definition of confidentiality and the scope of protection, afforded under the auspices of confidentiality, is not as clear as a business may desire.[439]

US courts, have used the doctrine of unconscionability, to limit arbitration clauses that require the award to remain confidential, when the parties are of unequal bargaining power. Although these cases, admittedly, draw on neither international nor business-to-business contracts, the emerging view in the USA remains important, because it shows the uncertainty of the term "confidentiality". Moreover, these cases begin to explore the "repeat player" concept, which recognizes the importance of arbitration participants, who are involved in numerous arbitrations.[440]

In the case of *Luna v Household Finance Corp. III*,[441] the court explained that a facially neutral confidentiality clause, which required the entire award to be kept confidential, contributed to the finding of substantive unconscionability, because one of the parties to the arbitration clause was a "repeat participant".

In *Lloyd v Hovensa*,[442] the court used the concepts set out in Luna, to strike the portion of the arbitration clause, that permitted one of the parties to unilaterally prevent the inclusion of its name in the award. The court reasoned that, the ability of a party, to unilaterally prevent the inclusion of its name in the award, favours the repeat participants and makes it difficult for potential plaintiffs to build a case of intentional misconduct, or to establish a pattern or practice of discrimination by a particular company. Clearly, the court's focus was on the shielding of a company's negative behavior from the public, i.e., in this case, the consumer public. However, there is nothing to prevent the repeat player concept, from being extended to the interpretation of a confidentiality term, in a commercial arbitration clause.[443]

US Courts have also recognised their independent duty, to examine the confidentiality of arbitration, when the parties seek their assistance to confirm or vacate arbitration awards.

In *Zurich American Insurance Co. v Rite Aid Corp.*,[444] an employment dispute and a resulting coverage controversy, arising out of a high-profile financial scandal, concerning Rite Aid Corporation, were submitted to confidential arbitration. Rite Aid's liability insurer, sued to vacate the confidential arbitration award that required it to indemnify, Rite Aid, for a separate multimillion dollar arbitral award, won by a former Rite Aid employee. Both the docket and record, in the court proceedings, were sealed by stipulation of the parties, who were negotiating

---

[439]Raymond (2005, pp. 495–496).

[440]Raymond (2005, p. 497).

[441]*Luna v Household Finance Corp. III*, 236 F. Supp 2d. 1166 (W.D. Wash. 2002).

[442]*Lloyd v Hovensa*, 243 F. Supp. 2d. 346 (2003).

[443]Raymond (2005, pp. 497–499).

[444]*Zurich American Insurance Co. v Rite Aid Corp.*, 345 F. Supp. 2d 497 (E.D. Pa. 2004).

a settlement of the underlying arbitration awards. In analysing, whether it was appropriate for the case to remain shrouded under seal, the district court, *sua sponte*, engaged in the balancing of interests, applicable to the sealing of judicial records and proceedings.[445] According to the Rite Aid court, neither the confidentiality of the arbitral forum, nor the federal policy of encouraging arbitration, trumped the clear law and policy standards, for maintaining open and accessible records of legal matters for public scrutiny. Instead, the significant public interest, in the case, required that the record be unsealed.[446]

Confidentiality clauses, in arbitration agreements, can impede potential plaintiffs from obtaining information necessary to build their cases, and may even restrict regulatory agencies from investigating and enforcing statutory rights. Courts may, thus, confront alternative dispute resolution confidentiality, when these potential litigants seek to discover arbitral decisions and awards, or information produced during an arbitration proceeding. In these cases, important public and private values again collide. On one hand, protecting the confidentiality of arbitration, furthers the strong public policy favouring ADR, by protecting party expectations and ensuring that parties in an arbitration proceeding get the protections for which they contracted. At the same time, however, courts must similarly protect the countervailing public and private interest, in affording a litigant the opportunity to broadly discover information in support of its case. As recently recognized in *Fireman's Fund Ins. Co. v Cunningham Lindsey Claims Mgmt., Inc.*,[447] "[a]n overzealous quest for ADR can distort the proper role of the court' by suppressing admissible evidence in the name of confidentiality".[448]

4.3.4.3 France

Aita v Ojjeh,[449] is a stringent defence of an implied duty of confidentiality and a clear deviation from similar English and American cases, which justify exceptions for judicial enforcement of a party's legal rights.[450]

The case, involved a party who sought annulment, in France, of an arbitral award rendered in London. The arbitration award disputed, in this case, was issued in England, between the parties, Mr Aita and Mr Ojjeh, concerning a loan agreement. Aita requested, in the Court of Appeal of Paris, that the award be dismissed, on the grounds that there was no valid arbitration agreement, as well as, on the basis that

---

[445] Kratky-Dore (2006, p. 508).

[446] Kratky-Dore (2006, p. 509).

[447] *Fireman's Fund Ins. Co. v Cunningham Lindsey Claims Mgmt., Inc.*, Nos. 03CV0531, 03CV1625 (DLI) (MLO), 2005 WL 1522783 (E.D.N.Y. June 28, 2005).

[448] *Fireman's Fund Ins. Co. v Cunningham Lindsey Claims Mgmt., Inc.*, Nos. 03CV0531, 03CV1625 (DLI) (MLO), 2005 WL 1522783 (E.D.N.Y. June 28, 2005) at *3; Kratky-Dore (2006, p. 509).

[449] *Aita v Ojjeh*, Judgment of 18 Feb. 1986, 1986 Revue de l' Arbitrage 583.

[450] Brown (2001, pp. 975–976).

they did not have the opportunity to pursue their claim during arbitration, and, on the grounds that the award was contrary to the French "ordre publique". Ojjeh, disputed the court's authority, and, also, claimed damages for Aita starting an unnecessary trial.

The Court of Appeal of Paris held, that it did not have authority to make a judgement and ruled against the party, holding that, the annulment proceedings violated the principle of confidentiality, by bringing the proceedings to a forum, known as with no authority. The act of seeking an annulment, in France, of an award rendered in London, was, merely, an act seeking to provoke a publication of confidential information. The action had caused a public debate that should have remained confidential, as this is the very nature of arbitral proceedings, i.e. to have the highest degree of discretion in the resolution of private disputes. By challenging the award, Aita caused Ojjeh damage, and he, therefore, had to pay a penalty.[451]

4.3.4.4 Germany

The OLG Frankfurt Court, in its decision of 22.10.2004,[452] where an arbitral tribunal's constitution was challenged as biased, on the basis that they had decided on issues based on partiality and had misjudged legal regulations, held that the above is no valid real reason, to challenge an arbitral tribunal as biased, and that, in any case, the alleged partiality of the arbitrators, does not constitute a breach of confidentiality and, as such, a valid reason to challenge and annul the respective arbitral award.

The court stated that, if the parties wished to have had such a right guaranteed, they should have expressly stated it, in a detail drafted confidentiality clause within the arbitration agreement.

4.4 The Treatment of Confidentiality by ICC Rules

Articles 1(1) and (2) of the ICC Court's internal rules, provide that the sessions of the Court are confidential and open to its member and to the Secretariat, and that, by invitation by the Chairman, other persons, which must respect the confidential nature of the Court, may be invited to attend. The documents to be submitted, are selected by the Secretariat. The parties to the proceedings, will not know what has been submitted to the ICC court, with respect to the decision sought. The ICC Court's desire, for confidentiality, has to be balanced against the need for potential users of ICC arbitration to understand how the ICC Court and ICC arbitration function. However, the issue of confidentiality, with respect to arbitration extends

[451] Brown (2001, pp. 975–976).

[452] OLG Frankfurt, Beschl. v. 22.10.2004 – Case 2 Sch 01/04 (2).

beyond the issue of confidentiality of the proceedings of the ICC Court, although there also exists a considerable overlap. As regards the proceedings of the ICC Court, it publishes articles, regarding types of decisions, and trends, but without identifying the parties involved.[453]

4.5 Conclusions

Within the last decade, the concept of confidentiality, in arbitration, has become a topic which has instigated a lot of academic writings and analyses. All this instigated debate, has resulted in the questioning of what were, up to then, perceived as common assumptions, and, has lead in the conclusion that the subject, is more complex, obscure and less settled than originally thought.

Confidentiality, is indeed given as one of the reasons to arbitrate a dispute, instead of litigating it. An empirical analysis and study,[454] conducted by Dr Christian Bühring-Uhle, in 1992, whereby data was collected from participants in international commercial arbitration, as to the advantages and disadvantages of this method of alternative dispute resolution, showed that, following "neutrality of the forum" and "international enforcement by treaty", the third most important reason for choosing arbitration, is its confidential character and nature.[455]

Secrecy, has never been a concept used in international commercial arbitration. Even the concept of confidentiality, which is not assumed anymore to be automatically applicable, has come under judicial attack, in a number of countries, such as in Australia, in *Esso/BHP v Plowman*,[456] or in Sweden, in *Bulgarian Foreign Trade Bank Ltd. v A.L. Trade Finance Inc.*[457] It is also to be noted that arbitral institutional rules, generally do not provide for any general duty of confidentiality,[458] and this means that confidentiality is, from the outset, to be treated only as a stochastic and relative concept in international commercial arbitration.

[453]Buehler and Webster (2008, pp. 14–15).

[454]Bühring (1996).

[455]Pryles (2008, pp. 501–502).

[456]*Esso/BHP v Plowman* (1995) 128 A.L.R. 391.

[457]*Bulgarian Foreign Trade Bank Ltd. v. A.L. Trade Finance Inc.*, Judgment of October 27, 2000, Swedish Supreme Court.

[458]The ICC Rules, article 21, only establishes the confidentiality of ICC hearings. However, the UNCITRAL Arbitration Rule 32(5), prohibits publication of awards without the consent of the parties. The LCIA Rules, in article 30, impose a duty of confidentiality on the parties, generally, unless they expressly agree to the contrary in writing, and the AAA International Rule 27, also, prohibits making the award public, unless the parties have consented, or because it is required by law. In contrast, the ICSID Rules, ICSID Arbitration Rule 48(4) and ICSID Financial and Administrative Regulation 22(2), prohibit the Centre from publishing awards, without the consent of the parties, but, at the same time, it is also submitted that parties are free to publish ICSID awards, unless they agree otherwise.

There is, of course, something to be said, in favour of confidentiality as well as transparency. While the potential for amicable solution, is one of the elements speaking for confidentiality, there are others, of a more general nature, such as the wish to not make a dispute public at all, or to protect business secrets, which are also valid.

On the other hand, it is obvious, that, not only, do arbitral institutions publish, more than ever, about arbitration cases, or that the law firms, and the parties they represent, speak more about it, but that the entire arbitration "community", is far better connected, resulting in more informal "sanitised" exchange, on cases of interest. This, in turn, means that the balance, between confidentiality and transparency, seems to tilt slightly more in favour of transparency, and the need for determining the right balance appears to be different, from case to case.

In addition, it is to be noted that, there are degrees of secrecy and confidentiality, depending on the function in question. At the one extreme, the internal deliberations of the tribunal, are and should remain secret. At the other extreme, it is difficult, or even inappropriate in some circumstances, to keep the arbitral award itself confidential, such as in the case of enforcing the award in domestic courts, where, obviously, the award cannot be kept secret.

All the above apart, it is notable that the non-respect for the confidentiality of awards, has certainly increased over the years. The trend, towards maintaining a balance between confidentiality and transparency, is also understandable. In weighing the concepts of confidentiality against transparency, one may bear in view, that, much of the reporting, done on arbitral proceedings, are not primarily made by the general media and with the intention of informing the public, as partly the case may be with major commercial litigation, but, rather, with the aim of keeping the professional circles informed of the developments. Further, the content of what is reported, of arbitral proceedings, is of some relevance. One gets the feeling that the intention, behind reporting of the arbitral developments, is to inform the professional circles, mostly, of the legal developments, rather than of detailed facts. That is, the reporting, made by the arbitration journals cited, should be seen in that light, without, however, denying the transparency effect of their publications.

However, it should also be accepted that, very often, the publication or circulation of arbitral awards, is by those individuals, or parties, who have an interest in certain views or philosophies being seen to be accepted in international arbitration. In this respect, scientific legal papers or articles, may only be based on a small number of arbitral awards, that have come into the public domain. It may also be that there are other awards, that have rejected, or, at least, eschewed, a particular view or philosophy, but have not been circulated, because their circulation serves no particular interest or view, and, therefore, the available corpus of published arbitral awards, should not be seen, as the equivalent of a fully reported body of case law, from a state court system, where all judgments are available.

Although the case law, on confidentiality, in commercial arbitration, has shown a disperse approach, in the treatment of the implied duty of confidentiality, nevertheless, it is accepted as essential that confidentiality be preserved, in certain situations, for business reasons, and, it is in this respect that, the courts attempt to create a safety net, in that they try to balance the public's need for openness, and the individual's need for confidentiality of sensitive information, and permit non-observance of confidentiality when the public interest demands it.[459]

From the examined jurisdictions, as far as common law is concerned, cases such as *Associated Electrics and Gas Insurance Ltd (Aegis) v European Reinsurance Co of Zurich*,[460] *Insurance Co v Lloyd's Syndicate*,[461] and *Ali Shipping Corporation v Shipyard Trogir*,[462] show that confidentiality agreements may not always be recognised, where the same issues and parties are involved. Similarly, the ruling in *United States v Panhandle Eastern Corp. et al*,[463] demonstrated that confidentiality need be provided for expressly, where it is not statutorily procured, and that, even where this is the case, public interest considerations may require it to be overruled. Contrary to the above, *Lincoln National Life Insurance Co v Sun Life Assurance Co of Canada*[464] demonstrated that confidentiality should be kept, in cases where third parties seek to rely on an award to which they have not been privy to.

In view of the fact that questions, on the preservation or not of confidentiality, are bound to be re-examined in future cases, it is highly probable that Courts will have to abstain, in the future, from their orthodox and rigid views on the duty to preserve confidentiality, in line also with the provision in s. 34 of the English Arbitration Act 1996, which encourages arbitrators to adopt an inquisitorial role in defining the facts of the case. Confidentiality, should not be an obstacle, when parties wish to use an earlier award in later proceedings, and where, to do so, would enhance the Court's powers, to define the issues accurately.[465]

In France, although there is a strong principle of confidentiality, there exists little, if any, case law on confidentiality in arbitration. Following *Aita v Ojjeh*,[466] in *Société True North et Société FCB Internationale v Bleustein et al*,[467] the French Court of Appeal restated that there exists an implied duty of confidentiality. However, recent case law, such as *Nafimco v Foster Wheeler Trading Company AG*,[468] shows that the attitude of the French Court of Appeal has been relaxed, as it does not categorically recognise the existence of such a principle.[469]

---

[459]Uff and Noussia (2009, pp. 1428–1449).

[460]*Associated Electrics and Gas Insurance Ltd (Aegis) v. European Reinsurance Co of Zurich* [2003] UKPC 11; [2003] 1 All E.R. (Comm) 253.

[461]*Insurance Co v Lloyd's Syndicate* [1995] 1 Lloyd's Rep. 272.

[462]*Ali Shipping Corporation v. Shipyard Trogir* [1998] 1 Lloyd's Rep. 643.

[463]*United States v Panhandle Eastern Corp. et al*, (D.Del. 1988) 118 F.R.D. 346.

[464]*Lincoln National Life Insurance Co v. Sun Life Assurance Co of Canada* [2004] EWHC 343; [2004] 1 Lloyd's Rep. 737, CA; [2004] EWCA 1660.

[465]Uff and Noussia (2009, pp. 1428–1449).

[466]*Aita v Ojjeh* (1986) Revue de'l Arbitrage 583.

[467]*Societe True North et Societe FCB Internationale v Bleustein et al*, Cour d'Appel de Paris 1999, Rev Arb 2003, 189.

[468]*Nafimco v Foster Wheeler Trading Company AG*, Cour d'Appel de Paris, 22.01.2004.

[469]Mueller (2005, pp. 218–219).

In Germany, the approach is similar. The OLG Frankfurt Court, in its decision of 22.10.2004,[470] stated clearly that there is a presumption towards the observance of confidentiality, but, that, where parties wanted to have specific effects, such as in the case to have an award annulled, because the alleged bias of the arbitrators impliedly pertained also an attack to the confidentiality, then they should have formulated a specific to this effect confidentiality clause.

The issue of disclosure, or not, of information of arbitral proceedings, to subsequent ones, or, of consolidation of arbitral proceedings, depends on the agreed the contractual confidentiality obligations. The right of an arbitral tribunal, to require production of documents, must be seen against the background of ZPO §§ 420–444 and 142, which allow only a limited production of documents. Depending on the agreement of the parties, the latter may be free, to use the information disclosed in arbitral proceedings for other purposes.[471]

Having in mind the Swedish Supreme Courts judgement, in *Bulgarian Foreign Trade Bank Ltd. v. A.L. Trade Finance Inc.*,[472] it is advisable for those who wish for confidentiality rather than transparency, to be very specific on confidentiality, when drafting arbitration clauses. Those who wish confidentiality, specifically, have to accept the burden of having to agree on that, especially since transparency and the risk of public display, generally, seem to work as a drivers for settlement, and, perhaps, mediation subject to complete secrecy, before even starting arbitration proceedings.[473] More specifically, parties drafting arbitration clauses, who are concerned to ensure a confidential arbitration process, should consider: (1) whether, the law of the location of the arbitration is a strong defender of confidentiality in arbitration, and, (2) if an arbitral institution has been chosen, what confidentiality provisions are contained in those rules.[474] If there remain concerns, about the level of confidentiality afforded by the chosen process, it will be prudent to include specific wording, in the arbitration clause, to ensure confidentiality.[475]

---

[470]OLG Framkfurt, Beschl. V. 22.10.2004 – Case 2 Sch. 01/04 (2).

[471]Rützel et al. (2005, pp. 133–134).

[472]*Bulgarian Foreign Trade Bank Ltd. v. A.L. Trade Finance Inc.*, Judgment of October 27, 2000, Swedish Supreme Court.

[473]Comment on Arbitration and Confidentiality, Transnational Dispute Management, Volume I, Issue 02 – May 2004.

[474]Herbert Smith Newsletter (2008).

[475]The lack of uniformity, amongst national laws, and the diverse treatment of confidentiality, raises a choice of law question. Usually the *lex cause*, will be the law applicable to the contract, which is the subject of the arbitration. Equally often, the law governing the arbitration agreement, will be the same as the law which governs the substantive contract, in which the arbitration agreement is usually found. However, an arbitration agreement is not invariably governed by the law of the substantive contract, as the law governing an arbitration agreement determines its validity and effect and this would not seem to encompass confidentiality of the arbitral proceedings themselves. Thus, the choices for the law governing confidentiality, would seem to lie between the *lex arbitri* or the *lex fori*. It is submitted, by many writers, such as Prof. Michael Pryles, that the *lex arbitri* is the law that should be chosen, as the law to apply. However, confidentiality may not always exist, under the applicable national law, but it may also arise as a result of contractual

A further remark, which needs to be made, is that confidentiality, in arbitration, derives from the applicable national law, or, from the party selected arbitration rules, or, from contractual provisions. As far as the applicable national law is concerned, there is no uniformity and the common assumption of confidentiality, albeit a somewhat vague concept, which is ill defined in extent and subject to diverse exceptions, was undermined by the High Court of Australia in *Esso/BHP v Plowman*.[476]

However, it is clear now that, this decision was not just an antipodean aberration, as it largely represents the law in the USA,[477] and has also been followed in Sweden.[478] In these circumstances, parties desiring confidentiality, in arbitration, should designate a particular set of arbitration rules, with appropriate and adequate, in number and extent of coverage, confidentiality, provisions within; or, absent or limited such provisions, conclude a confidentiality agreement, in the arbitration clause or elsewhere, dealing with all the existence of the arbitration, the award, as well as documents and information, obtained in the arbitration.

Due to the fact, that possible limitations, to the effectiveness of confidentiality agreements, exist, additional required measures, pertain that, both parties must agree to the terms of the agreement. Because a confidentiality agreement, only binds the parties to it, special provisions are required for the arbitrators, witnesses and any administering arbitral centre.

Not least, it should be noted that mandatory provisions of law, which provide for disclosure of information, will override confidentiality agreements.[479]

---

provisions concluded between the parties to arbitration, incorporated by reference, such as in the case of a set of institutional arbitration rules, whereby case any provision therein on confidentiality will also apply to the arbitration. International arbitration rules, either contain no provisions on confidentiality, such as the UNCITRAL Arbitration Rules, which contain a provision on privacy in Art. 25(4) but do not deal with confidentiality, or the ICC Rules, which deal with privacy in Art. 21 (3), and only contain an implicit provision on confidentiality, in Art. 20(7), whereby they state that the arbitral tribunal, may take measures, to protect trade secrets and confidential information, or, contain limited provision on confidentiality, such as the International Arbitration Rules of the American Arbitration Association, Art. 34, or contain extensive provisions on confidentiality, such as WIPO Arbitration Rules Art. 73, 74, 76, the Rules of the London Court of International Arbitration (LCIA), Art. 30, the Rules of the Australian Centre for International Commercial Arbitration (ACICA), Art. 18, or the 2007 Singapore International Arbitration Rules, Art. 18, or the "IBA Rules on Arbitration", Art. 3(12), 9); Pryles (2008, pp. 535–540).

[476] *Esso/BHP v Plowman* (1995) 128 A.L.R. 391.

[477] *US v Panhandle Eastern Corp.* (D.Del.) 1988, 118 F.R.D. 346.

[478] *Bulgarian Foreign Trade Bank Ltd. v. A.L. Trade Finance Inc.*, Judgment of October 27, 2000, Swedish Supreme Court.

[479] Pryles (2008, pp. 551–552).

Chapter 5
Critical Analysis, Overall Assessment and Discussion

5.1 Overall Analysis of Arbitration and Confidentiality Within It

5.1.1 Critical Assessment and Analysis of the Purpose of Arbitration and Its Interplay with Confidentiality

"Globalization" is categorically with us. It has affected the world's economies, popular cultures, languages and legal systems. Indeed, in this last regard, globalization has contributed directly to the rapid and broad growth of international arbitration.

As many businesses have become inherently international, they have sought more effective and efficient means of resolving disputes without having to utilise national litigation systems that are often expensive and slow, or perhaps rife with national bias and political considerations. Often, these businesses have chosen the dispute resolution mechanisms embodied in international arbitration.

As international arbitrations have grown both in number and prominence, so too have they evolved in terms of procedure, style and content. Effective and efficient practices have tended to be incorporated into the international arbitral landscape while defective, inefficient or biased experiments are likely to be discarded. As gaps in international arbitration's capabilities have been identified, arbitral practices have evolved to fill them, and the result has positioned international arbitration as an efficient alternative to the perceived problems of domestic courts. In recent years, this evolutionary process has operated at an accelerated pace.[1]

With regards to confidentiality, as with numerous other considerations in the arbitral context, parties are generally free to tailor their agreements to fit specific needs and expectations. Courts generally enforce the terms of an arbitration agreement relating to confidentiality. Parties may include confidentiality provisions in

[1]Leahy and Bianchi (2000, p. 19).

K. Noussia, *Confidentiality in International Commercial Arbitration*,
DOI 10.1007/978-3-642-10224-0_5, © Springer-Verlag Berlin Heidelberg 2010

arbitration agreements, because they appear to use arbitration as a means to resolve disputes or because they assume, often incorrectly, arbitration to be private and confidential.[2]

Most national courts agree that arbitrations are intended to be private means of dispute resolution, in the sense that the general public has no right of access to the proceedings. For example, English and Australian courts have expressly held that arbitrations proceed under an implied condition of privacy.[3] More controversial is the issue of whether the proceedings are confidential, so that one party can restrain the other from divulging facts or documents relating to the arbitration. In the United States, confidentiality is not a rule of law,[4] but the longstanding arbitral practice is to observe confidentiality.[5] In England, courts have made confidentiality a legal requirement.[6] In Australia, the opposite position was established in the infamous to the arbitration world case of *Esso/BHP v Plowman*[7] and in other jurisdictions, such as Sweden, confidentiality is only exceptionally implied.[8] Thus, some national courts consider arbitration to be impliedly confidential. The exact scope of the obligation and the extent to which it applies to different participants in the arbitral process, i.e. the parties, their counsel, witnesses, experts, the administrative body, can vary considerably from one jurisdiction to the next.[9]

---

[2]Leahy and Bianchi (2000, p. 36).

[3]*Esso/BHP v Plowman* (1995) 128 A.L.R. 391; *Hassnesh v Mew* [1993] 2 Lloyd's Rep 243.

[4]*United States v Panhandle Eastern Corp.* 118 F.R.D. 346 (D. Del. 1988).

[5]Domke (1999, § 24:07): "[t]he arbitrator should not give out any information about the proceeding or even make known the result of the arbitration to persons other than the parties. Though this is not a legal requirement, it has been sanctioned by long-standing practices. Privacy of arbitration is one of the essential factors carefully observed in institutional arbitration where no one other than the parties is allowed to gain any knowledge of the records and files".

[6]In *Hassneh Insurance Co. of Israel v Mew* [1993] 2 Lloyd's Rep. 243, where material introduced into evidence in a reinsurance contract arbitration was sought by one of the parties to be held in confidence, an English court found that there was an implied right of confidentiality in every arbitration. This implied right was the foundation upon which the court eventually required the materials to be held confidential. The court, citing *The Eastern Saga*, [1984] 2 Lloyd's Rep. 373 (Q.B.) stated, at 379: "... the concept of private arbitration derives simply from the fact that the parties have agreed to submit to arbitration particular disputes arising between them and only them. It is implicit in this that strangers shall be excluded from the hearings and conduct of the arbitration...."; Leahy and Bianchi (2000, pp. 35–37).

[7]In *Esso/BHP v Plowman* (1995) 128 A.L.R. 391 the High Court of Australia held that arbitrations are not *per se* confidential, whether on the basis of an implied term or as being inherent in the subject matter of the agreement; Leahy and Bianchi (2000, pp. 35–37); However, more recent case law – such as *Transfeld Philippines Inc & Ors v Pacific Hydro Ltd & Ors [2006] VSC 175* – has demonstrated that confidentiality is observed, as the cases where documents will not be treated as confidential are rare; Derrington (2007, pp. 188–190).

[8]The Swedish Supreme Court in *Bulgarian Foreign Trade Bank Ltd. v A.L. Trade Finance Inc.* [Judgment of October 27, 2000, Swedish Supreme Court] ruled that that a party in arbitration proceedings governed by Swedish law is not bound by confidentiality, unless the parties have entered into a specific agreement to that effect; Leahy and Bianchi (2000, pp. 35–37).

[9]Leahy and Bianchi (2000, pp. 35–37).

5.2 Critical Analysis on the Basis of the Examined Case Law in the Chosen Jurisdictions

5.2.1 The Current Position

In order to critically assess and analyse the stand of arbitration – on the basis of our study of the selected jurisdictions – we need to pose several questions, such as, for example: what is the position nowadays in relation to confidentiality in arbitration? Or what are the basic problems and the possible solutions detected and what does the future hold, i.e. will the problems encountered on confidentiality affect arbitration in all or in some of the examined jurisdictions?

To begin answering the above questions, one need ask a subsequent precedent one, i.e. which elements of arbitration fall under the confidentiality umbrella and to what extent is their protection guaranteed?

It has been standard practice to include the word "confidentiality" in any list of supposed benefits of arbitration.[10] The very existence of an arbitration may be protected by a duty of confidentiality as the mere fact that an arbitration is pending may be viewed as a secret.[11] Moreover, even more in the modern era, the concept of secrecy may no longer vary from country to country. The burden of the proof is on the party claiming that the information he wants to see protected is actually secret, or was before the wrongful disclosure occurred.

However, documents pre-existing to the arbitration are not necessarily secret. They may be stamped as confidential, or they may have been compiled in such circumstances that it is most likely that they were considered as confidential. Otherwise, no automatic protection should attach to them. The onus of proof rests with the party contending that there is a need for protection.

Nonetheless, as no firm evidence can be brought as to the fact that no publication ever occurred, a *prima facie* showing of confidentiality will shift the burden of proving confidentiality to the other party. If that party alleges that the information is no longer secret by reason of some specific disclosure to the public, it will usually be easy for him to produce evidence in that respect.[12]

In *Esso/BHP v Plowman*[13] the test for confidentiality of documents was clothed in the question whether it is proper to request its production in a subsequent case and as such constituted a rather inductive method of defining secrets.

Under continental law the arbitral tribunal or the supporting judge might deduce, from the fact that the information in question is not secret, the legal consequence that it has to be produced. It is submitted, thus, that the continental deductive method may yield more predictable results, especially as far as third parties are

[10]Paulsson and Raeding (1995, pp. 303–304).

[11]*Hassnesh v Mew* [1993] 2 Lloyd's Rep 243, 247.

[12]Dessemontet (1996, p. 16).

[13]*Esso/BHP v Plowman* (1995) 128 A.L.R. 391, High Court of Australia.

concerned, by the request for production of evidence.[14] However, courts have not articulated a general rule on this issue for reasons such as the fact that the involvement of courts may detect that arbitration will become a public record.[15] In addition, the fact that lawyers and arbitrators may disclose the participation to arbitration, or that financial considerations, ethical duties and public policy issues may detect so, or that third parties participating in arbitration, such as expert witnesses, may form the grapevine through which arbitration is spread.[16]

Notwithstanding the above, the general rule remains that documents and evidence of the arbitration are protected by confidentiality.

In this respect *Ali Shipping v Shipyard Trogir*[17] provided the leading rule on this point and stated that not only parties directly connected to the arbitration are bound by confidentiality, but also third parties which are bound by a duty implied in law towards the observance of the obligation of confidentiality. Contrary to *Ali Shipping v Trogir*,[18] *Esso/BHP v Plowman*[19] – a decision with significance far beyond the shores of Australia[20] – shocked the arbitration world and at the same time created a totally antipodean precedent by stating that documents or other evidence of the arbitral proceedings are unlikely to remain confidential unless this is expressly and particularly stipulated. Up to that point in time, and although it was accepted that a general obligation of confidentiality in arbitration does not exist *de lege lata* but only *in statu nascendi*, a general rule of confidentiality *de lege ferenda*, was favoured.[21] However, the decision in *Esso/BHP v Plowman*[22] cast severe doubts with regards to the duty to observe confidentiality, more specifically with regards to the question whether, as a general principle, international commercial arbitration is to be considered as truly encompassing the feature of a confidential element as one of its basic characteristics which are embedded in its nature, and it has also raised the question of the extent of the exceptions to it.[23]

---

[14]Dessemontet (1996, pp. 19–20).

[15]Parties frequently involved in arbitration may not be able to withhold the fact of such involvement because although third parties are excluded from most types of international arbitration, nevertheless it does not necessarily follow that parties will not to disclose what has transpired in the process of an arbitration nor that there exists a positive and unlimited duty on the part of participants in arbitral proceedings to maintain confidentiality; Paulsson and Raeding (1995, pp. 303–304).

[16]Brown (2001, pp. 1000–1004).

[17]*Ali Shipping v Shipyard Trogir* [1998] 1 Lloyd's Rep 643.

[18]*Ali Shipping v Trogir* [1999] 1 W.L.R. 314.

[19]*Esso/BHP v Plowman* (1995) 128 A.L.R. 391, High Court of Australia.

[20]Editorial (1995, pp. 231–233).

[21]Paulsson and Raeding (1995, pp. 303–304).

[22]*Esso/BHP v Plowman* (1995) 128 A.L.R. 391, High Court of Australia.

[23]In England in *Oxford Shipping Co v Nippon Yesen Kaisha [The "Eastern Saga"]* [1984] 2 Lloyd's Rep. 373 (QB), *Dolling-Baker v Merrett* [1990] 1 WLR 1205, and in *Hassnesh v Mew* [1993] 2 Lloyd's Rep 243, it was demonstrated that the nature and the extent of the duty of confidentiality in arbitration is by no means fully chartered but subject to certain limitations and exceptions. The possible exceptions, as articulated in the cases of *Ali Shipping v Shipyard Trogir*

Notwithstanding the initial impact of the decision in *Esso/BHP v Plowman*[24] and the statement that "... the best method of driving international arbitration away from England ... would be to reintroduce all the court interference that was swept away or ... for the House of Lords to overthrow Dolling-Baker and to embrace the majority judgment of the High Court of Australia in Esso/BHP ... as this would be to announce that English law no longer regards the privacy and confidentiality of arbitration proceedings ... as a fundamental characteristic of the agreement to arbitrate",[25] the implications of *Esso/BHP v Plowman*[26] seem to have lessened in the light of latest Australian case law. More specifically, *Transfeld Philippines Inc & Ors v Pacific Hydro Ltd & Ors*[27] has demonstrated that there is no real danger to confidentiality, because the circumstances in which documents will not fall under the cloak of confidentiality for having been produced outside the usual discovery process or pursuant to subpoena will be relatively rare. Even in those cases, Australian courts are likely to hold that such documents have been produced subject to an implied undertaking not to use them other than for the purposes of the arbitration. Moreover, they will be reluctant to relieve a party from that undertaking – either pursuant to their supervisory powers, if they are applicable, or pursuant to any supposed head of inherent jurisdiction – in accordance with the view of the House of Lords in the decision of *Bremer Vulkan v South India Shipping Corpn Ltd*,[28] namely that the source of judicial powers over arbitrators is wholly statutory and not inherent.

Thus, following *Transfeld Philippines Inc & Ors v Pacific Hydro Ltd & Ors*,[29] the practical effect of the distinction between the English and the Australian approaches to confidentiality in arbitration would appear as largely illusory.[30]

Another critical question which needs to be posed is in which ways can a duty of confidentiality be enforced and what are the sanctions for such a breach?

Equally to the case of *Esso/BHP v Plowman*,[31] the arbitration world was shocked by the harshness of the ruling of the City of Stockholm Court at first instance in *Trade Finance Inc v Bulgarian Foreign Trade Bank Ltd*,[32] which stipulated stringent sanctions against those who breach the duty to observe confidentiality.

[1998] 1 Lloyd's Rep 643, *Esso/BHP v Plowman* (1995) 128 A.L.R. 391, High Court of Australia and *Trade Finance Inc v Bulgarian Foreign Trade Bank Ltd* Case No Y 1092-1098, SVEA Court of Appeal, relate to documents and evidence (parties may agree to disclosure of documents or evidence); Brown (2001, pp. 1008–1014); Editorial (1995, pp. 231–233).

[24] *Esso/BHP v Plowman* (1995) 128 A.L.R. 391, High Court of Australia.

[25] Lord Neil (1996, p. 316).

[26] *Esso/BHP v Plowman* (1995) 128 A.L.R. 391, High Court of Australia.

[27] *Transfeld Philippines Inc & Ors v Pacific Hydro Ltd & Ors [2006] VSC 175.*

[28] *Bremer Vulkan v South India Shipping Corpn Ltd* 18 [1981] AC 909.

[29] *Transfeld Philippines Inc & Ors v Pacific Hydro Ltd & Ors [2006] VSC 175.*

[30] Derrington (2007, pp. 188–190).

[31] *Esso/BHP v Plowman* (1995) 128 A.L.R. 391, High Court of Australia.

[32] *Trade Finance Inc v Bulgarian Foreign Trade Bank Ltd*, Case T-6-11-98, Stockholm City Court.

It may be thought that the Swedish Court went too far in invalidating the entire arbitration agreement on the basis of a breach of an implied duty to confidentiality. However, logic dictates that if confidentiality is perceived as an essential attribute of an arbitration agreement, then its breach should be treated as the breach of any other contractual provision. If the arbitration world wants the duty of confidentiality to be implied and as such give to arbitration proceedings integrity and a genteel nature, then it should not judge such sanctions as harsh, but it should instead seek to promote the notion of serious sanctions for parties who breach this duty.[33]

Another critical issue, involves the case where a party withholds evidence on the basis of a right to confidentiality. Equally, sanctions are imposed where parties exercise misconduct in that they withhold evidence, claiming a confidentiality justification for such conduct. Although all arbitral regimes allow arbitrators discretion in formulating measures to deal with such misconduct, nevertheless such sanctions are not universally without teeth. In this respect, in December 1998, the First Commercial Court of Istanbul, Turkey in *Technics Engineering Architecture Marketing Srl. (Italy) v Degere Enterprises Group AS (Turkey)*[34] enforced an ICC arbitration award made without considering expert evidence. The decision is significant in that it evidences the widening acceptance of arbitration decisions made without withheld evidence. Another option is for arbitrators to draw a negative inference on the withholding party. Such an inference, although it appears contrary to the UNCITRAL Rules, is expressly allowed under the Rules of the Stockholm Chamber of Commerce.[35]

Another critical aspect of confidentiality in arbitration – where there is also a judicial spilt – is with regards to whether the implied privacy of arbitration prohibits multi-party joinder in arbitrations.[36] Until the decision in *Oxford Shipping Co v Nippon Yesen Kaisha [The "Eastern Saga"]*,[37] multi-party joinders were allowed and encouraged in England. However, in *Oxford Shipping Co v Nippon Yesen Kaisha [The "Eastern Saga"]*[38] it was held that absent any inherent power of arbitrators, and due to the principle of privacy, such joinders are prohibited.[39]

---

[33]Brown (2001, pp. 1015–1017).

[34]JCC Award, 1998; Case Comment (1999) JCC Award Upheld Doesn't Conflict With Turkish Law, Mealey's Int. Arbitration Report, 14(3):7.

[35]Lindahl and Avokatbyra (1983, pp. 12–13); Leahy and Bianchi (2000, pp. 43–44).

[36]Parties may wish to join multiple parties due to joint and several or imputed liability and subcontracting issues. Likewise, arbitrators, encouraged by Courts might seek to join parties for reasons of efficiency and reasons of *res judicata*; Leahy and Bianchi (2000, p. 40).

[37]*Oxford Shipping Co v Nippon Yesen Kaisha [The "Eastern Saga"]* [1984] 2 Lloyd's Rep. 373 (QB).

[38]*Oxford Shipping Co v Nippon Yesen Kaisha [The "Eastern Saga"]* [1984] 2 Lloyd's Rep. 373 (QB).

[39]The court in *Oxford Shipping Co v Nippon Yesen Kaisha [The "Eastern Saga"]* [1984] 2 Lloyd's Rep. 373 (QB) at 384 stated: "[i]t seems to me that, as is graven upon the heart of any commercial lawyer, arbitrators in the position of these arbitrators enjoy no power to order concurrent hearings, or anything of that nature, without the consent of the parties. The concept of private arbitration derives simply from the fact that the parties have agreed to submit to arbitration particular disputes

Although confidentiality is an undisputable feature of the nature of arbitration and constitutes an attraction for those opting to arbitrate their disputes, at the same time exceptions to its observance should be recognised, because the notion of an absolute confidential character of arbitration contributes to a broader concern that arbitration itself cannot vindicate important deterrent, declarative, and normative policies underlying various public rights.

Arguably arbitration can serve remedial and deterrent functions. However, without public knowledge of a dispute or its resolution, private arbitral decisions affect only the conduct of the participants and cannot guide the primary behaviour of others, making it difficult if not impossible for prospective violators to appreciate fully the costs of engaging in prohibited conduct as – unlike publicly available court decisions – unpublished arbitral awards do not communicate public values or educate the community about the underlying law. Thus, parallel to the existence of a need to preserve the duty of confidentiality, there are also advantages to be seen in limiting such a duty so that exceptions to it may help to fulfil the normative and declarative functions of litigation.[40]

5.2.2 *Critical Assessment, Analysis and Justification of the Interplay of Arbitration and Confidentiality*

Rightly or wrongly, parties expect arbitrations to be confidential, as confidentiality is widely perceived as an advantage over litigation where matters become public record.

In today's global market arena, corporations expand globally and as such they face greater challenges, complexities and risks. Consequently, cross-border disputes and regulatory investigations almost inevitably involve more than one legal system and parties, lawyers and arbitrators, judges or regulators from diverse legal, commercial and cultural backgrounds.

What does this mean for expectations of confidentiality in international disputes where very different, often ill-defined and sometimes contradictory notions of confidentiality or privilege interact? Has the recent approach of the judiciary in England and the European Union affected the provision of legal advice and assistance by eroding the confidentiality of arbitration and diminishing the role of legal privilege?

arising between them and only them. It is implicit in this that strangers shall be excluded from the hearing and conduct of the arbitration and that neither the tribunal nor any of the parties can insist that the dispute shall be heard or determined concurrently with or even in consonance with another dispute, however convenient that course may be to the party seeking it and however closely associated with each other the disputes in question may be. The other powers which an arbitrator enjoys relate to the reference in which he has been appointed. They cannot be extended merely because a similar dispute exists which is capable of being and is referred separately to arbitration under a different agreement."; Leahy and Bianchi (2000, p. 40).

[40]Kratky-Dore (2006, p. 492).

Case law shows that questions of privilege and confidentiality can be a legal minefield in contentious proceedings at national level and even more so in international proceedings. Confidentiality in documents produced or divulged for the purpose of arbitration stem from an implied right of privacy in the arbitration process keeping matters private between the parties involved. The existence, extent and the basis of confidentiality in international commercial arbitration is a matter of scholarly debate and occasionally the focus of decisions of arbitration tribunals and state courts, and should not be automatically assumed.

In *Emmott v Michael Wilson & Partners Ltd*,[41] the decision of the Court of Appeal provided an in-depth analysis of the law on the private and confidential nature of commercial arbitration in England. The court acknowledged that there is a well-settled obligation, implied by law in England, not to disclose any documents prepared for and used in arbitration for any other purpose, but also recognised a concurrent and sometimes overriding public interest that means in certain circumstances disclosure may be permissible, albeit determinable only on a case-by-case basis.

Parties to arbitration in England may generally be allowed, and may even be required, to disclose details of the arbitration where parties to the arbitration expressly or impliedly consent; or where disclosure is reasonably necessary to protect legitimate interests of an arbitrating party – including requirements of public reporting, fiduciary obligations, auditing requirements, disclosures to insurers and disclosure in court applications; or where a court permits disclosure – by order or leave; or where the interests of justice require disclosure and perhaps where public interest requires disclosure.[42]

Importantly, the court in *Emmott v Michael Wilson & Partners Ltd*,[43] decided that "the interests of justice" were not confined to the interests of justice in England. The international nature of the dispute in the case demanded that the court take a broader view, considering whether the interests of justice would be served in another jurisdiction by permitting disclosure there.

Additional uncertainties arise as there is no single international code of commonly accepted principles on privilege though all professional privileges have the same rationale (to encourage frank and open communications between professionals and their clients). Legal professional privilege is intended to promote law-abiding behaviour by allowing business people to seek legal advice without the risk of it causing them prejudice. The right to proper legal advice is reflected in the principles of "legal privilege", as it is known in common law countries, and the principle of "professional secrecy" of civil law countries. While in common-law countries privilege is a right which also extends to in-house counsel – and it is only the client who can waive the privilege – the general civil law concept of professional secrecy is based on professional ethics, meaning only the lawyer, not the client, can invoke the privilege and only information in the lawyer's possession

[41] *Emmott v Michael Wilson & Partners Ltd* [2008] EWCA Civ 184.

[42] Sindler (2008).

[43] *Emmott v Michael Wilson & Partners Ltd* [2008] EWCA Civ 184.

created as part of the exercise of their profession is protected. The same information or advice attracts no protection in the hands of the client.

The European Court's decision in *AkzoNobel Chemicals v Commission of European Communities*[44] reaffirmed that in-house legal counsel cannot claim legal professional privilege protection when under investigation by the European Commission, going even further by holding that only communications emanating from independent lawyers qualified to practice in a member state within the EU can be privileged, meaning privilege of in-house and non-EU qualified lawyers is not respected at the EU level. English in-house lawyers might be protected in England, but not at EU level. Advice from non-EU qualified lawyers is similarly not protected at EU level.[45] What then of parties' and counsel's expectations about their communications in cross-border deals or disputes? If different rules of privilege are applied than those which the parties may reasonably expect – that they be accorded at least the same privilege rights as in their own domestic proceedings – parties and counsel may find they have to reveal information that was reasonably expected to be protected. Advice that is privileged in the country where it is given or from which it is sent may, however, not be protected everywhere a client operates or everywhere the advice is intended to be received. The importance of due process and equal treatment in arbitration means arbitrators are likely to look for the widest form of privilege to give parties equal protection. Where a person expects to enjoy additional evidentiary privileges before its national courts, a tribunal would allow the other party to benefit from such additional privileges, in the sense of "most favoured privilege treatment". The result is then more predictable, allowing parties to be confident that they would never be required to produce information that is considered privileged under the law of their home jurisdiction.

The case of *AkzoNobel Chemicals v Commission of European Communities*[46] and the case of *Emmott v Michael Wilson & Partners Ltd*[47] are useful reminders

[44] *AkzoNobel Chemicals v Commission of European Communities*, Joint Cases T-125/03 and T-253/03, European Court of First Instance of 17 Sept. 2007.

[45] Allowing the advice of internal counsel to be used against a company goes squarely against the very philosophy of privilege as corporate counsel are useful precisely because they help companies navigate legal risks. The same of course for non-EU qualified counsel. Advice from the best lawyer may not be protected if it is not also from the right lawyer. The very purpose of privilege should be to allow clients to confer openly about issues with the best person for the job both in-house and external counsel and should not be limited by the formality of Bar membership on which the court in *AkzoNobel Chemicals v Commission of European Communities* [Joint Cases T-125/03 and T-253/03, European Court of First Instance of 17 Sept. 2008] focused.

[46] *AkzoNobel Chemicals v Commission of European Communities* [Joint Cases T-125/03 and T-253/03, European Court of First Instance of 17 Sept. 2007], which held that only communications of independent EU qualified lawyers can be privileged, in other words that privilege of English in-house lawyers protected in England, but not at EU level and that privilege of non-EU qualified lawyers is not respected at EU level.

[47] *Emmott v Michael Wilson & Partners Ltd* [2008] EWCA Civ 184, whereby the court found that the notion of "interest of justice" had an international character which extended outside the English jurisdiction and as such could justify its serving in other jurisdictions by permitting disclosure in them.

that care is needed when negotiating arbitration agreements or when preparing documents in the context of seeking legal advice from external lawyers or even internal lawyers in connection with investigations, international transactions, international arbitrations and cross-border litigation.

Legal inconsistencies across jurisdictions and different treatment by institutional arbitration rules mean parties to arbitration should not assume that confidentiality is absolute even where a confidentiality obligation is said to exist. Being proactive in preserving confidentiality by incorporating express confidentiality provisions in arbitration agreements, stipulating confidentiality terms in procedural directions or orders from the arbitral tribunal and opting for arbitration rules which provide for confidentiality protection, will help protect the confidentiality of business secrets and ensure their dispute and arbitration remain as confidential as possible. Parties should ensure arbitration agreements contain appropriate confidentiality clauses, covering all aspects which need remain confidential. Managing privilege and confidentiality is also about managing expectations and managing risks. It necessitates negotiating appropriate confidentiality protection at the outset of all transactions where needed and ensuring an awareness of the complexities that questions of privilege protection entail in a globalized world. Safeguards are available to assist in keeping protection where it is expected and maintaining confidentiality and secrecy where possible. While multinational cross-border corporations that participate in international dispute resolution processes cannot maintain a firewall between different procedures in different countries, managing interactions and foreseeing the effect of a seemingly prudent communication in one jurisdiction on another, is an important though difficult aspect of modern commercial and legal practice.[48]

5.2.3 Critical Assessment, Analysis and Justification of the Desired Level of Confidentiality to Be Preserved

As stated above, confidentiality is implied into arbitration in some legal systems, although its exact scope and extent varies considerably from one jurisdiction to the next. Thus, national courts are split as to whether documents used in or produced during an arbitration should maintain their confidentiality outside the arbitral process and the courts of some nations have found that the confidentiality of such documents is absolute except where consent of both parties has been given or pursuant to court order,[49] while other courts have found that no special confidentiality should be afforded[50] or that as a general principle, arbitration documents

---

[48]Sindler (2008).

[49]*Hassneh Insurance Co. of Israel v Mew* [1993] 2 Lloyd's Rep. 243.

[50]*United States v Panhandle Eastern Corp. et al* (D.Del. 1988) 118 F.R.D. 346.

should be considered confidential, but the application of that principle may vary depending upon the factual circumstances.[51]

The English view[52] is that the implied right of privacy of arbitration extends to the confidentiality of documents which are incidental to arbitration.[53] In contrast, the American view, by and large, appears to be that unless the parties agree, no confidentiality attaches to documents used or produced in the arbitration.[54] In Sweden, in *Bulgarian Foreign Trade Bank Ltd. v A.L. Trade Finance Inc*,[55] it was held that confidentiality of arbitration documents is an implied characteristic of arbitration, but that the extent of this confidentiality may vary depending upon the reason for disclosure and the nature of the information sought to be disclosed.[56] The approach of the Swedish judiciary in *Bulgarian Foreign Trade Bank Ltd. v A.L. Trade Finance Inc* which recognises an implied duty to observe confidentiality subject to fact-intensive factors, is a tentative solution. One of the pitfalls of absolute confidentiality would be that parties could then opt to use arbitration to protect damaging or incriminating documents from use in subsequent litigation by having such documents entered into evidence during an arbitration.[57] Obviously, such patent manipulation cannot be tolerated. Still, parties do appear to opt for arbitration as an alternative to litigation precisely because arbitration is private and confidential. Because domestic judicial systems have an interest in promoting arbitration, e.g. to encourage judicial efficiency, confidentiality of arbitration documents should be recognised by courts, at least in a limited capacity, in order to encourage use of the arbitration system.[58]

5.2.4 Possible Solutions as to the Way Forward

With regards to the issue of confidentiality in arbitration its future ramifications and any predictions for what the future holds, there are further questions which need be posed.

How do we assess the significance of the confidentiality problem? Is it a matter of practice only or does it have a systemic reach? Which interpretation has the greater appeal? What is the reason for privacy and confidentiality? Does the

---

[51]*Bulgarian Foreign Trade Bank Ltd. v A.L. Trade Finance Inc.*, Judgment of October 27, 2000, Swedish Supreme Court.

[52]Espoused in *Hassneh Insurance Co. of Israel v Mew* [1993] 2 Lloyd's Rep. 243.

[53]Leahy and Bianchi (2000, pp. 38–39).

[54]*United States v Panhandle Eastern Corp. et al* (D.Del. 1988) 118 F.R.D. 346.

[55]*Bulgarian Foreign Trade Bank Ltd. v A.L. Trade Finance Inc.*, Judgment of October 27, 2000, Swedish Supreme Court.

[56]Leahy and Bianchi (2000, p. 39).

[57]Leahy and Bianchi (2000, pp. 39–40).

[58]Leahy and Bianchi (2000, pp. 39–40).

antipathy towards public scrutiny indicate a motive or the need to hide certain types of conduct? Why should the adjudication of commercial disputes lurk in the shadows?[59] Is the public interest a factor in the issue and if so can a viable form of equilibrium be restored and maintained between public and private adjudication? What is the best solution and the way forward?

When reviewing the confidentiality issue in the context of an arbitration, a court will likely defer to the applicable rules of the arbitration institution chosen by the parties. The rules of the various institutional bodies vary significantly. Some are complete and comprehensive, while others simply touch upon the issue of confidentiality.[60] Where a reviewing court finds that institutional rules applicable to an arbitration agreement either do not address confidentiality or, for some reason, do not apply, a court will most likely apply the national default rules.[61]

Although uncertainty remains in respect of much with regards to confidentiality in arbitration, parties should strive for more definitive rules from institutional arbitration bodies and national sources in the near future, as institutional arbitration bodies will likely model future versions of their rules in order to increase certainty and comprehensiveness concerning confidentiality and privacy.

Likewise, national courts will likely look to the Swedish case of *Bulgarian Foreign Trade Bank Ltd. v A.L. Trade Finance Inc.*[62] and conclude that confidentiality should be qualified by the type of information sought to be protected and the reasons for disclosure. The Swedish rule is a logical extension of the qualified

[59]Carbonneau (2005, pp. 715–716).

[60]For example, the AAA Rules require only that the members of the arbitration panel and the arbitration administrator keep the proceeding in confidence – See AAA International Arbitration Rules, Art. 34. The AAA Rules make absolutely no mention of any duty of confidentiality applicable to parties or witnesses. Likewise, the UNCITRAL Rules do not even mention privacy or confidentiality of arbitrations. The Rules of Arbitration of the ICC assign slightly greater importance to confidentiality, but, where explicit, govern only the internal workings of an arbitration – *Rules of Arbitration of the International Chamber of Commerce*, Appendix II, Article I. – and are ambiguous as to their potential application to the parties to an arbitration – *Rules of Arbitration of the International Chamber of Commerce, Statutes of the International Court of Arbitration of the ICC*, Appendix I, Article 6: "The work of the Court is of a confidential nature and must be respected by everyone who participates in that work in whatever capacity. The Court lays down the rules regarding the persons who can attend the meetings of the Court and its Committees and who are entitled to have access to the materials submitted to the Court and its Secretariat". The WIPO Rules provide for complete confidentiality except where both parties expressly agree to the disclosure of information, or where the law, or a court or other competent authority, so orders – and then only to the extent necessary – World Intellectual Property Organization Arbitration and Mediation Center, *Complete Listing of the Arbitration Rules*, Articles 73–76; Leahy and Bianchi (2000, pp. 40–41).

[61]In *United States v Panhandle Eastern Corp.* (D. Del. 1988), 118 F.R.D. 346, at 349–350 the court applied US law concerning protective orders after determining that ICC rules concerning confidentiality did not apply to the parties, only to the internal ICC mechanism.

[62]*Bulgarian Foreign Trade Bank Ltd. v A.L. Trade Finance Inc.*, Judgment of October 27, 2000, Swedish Supreme Court.

confidentiality found by English courts in *Hassneh Insurance Co. of Israel v Mew*,[63] and will likely garner international interest.

At the same time, calls for public disclosure may become pertinent. The impact of public disclosure upon the institution of arbitral adjudication should be carefully weighed before allowing such disclosure aiming to fulfil normative and declarative functions, for the courts' dominant concern is to allow access to information for the purpose of building a record in another action. On the one hand, maintaining the confidentiality of private arbitral justice may be outweighed by the needs of the public interest in adjudication, but, on the other hand, a balance between the imperatives of private and public justice should, therefore, be drawn. However, it should also be borne in mind that the challenge to arbitral confidentiality may reflect a communitarian need for public debate and scrutiny of justice determination.[64] If indeed public proceedings are instrumental to adjudication, the movement toward privatised justice may be confronting its first significant hurdle. It may also have come full circle as the difficulty to articulate adequate regulatory provisions on the question may indicate a need to return to the prior form of judicial adjudication via state court litigation. Having said that, there may exist another interpretation. In other words it may simply be the case that problems with arbitral confidentiality, due to their infrequency, are nothing more than a momentary difficulty. The courts may not have had, so far, the opportunity really to focus on the problem and are likely to respond appropriately as more cases will arise.

In addition, there remains always a possibility that national courts may abandon confidentiality and opt for full disclosure of awards and proceedings in order to develop a form of arbitration case law, or at the very least, a solid record of patterns and practices in arbitrations. The existence of arbitration reporting services[65] establishes this as a distinct possibility. Those calling for a record of arbitration opinions point to the importance such a record can have in increasing the certainty that arbitration parties enjoy when contemplating or planning to defend a claim in arbitration and of the increased accountability such records impose upon arbitrators.[66] They are also critical of the publication of awards in edited forms which leave the basis of the arbitrators' decisions unclear. However, although understandably valid, if such a public record of awards were to be created, the possibility of publicising edited awards seems to be the only workable solution in order to satisfy those fearing the loss of confidentiality. Still, though sanitized and edited, such awards would allow the development of the law and practice of international commercial arbitration and provide a guide to future parties and arbitrators facing similar legal issues, as well as bring consistency and predictability to the system. Not least, the sharing of experiences, the greater transparency and the referral to

[63] *Hassneh Insurance Co. of Israel v Mew* [1993] 2 Lloyd's Rep. 243.

[64] Carbonneau (2005, pp. 715–716).

[65] Such as Mealey's International Arbitration Report.

[66] Leahy and Bianchi (2000, pp. 41–42).

established principles from prior decisions would help further develop the notion of a *lex mercatoria* in international commercial arbitration.[67]

The protection of confidentiality in the arbitration derives not only from the law of arbitration but also from the law of proprietary information and the law of trade secrets. There is no use in debating whether there exists a worldwide principle of confidentiality in the arbitration proceedings as it is accepted that not only the national traditions differ, but also that the legal or institutional rules are generally scant. Meanwhile, multinational corporations having recourse to arbitration will long for certainty. The public domain is not defined in relation to a given country but on a worldwide basis, for the word wide web bridges regional or national barriers to the free flow of information. Thus, there is no presumptive secrecy. The party who contends that an arbitration is confidential in whole or in part has to show it.[68] A handful of cases in the last decades, in a number of national jurisdictions, have demonstrated that the issue of the observance of the duty of confidentiality and of the sanctions that should exist is complex and that there exists the paradox that parties may in practice find it undesirable for the rule to be as comprehensive as they vaguely suppose it to be.[69] These national differences generate uncertainty. Our world has not evolved to the point where a supranational court is available to resolve these national differences. Moreover, relying on institutional rules will not solve the problem as simply incorporating the rules of an arbitral institution is not likely to resolve uncertainties about confidentiality because although institutional rules commonly provide that the arbitrators shall maintain the confidentiality of the proceedings, some, however, prohibit disclosure by the parties.[70]

---

[67]Ong (2005, pp. 177–180).

[68]Dessemontet (1996, pp. 27–31).

[69]In Australia it was held in *Esso/BHP v Plowman* (1995) 128 A.L.R. 391, High Court of Australia that confidentiality, unlike privacy, is not "an essential attribute" of commercial arbitration. In the United States, in the leading case of *United States v Panhandle Eastern Corp. et al* (D.Del. 1988) 118 F.R.D. 346 the court held that there is no inherent duty of confidentiality unless the parties contract for it, and that the ICC Rules place no obligation of confidentiality on arbitrating parties and granted the government's request to compel production of the documents. English law holds that arbitral parties are subject to an implied duty of confidentiality. In the leading case of *Ali Shipping v Shipyard Trogir* [1998] 1 Lloyd's Rep 643 the court held that such an obligation is implied in every arbitration agreement as "an essential corollary of the privacy of arbitration proceedings". However, English law also recognises certain exceptions. French law appears to provide even more stringent protection for the confidentiality of arbitral proceedings and awards. In *Aita v Ojjeh*, Cour d' Appel de Paris, February 18, 1986 the French court of Appeal dismissed an action to annul an arbitral award rendered in London, penalizing the party bringing the annulment action for thereby breaching the principle that arbitral proceedings are confidential. The decision does not even appear to allow for the narrow exceptions recognised by English law; Editorial (1995, pp. 231–233).

[70]For example, Article 25(4) of the Arbitration Rules of UNCITRAL provides that hearings shall be held "in camera" but it does not say what the parties may or may not reveal outside the hearing. The rules of the ICC, though excluding from hearings "persons not involved in the proceedings" and permitting the arbitral tribunal to "take measures for protecting trade secrets or confidential

A ready solution to the problem of duelling confidentiality laws and rules is not at hand. Moreover, although the existence of a consistent judicial approach would be the best way to achieve the observance of the duty of confidentiality,[71] nevertheless case law such as *Esso/BHP v Plowman*[72] and *Transfeld Philippines Inc & Ors v Pacific Hydro Ltd &* Ors[73] constitute a vivid proof of the contrasting practical difficulty to achieve and guarantee such a judicial consistency[74] and also further validate the presumption that a solution is not likely to come from the courts because they are often bound by prior decisions and face competing incentives. On the one hand, upholding an implied duty of confidentiality may attract arbitrations and the business they bring to the host country. On the other hand, courts may view the confidentiality of arbitral materials as interfering with the search for truth in judicial proceedings. In addition, courts cannot easily enforce confidentiality duties or agreements, in part because damages are often nonexistent or difficult to prove. Nor can one count on national governments to step in and resolve their differences on this issue.

Given the difficulties in getting the necessary consensus for even "modest treaties", amending existing arbitral enforcement treaties like the New York Convention or entering into a new treaty is far from likely.

Similarly, a solution is most likely not to come from the arbitral institutions or the arbitration participants themselves,[75] simply because their differences reflect competition for the lucrative arbitration business.

One might think that the parties themselves hold the key to a solution because they may include a provision in their agreement expressly specifying whether and to what extent the arbitral proceeding and award are to be kept confidential. That may help, but it does not provide any certainty. First, disputes subject to arbitration often arise years after the contract was negotiated. It is difficult to predict so far in advance where one's interest will lie on the confidentiality spectrum. Second, a clause that would cover all contingencies would have to be quite detailed and lengthy, raising the transactional costs of entering into the agreement at a time when the parties prefer not to focus on contingent future disputes. Finally, it is not clear that a particular national court would respect the entirety of the parties' agreement, especially those aspects that may conflict with the public policy of the forum country. Similarly, the parties cannot obviate the difficulties by simply incorporating the rules of an arbitral institution with strong confidentiality protections into their agreement. None of these rules specify what

information", are silent on the confidentiality of awards and of materials produced and information divulged in the proceeding.

[71]Brown (2001, pp. 1015–1017).

[72]*Esso/BHP v Plowman* (1995) 128 A.L.R. 391, High Court of Australia.

[73]*Transfeld Philippines Inc & Ors v Pacific Hydro Ltd & Ors [2006] VSC 175.*

[74]Editorial (1995, pp. 231–233).

[75]Dessemontet (1996, pp. 21–23).

recourse a party would have if confidentiality is breached after the arbitration is concluded.[76]

Nevertheless, if the question of confidentiality was to be left to the parties in their commercial agreement or arbitration agreement, a draft form of a detailed confidentiality clause that would serve as a basis for discussion and negotiation when confidentiality is important to the parties and a version of an extensively drafted confidentiality could possibly have the following format:[77]

Draft Confidentiality Agreement
Subject to any applicable and overriding law and duty, the parties agree for themselves and any persons or companies under their control and direction that any arbitration conducted under the authority of this agreement will be private and confidential, and all documents, evidence, orders and awards, whether electronic or otherwise, will be kept private and secret and will not be disclosed to persons who are not participating in the arbitration proceeding. This obligation continues during the course of the proceeding and thereafter unless all parties otherwise agree. If a party concludes that its legal duty requires disclosure of such material, it will give the opposing party notice of its intention to disclose before making any such disclosure. If the opposing party will not consent to the disclosure, the parties agree that the question of whether there is any applicable and overriding law and duty in relation to the material under consideration will be presented for decision to the arbitrator who is appointed under this agreement. The parties agree to be bound by the ruling of the arbitrator whose decision will be final and binding. The arbitrator may determine the timing, nature and extent of disclosure. The parties agree that any failure to abide by the decision of the arbitrator may give rise to a claim for an injunction.

The parties agree that they will expect and require a person who is appointed as an arbitrator under this agreement to agree with, and for the benefit of, all parties that all documents, evidence, orders and awards, whether electronic or otherwise, in relation to this arbitration will be kept secret, private and confidential by the arbitrator; will be not be disclosed by the arbitrator to anyone who is not a participant in the proceeding; and will be destroyed by the arbitrator at the conclusion of the proceeding.

The parties agree that they will expect and require the person who is appointed as a court reporter or clerk under this agreement to agree with and for the benefit of all parties that all documents, evidence, orders and awards, electronic or otherwise, in relation to the arbitration will be kept secret, private and confidential by him or her and will not be disclosed to anyone who is not a participant in the proceeding.

The parties agree that they will expect and require all counsel and their staff who are retained or appointed to act for a party in an arbitration under this agreement will be expected and required to agree with, and for the benefit of, all parties that all documents, evidence, orders and awards, whether electronic or otherwise, in relation to the arbitration will be kept secret, private and confidential by them and will not be disclosed by them to anyone who is not a participant in the proceeding unless the counsel is bound by an overriding law or duty.

---

[76]Presumably, a party would have to go to court, where the vagaries of national law would come into play. But, if this were the case, would a court in the USA hold that the parties' incorporation of the rules of the LCIA Arbitration International represents a binding agreement to keep proceedings confidential? Perhaps, but the dearth of authority on this issue makes reliance on such an outcome hazardous.

[77]Thompson and Finn (2007, pp. 75–78).

> The parties agree that they will expect and require a person who is retained as a consultant/expert witness by a party to this arbitration to agree with, and for the benefit of, all parties that all documents, evidence, orders and awards, electronic or otherwise in relation to the arbitration will be kept secret, private, and confidential by the consultant/expert witness and will not be disclosed by the consultant/expert witness to anyone who is not a participant in the proceeding unless the consultant/expert witness is bound by an overriding law or duty.
>
> The parties agree that they will expect and require a person whom they present as a witness at any hearing held pursuant to this arbitration to agree with, and for the benefit of, all parties that all documents, evidence, orders and awards, electronic or otherwise, in relation to the arbitration will be kept secret, private and confidential by the witness and will not be disclosed by the witness to anyone who is not a participant in the proceeding.[78]

Notwithstanding the above suggestion, whether formed separately or as part of the arbitration agreements, when devising a confidentiality agreement it should be borne in mind that the fact that confidentiality has different value to different parties in different contexts and the fact that the shear fact of a lack of consistent methods of framing such confidentiality agreements, denote the possibility of disparate interpretations. Thus, consideration and special attention should be given, when drafting confidentiality agreements, to that which should be rendered confidential, the reason for doing so, the extent of confidentiality desired and the means of so providing, as well as to the nature of applicable law and its connection and relation to arbitral confidentiality, as it may be needed to vary confidentiality provisions to accommodate differences in applicable laws and business practices. Finally the cost of devising a confidentiality provision or agreement need be considered, and more specifically the cost of negotiating and the concessions that parties may need to do, should be calculated.[79] Moreover, parties should adopt interpretative aids to avoid disparate interpretations and evaluate the nature of the law governing confidentiality in arbitration and, at the same time, arbitrators should be willing to scrutinise confidentiality agreements in light of the applicable law each time in best serve the interests of the parties involved as well as consider the delicate balance that exists between freedom of contract and the regulation of contract, including contracts regulation of confidentiality provisions.[80]

5.2.5 Tentative Conclusion

The confidentiality problem appears so pressing and intractable as to demand some sort of joint resolution, if only to prevent discontent with the arbitral process from becoming endemic. Because no one can be sure of the scope of confidentiality protections today, there is an urgent need for a uniform rule.

---

[78]Thompson and Finn (2007, pp. 75–78).

[79]Trackman (2002, pp. 12–13).

[80]Trackman (2002, pp. 17–18).

However, what should it look like and how can it be achieved?

What is needed is a universally accepted default rule, i.e. a rule binding in the absence of mutual assent otherwise.[81] Although the existence of a consistent judicial approach would be the best way to achieve the observance of the duty of confidentiality,[82] nevertheless, and due to the fact that case law such as *Esso/BHP v Plowman*[83] and *Transfeld Philippines Inc & Ors v Pacific Hydro Ltd &* Ors[84] constitute a vivid proof of the contrasting practical difficulty to achieve and guarantee such a judicial consistency, it is submitted that a pertinent solution could be best achieved via the means of a statutory remedy.[85]

[81]Sarles (2002).

[82]Brown (2001, pp. 1015–1017).

[83]*Esso/BHP v Plowman* (1995) 128 A.L.R. 391, High Court of Australia.

[84]*Transfeld Philippines Inc & Ors v Pacific Hydro Ltd & Ors [2006] VSC 175.*

[85]Editorial (1995, pp. 231–233).

Chapter 6
Transnational Law and Arbitration

In recent years "transnational law" has become a term often used in legal terminology especially in the context of international commercial arbitration whereby expressions such as "transnational law" or "new *lex mercatoria*" denote non-national or supra-national legal rules or principles employed by arbitration tribunals in the course of disputes settlement.[1]

This chapter discusses the impact of transnational law on international commercial arbitration and its interconnection with confidentiality. More specifically, we address the modern European and global character of arbitration and the way in which the various levels of protection of confidentiality affect it, before discussing the advantages and disadvantages as well as the possibility of achieving a uniform transnational arbitration law.

6.1 The Need for Transnational Law

6.1.1 In Relation to International Commercial Law

In the context of international commercial law, transnational law denotes the following: Firstly, it denotes the general legal regime of an international commercial transaction, which includes the applicable law of the transaction together with all other norms which impinge on the transaction. Secondly, it denotes the factual uniformity or similarity in contract laws applicable to or contractual patterns used in international commercial transactions – whereby transnational law denotes the noticeable and considerable similarity of the norms, principles, rules, contractual documents and clauses employed in international commercial transactions irrespective of the geographical location of the transaction. Thirdly, it denotes the international sources of commercial law, i.e. the laws which are the product of a conscious

[1]Bamodu (2001, pp. 6–16).

K. Noussia, *Confidentiality in International Commercial Arbitration*,
DOI 10.1007/978-3-642-10224-0_6, © Springer-Verlag Berlin Heidelberg 2010

and concerted effort by the international business community in respect of matters of a transnational nature in respect of activities with cross-state elements and apply to the respective activity regardless of its place of occurrence or of the place where any disputes fall to be resolved.

All of the above definitions embody a conception of a law applicable in respect of transactions of a private nature,[2] which transcend national frontiers[3] in that are concerned with more than one territorial entity or State.

Regarding its sphere of operation, transnational law does not operate *per se* but is an autonomous system of law the rules of which can operate within an individual national legal system by permission of the latter and which derive from international or transnational sources rather than exclusively from the legislative processes of a particular national legal system.

With respect to commercial contracts, transnational law might result from special conventions, establishing standard type contracts, or from general principles of law. Although disputes involving private persons or entities of different national law systems have been traditionally regarded as subject to national laws, in many legal systems certain rules developed on an international level for application to transnational relationships, including international conventions, model laws or uniform principles, particularly in the context of international commercial transactions.

The efforts to adopt a system of transnational law is clearly elaborated via the efforts to harmonise or unify the latter by means of international conventions or treaties through which states agree to adopt uniform principles in relation to aspects of international private law or through the adoption of a new *lex mercatoria*, i.e. general principles and international business customary rules which can be further defined according to a geographical, political, economic, legal or commercial criterion.[4]

It is argued that such a harmonisation based on the adoption of universally accepted standards of business conduct, would serve as a common platform for commercial parties from all countries enabling them to co-operate in the perfection of the mechanism of transnational "law trade" and would offer many advantages. First, it would permit the application of international principles of commercial law applicable in a uniform manner and independently from the particularities of domestic laws. Second, it would take into account the needs of international commercial relations and allow a fruitful exchange between legal systems. Third, it would in this way allow the establishment of a new *lex mercatoria*.[5]

There are many economic and legal factors, which purport to the current climate for the transnationalisation of commercial law. For once, the need for the existence of a new *lex mercatoria* as an autonomous legal order nowadays cannot solely be

[2]Though it may also extend to private nature transactions of States.

[3]Bamodu (2001, pp. 7–8).

[4]Bamodu (2001, pp. 12–14).

[5]Berger (2000a, p. 91–92).

attributed to the general contract conditions existing or to the normative value of trade usages. It also has to be justified by modern economic and geo-political factors, which further reflect the need of its existence. These factors are: the progress of European integration towards the creation of a single European market; the establishment of a global corporate culture through the spreading of transnational corporations and global financial flows and capital markets; the wide evolution of global electronic communication technology and of the internet; the dominance of the party autonomy doctrine; the realization of unfitness of domestic legal rules for international commercial transaction and any potentially arising disputes; the frequent application of international uniform law instruments; the gradual convergence of civil and common law – not least elaborated in the efforts towards a modern European *ius commune*; the extreme growth in the use of arbitration and alternative dispute resolution mechanisms in international commercial disputes; and, the wide recognition that arbitration enjoys parallel to state courts adjudication procedures.

In short, the establishment of a trend towards a global civil society, the declination of sovereignty and national boundaries in global markets and of the ability of state power to influence or steer national or international economic developments and the strong trend towards informal approaches to international rule- and decision-making demonstrate nowadays the need for the establishment of a transnational uniform law, even more in the field of international commercial transactions and of related disputes.[6]

6.1.2 In Relation to Arbitration

The combined effect of the phenomena of trans-nationalism and of the decrease of state sovereignty and territoriality assist the notion of the evolution of a global civil society where, at a global level, there would be few, if any, territorial limits of law-making and law enforcement which would further ensure the decentralisation of the rule-making process and of the society's active role, as opposed to the state sovereign. In effect, the creation of a global marketplace would provide the breeding ground for a modern theory of transnational commercial law[7] applicable not only to state court but also to arbitration proceedings.

It is therefore widely accepted that arbitrators may apply transnational law and the *lex mercatoria*, particularly in cases where the applicable national law gives no answer or no reasonable answer. In relation to the latter use of it, it entails the significant advantage that it allows the parties involved to plead on an equal footing, because in this way no-one is favoured by the application of any national law.

---

[6]Berger (2000a, p. 98).

[7]Berger (2000a, p. 102).

However, there is a dichotomy of opinion as to whether arbitrators should be allowed to apply transnational law and the new *lex mercatoria* where the parties have not opted for its use. Whilst some legal systems – such as those of France, Italy and the Netherlands – have procedural laws which allow arbitrators to apply transnational law and the new *lex mercatoria* even where the parties have not opted for it, other legal systems – such as the English and others incorporating the UNCITRAL Model Law – permit arbitrators to apply non national rules of law only when the parties have chosen them as applicable to the substance of the dispute.[8]

6.2 Transnational Law and Arbitration

Transnational law has had a huge impact on the modern European and global character of arbitration in that the latter favours the application of the former even where parties have not explicitly opted for it.

Does an arbitral tribunal have the power or duty to apply public law or mandatory rules, or public policy, or general private law principles or national laws which themselves identify transnational rules, different from the substantive law which is applicable to the dispute involved? Although a choice of law made by parties could be thought to set the rules to be applied by the arbitral tribunal in its decision on a dispute arising out of a relationship which is governed by that law, a large number of cases exist where other provisions of law not directly stemming out of the legal system chosen by the parties are often invoked. The results as shown in case law are disperse.

6.2.1 Public and Mandatory Rules Functioning as Transnational Law Applied to Arbitration

In cases where the parties have agreed on a choice of law clause in favour of one particular national law or where the conflicts of law rules applied by the arbitral tribunal designate this law but foreign public mandatory rules are invoked to be used, the issue is whether the parties choice of law limits the arbitral tribunal with respect to the applicable law to provisions which are classified as the *lex contractus*.[9]

Arbitral case law has shown a change of attitude towards the application of public mandatory law which interferes with the validity or the performance of the contract concluded by the parties to the dispute. The mere invocation of a

[8]Lando (2000, pp. 401–402).

[9]Hochstrasser (2005, pp. 7–8).

mandatory rule by a party does not automatically result in the non-arbitrability of the dispute involved. However, some awards will apply mandatory law whilst others will not do so.[10] For example, in the ICC Award of 14 April 1966 it was held that Mexican custom regulations did not have extraterritorial effect and could not govern the performance of the contract in France. Again, in the Award in the ICC Case No. 1512, of 1971, a Pakistani bank was found to be not liable for non-performance of a guarantee issued in favour of an Indian party not because a Pakistani decree declared payments to Indian parties as illegal but only because, in accordance with the terms of the guarantee, payment was to take place in India and as a result of the above contract stipulation Pakistani law had no application, and, thus, Indian law was the mandatory applicable law.[11] But in *Mitsubishi v. Soler Chrysler-Plymouth*[12] the accepted rule that arbitrators should not be able to decide on questions on anti-trust law was held not to apply to international arrangements and, thus, arbitrators were clearly able and willing to apply mandatory law.

In short, whilst arbitrators should seek to respect the contractual intention of the parties, they should also secure in the best way the efficacy of the rendered award and the avoidance of its annulment by counterbalancing the mandatory rules of the place of performance and of the country of enforcement of the award.[13]

The application of mandatory rules in the form of law of another country than the one chosen by the parties or of transnational character rules, seems imperative in cases where the mandatory rule in question:

(a) Is a provision with mandatory effect; or
(b) Is applicable irrespective of the law chosen by the parties or the law as this is determined by conflict of laws rules; or
(c) Is applicable to the dispute involved in accordance with its own terms and there is a close connection between the dispute involved and the jurisdiction from which the mandatory rule arises from; or
(d) Is judged by the arbitral tribunal as worth to be applied and its application leads to a logical result; or

[10]Hochstrasser (2005, p. 17).

[11]Hochstrasser (2005, pp. 9–10).

[12]*Mitsubishi v. Soler Chrysler-Plymouth* 473 U.S. 614 (1985). In this case the petitioner, Mitsubishi Motors Corp., a Japanese automobile manufacturer, brought suit against the respondent, Soler Chrysler-Plymouth, Inc., a Puerto Rican automobile dealer, seeking an order compelling arbitration of certain disputes arising out of a sales agreement between the companies. The respondent answered, asserting various counterclaims against petitioner, including antitrust claims under the Sherman Act (15 U.S.C. §§ 1–7 (1982)). The US District Court for the District of Puerto Rico ordered arbitration of most of the issues between the parties pursuant to an arbitration clause contained in the sales agreement which provided that all disputes, controversies or differences which might arise between Mitsubishi and Soler out of or in relation to that agreement or for the breach thereof, would be finally settled by arbitration in Japan, in accordance with the rules and regulations of the Japan Commercial Arbitration Association.

[13]Hochstrasser (2005, p. 20).

(e) Is attempted to be circumvented via the parties choice of application of a certain *lex contractus*; or
(f) Affects the performance of the contract and where there is a close connection of the performance of the contract and of the mandatory rule in question; or
(g) Would secure enforcement of the award which would otherwise be doubted.[14]

6.2.2 Arbitral Case Law, International Legal Instruments and National Laws Functioning as Transnational Law Applied to Arbitration

Arbitral case law, international legal instruments and national laws embody and at the same time formulate new transnational law which is applicable to arbitration.[15] Although doubted in the past,[16] it is nevertheless nowadays accepted that there exists a body of arbitral case law. Of course precedent does not apply to arbitration and in that sense the existence of arbitral case law is only perceived in that a set of solutions exists by reference to arbitral awards which can act as an instructive corpus and a useful instrument for arbitrators.[17] The existence and study of this arbitral case law allows us also to reinforce the beneficial use of general and specific transnational rules which can be applicable to the resolution on the merits of a dispute. Moreover, because the arbitrators are to be seen as expert international jurists, the arbitration agreement can provide guidance as to the manner in which they will apply the conventional rules of law to the merits of the dispute and in doing so they may be directed into taking into account certain international principles,[18] or the trade usages existing in a specific industry or a specific code of conduct which reflects trade usages and customs which would apply in the same way as statutory provisions.[19] In that sense, general transnational principles are established, which emanate either from the idea of the establishment of immanent principles of international arbitral justice or from a comparative analysis of national laws or an analysis of international conventions or of private codifications.[20]

Arbitral case law such as the Award in ICC Case No. 8385 has restated the above by holding *inter alia* that the application of international principles is highly

[14]Hochstrasser (2005, pp. 33–35).
[15]Henry (2005, p. 41).
[16]Thompson and Derains (1974, p. 879).
[17]Henry (2005, pp. 43–44).
[18]Such as for example the "UNIDROIT Principles of International Commercial Contracts" or the "Principles of European Contract Law".
[19]Gelinas (1999, p. 63).
[20]Henry (2005, pp. 43–44).

beneficial, not least in that those principles permit uniformity of application irrespective of national laws.[21]

General legal principles may also be applied and used as transnational law, so as to promote and enhance interpretation of the contracts in question, such as the principle of the binding nature of contracts otherwise stated as the "pacta sunt servanda" principle[22] or the principle of good faith[23] or the principle of the "useful effect" otherwise stated as "effet utile" or the "contra proferentem"[24] rule. Most of these principles feature also in the UNIDROIT Principles of International Commercial Contracts or the Principles of European Contract Law.

National laws also assist the establishment of transnational laws and rules to be used in arbitration, simply by their existence which allows a comparative analysis and an identification of rules common to countries outside national frameworks as well as in their contribution to the drafting of international instruments which in their turn conceptualise the drawing up of common norms which lead to the creation of transnational rules.[25]

Not least, the creation and application of transnational rules in arbitration and their existence in arbitral awards promotes the re-genesis of a *Lex Mercatoria* which could exist via the corpus of the judicial activity of arbitrators.[26]

6.3 Transnational Arbitral Law and Its Interplay with Confidentiality

The existence of transnational rules which apply to arbitration is affected and interconnected with the concept of confidentiality in arbitration in many ways. Firstly, it is connected in the sense that rules and practices in the taking of evidence may differ widely between various legal systems, in particular in contexts such as that of document production, witness hearings and expertise. International commercial arbitrations which often involve parties and counsel from widely different legal systems and traditions highlight even more the above differences. Although the flexibility of the arbitration process allows parties to determine the procedural rules applicable to their dispute, in cases where parties do not use this flexibility will mean that their expectations in relation to evidentiary matters may differ and may, thus, create conflicts. Such conflicts will often also touch on the issue of confidentiality as there will be diverse approaches as to what is permitted to be disclosed

---

[21]ICC Case No. 8385, 124 J.D.I. 1061, 1066 (1997).

[22]1996 Award in ICC Case No. 8486, 125 J.D.I. 1047 (1998).

[23]1993 Award in ICC Case No. 7105, 127 J.D.I. 1062 (2000); 1991 Award in ICC Case No. 6519, 118 J.D.I. 1065 (1991).

[24]1995 Partial Award in ICC Case No. 7710, 128 J.D.I. 1147, 1151 (2001).

[25]Henry (2005, pp. 49–54).

[26]Henry (2005, p. 62).

under the different procedural laws, and evidentiary practices.[27] However, the existence of some common standard practices which have been followed in arbitration proceedings allows us to identify some standard evidentiary practices, such as the exchange of detailed written submissions and the accompanying documentary evidence, the submission of written testimonies, the holding of witness hearings which may include an examination or cross examination of witnesses, the keeping of transcripts from the oral evidence given by witnesses, all of which combine elements from common law and civil law evidentiary practices.[28]

Following the above remark, one wonders if the aforementioned common practices have been codified. The answer is in the negative. The UNCITRAL Notes on Organising Arbitral Proceedings do not constitute anything more than guidance notes and certainly should not be perceived as codified (transnational) principles and rules for the taking of evidence. At the opposite end, the 1999 IBA Rules on the Taking of Evidence in International Commercial Arbitration represent an increasingly popular practice in the taking of evidence in international arbitration and in that sense could be perceived as a successful attempt to codify the general rules on the taking of evidence in international arbitration and at the same time prove the emergence of transnational rules on the taking of evidence and the need for further codification of transnational rules and principles in this field.[29]

Secondly the existence of transnational rules which apply to arbitration is affected and interconnected with the concept of confidentiality in arbitration in the sense that third-party intervention may occur in arbitration, either in the form of forced intervention – where a party to the arbitration wishes to join a third party in it so as to raise claims against it, or in the form of voluntary intervention – where a third party has personal interests in proceedings between other parties and wishes to intervene in them and seek relief or where a third party intervenes in proceedings merely to support the case of one of the parties. Often the intervening party is termed as "amicus curiae".

Accepting an *amicus curiae* without limits jeopardizes any duty of confidentiality. Thus third parties should abide by the confidentiality duties decided by the arbitral tribunal or the parties. To do so, any *amicus curiae* should be governed by rules and clearly designated procedural rules. Such rules may be perceived as transnational arbitral rules.[30]

Different levels of confidentiality affect the European and global character of arbitration. A careful drafting of arbitration agreements and of the clause of confidentiality therein affords the parties protection of their confidentiality right whatever the level of confidentiality duty may be. To this end, the emergence of transnational rules applied on arbitration promote the goal of respecting the duty to

---

[27]Gunter (2005, pp. 129–132).

[28]Gunter (2005, p. 138).

[29]Gunter (2005, pp. 148–149).

[30]Favre Bulle (2005, p. 232).

confidentiality, save the parties involved time and effort and overall further promote arbitration as a means of alternative dispute resolution.

6.4 The Notion of a Uniform Arbitral Law

The emergence of the decided arbitral cases on the basis of the application of transnational rules reinforces the notion of the establishment of a uniform arbitration law. Codification efforts mirroring this trend also exist in the form of the UNIDROIT Principles of International Commercial Contract, or in the Principles of European Contract or in the Central List of *Lex Mercatoria* Principles, Rules and Standards, all of which reflect the tendency to codify transnational law. In the future it seems that there will be an even more increase in the reliance by arbitrators on notions of *lex mercatoria*, general law principles and trade usages and customs enunciated via codification attempts such as the afore mentioned the UNIDROIT Principles of International Commercial Contract, or in the Principles of European Contract or in the Central List of *Lex Mercatoria* Principles, Rules and Standards. All these codification attempts are new and progressive in that they advance the creation of a uniform private law, and in turn also that of a uniform arbitration law, which will have benefits such as the reduction of transaction costs and the creation of a level playing field for parties to cross-border contractual transactions and disputes arising therein.[31]

[31]Berger (2001a, p. 26).

Chapter 7
Towards a Uniform Arbitration Law?

Arbitrators nowadays rely more and more on *lex mercatoria*, general law principles and trade usages and customs, when adjudicating. The increase in arbitral cases, decided on the basis of the application of transnational rules, reinforces the notion of the establishment of a uniform arbitration law, which entails many advantages. However, there are equally voices raised against such a notion of a uniform arbitral law.[1]

7.1 The Uniformity Debate

7.1.1 The Process of Internationalisation of Arbitration: A Newly Emerging Lex Mercatoria

The internationalisation of modern commercial law is conducted, *inter alia*, via international arbitrations. Arbitrators tend to enjoy greater freedom in conducting proceedings, and, in doing so, develop the applicable transnational law and custom and, frequently, rely more freely on transnational principles, where necessary and appropriate. Traditional litigation courts should do the same, with regards to international commercial cases, but often hesitate.

The transnational *lex mercatoria* disappeared, as a result of the nationalisation of all law from the early nineteenth century onwards, which made all law purely national and at the same time territorial. However, strong sociological and economic features continued to strive for a transnational substantive system of law. In modern times, the emergence and operation of different legal orders, the application and impact of fundamental or more general legal principles and newly developing customs in the international commercial and financial legal order, argue, for the

[1] Such as, the reduction of transaction costs and the creation of a level playing field, for parties to cross-border contractual transactions and disputes arising therein. See Berger (2001a, p. 26).

K. Noussia, *Confidentiality in International Commercial Arbitration*,
DOI 10.1007/978-3-642-10224-0_7,

creation and establishment of a modern *lex mercatoria*, or law merchant, as the new transnational law.[2] Not least, the result of a new *lex mercatoria* is even more apparent, within the modern world. The new *lex mercatoria* is neither static nor territorial, but emanates from the international commercial and financial legal order, which is maintained amongst businessmen.[3]

Domestic courts, find the *lex mercatoria* and directly apply the hierarchy of norms, inherent in it, to commercial disputes. Within this new and modern *lex mercatoria*, the search for better law, or for what makes more sense in the circumstances is preferred to the application of domestic rules that were never intended for international transactions and, thus, are sometimes erratically applied. Especially, in the commercial sphere and in the sphere of international commercial arbitration, the *lex mercatoria* or transnational approach is generally preferable and likely to reach better results.[4]

Nowadays, whilst the notion of causality has suffered re-evaluation in quantum mechanics, territorial and temporal confines of the law, and its static character or systematic nature, are more confidently to be questioned, at the same time, a functional, dynamic and self-propelling approach, in law formation and application, regains an important place.

Globalisation needs a new legal framework, more flexible, aware of and adaptive to reasonable needs. Thus, an apparent need for the establishment and recognition of the emerging new *lex mercatoria* is, more than ever, apparent. However, because of the ambivalence on the subject of *lex mercatoria*, and due to a lack of a clear idea of what the modern *lex mercatoria* really is, direct references to the *lex mercatoria* remain rare, in statutes or official commentaries, whilst courts and arbitrators usually use different terminology in an effort also to limit theoretical controversy. Equally, a contractual choice of law favouring *lex mercatoria*, remains uncommon. There are also voices raised against *lex mercatoria*, stating that it is impossible to develop law outside a state framework or that the new *lex mercatoria* provides too little certainty. Notwithstanding the above, the new *lex mercatoria* is an emerging reality which, despite its drawbacks, establishes itself more and more.[5] International commercial activity, unavoidably engenders transnational disputes and argues for the development of a uniform commercial law and workable procedural framework, for resolving disputes arising from international commercial activity.[6] While maintaining pluralism in the community of nations, the international legal order, in an effort to facilitate the resolution of disputes with an international character, seeks to unify substantive law. Effective harmonization and unification

---

[2]Dalhuisen (2007, pp. 141–143).

[3]Dalhuisen (2007, pp. 210–211).

[4]Dalhuisen (2007, pp. 166–167).

[5]Dalhuisen (2007, pp. 170–244).

[6]Carbonneau (1989, pp. 42–43).

of substantive standards and norms, can reduce the conflict among and attenuate the impact of national variations.[7]

However, the fact that all discussions on the prospect of a new *lex mercatoria*, in particular with regards to the conduct of parties in contract drafting and dispute settlement, are based, to a large extent, on assumptions, about its utility, makes any of the above or other arguments, exchanged within the debate on transnational commercial law, highly speculative or of a predominantly prognostic character. The lack of empirical data has often been the route for so many misunderstandings and irreconcilable antinomies of points of view. Even where enquiries have been conducted,[8] the results were unreliable, due to the very small sample of data. The UNIDROIT enquiry was a project, which may have had a large data sample, and which may have provided an insight to the UNIDROIT principles that also referred to the *lex mercatoria*; however, due to the fact that the principles were merely pre-statements of transnational commercial law, and did not codify the legal system, therefore, data about their use, is not a good indicator for the acceptance or not of a transnational commercial system.

However, the CENTRAL enquiry of 1999 was a better effort, as it comprised a world-wide large scale data sample for study, and, consequently, the "food" for the examination of a comprehensive concept on the viability of transnational commercial law.[9] The study showed that there is a high awareness of the use of transnational law in practice, together with a high use of the term *lex mercatoria*. In addition, it was noted that transnational law was used in connection with domestic law, which further indicates the flexibility of the character of transnational law and reveals the "Cartesian pragmatism" with which international legal practice is approaching the issue of transnationalisation of the global legal process today. Also, a high response rate, indicated the use of transnational law to supplement or interpret international uniform instruments, and as a means to improve the understanding between parties from different legal systems and with different languages.

The study also showed, that those negatively responding to the notion of the establishment of a *lex mercatoria*, were not so much arguing for its alleged incompleteness – which was the perceived notion until the point of the CENTRAL enquiry – but that their objections were based upon a lack of practical experience and the unavailability of information on the subject of transnational commercial law. Thus, it seems that it is more pragmatic reasons, rather than dogmatic reservations, which lie against the use of the concept of transnational commercial law. Overall, the CENTRAL Enquiry generated data showing that transnational commercial law, though not widely recognized, is nevertheless widely used in international legal practices, and that there is a considerable gap between the assumptions of lawyers, who discuss the theory of transnational commercial law, and the assumptions and viewpoints of international legal practice. Not least, the

---

[7]Carbonneau (1989, p. 59).

[8]Such as, the SELDEN and GORDON enquiries.

[9]Berger (2003, pp. 91, 94–95).

CENTRAL Enquiry, proves the existence, in practice, of a new *lex mercatoria*, whilst urging for marketing strategies, which will help to achieve its successful establishment or, equally, for the adoption of pragmatic solutions, to make the contents of transnational law more visible.[10]

7.1.2 The Debate Over the Emerging New Lex Mercatoria

There are many views opposed, equally for and against the notion of *lex mercatoria* and the idea for a uniform law in arbitration.[11] In England, the notion of *lex mercatoria* has been regarded as a slightly wicked misnomer, on the ground that it is not law at all. However, the notion of *lex mercatoria* entails that the latter is not a complete and self-contained legal system, but rather a source of law made up of custom, practice, convention, precedent, and many national laws, and, at the same time, an alternative to a conflict of laws quest and a way out of applying inconsistent rules.[12] The point, also, that *lex mercatoria* is not universal, and thus should be discarded, is invalid, as *lex mercatoria* does not depend on the proof of universality, but, is, in itself, a factor, towards a common law of international private trade.[13]

7.2 A Uniform Law?

The task today is to revive the old concept of universal standards in private law, and adapt it to the exigencies of the modern world. International commercial arbitration has shown that this goal is achievable, because, despite of the many problems to be solved, international arbitral proceedings are effective only if they embrace universal standards, as practical considerations and matters of principle have shown. The end of the division of the world into antagonistic political, economic and legal systems, and the globalisation of the market economy have provided a fresh impetus to make arbitration law universal. Harmonization efforts of the past, including the draft Uniform Law on Arbitration of 1954, the European Convention Providing a Uniform Law on Arbitration of 1966, and the Model Law on International Commercial Arbitration of 1985. The last one, which was adopted by the UNCITRAL, is highly successful, in that it sought to harmonise and improve legislation, and emphasized the freedom of the parties and other modern trends in

[10]For example, a restatement of international contract law published by UNIDROIT and the Lando Commission on European Contract Law, or the publication of a legal database to provide international legal practitioners with an easy-to-access and up-to-date working tool, in the area of international commercial law. See Berger (2003, pp. 100–113).

[11]Von Breitenstein (2000, pp. 115–135); see Schroeder (2007, pp. 449–455).

[12]Lowenfeld (1998, pp. 75, 83–85).

[13]Lowenfeld (1998, pp. 85–87).

arbitration. However, the conceptual link between the substantive law of international contract and the law of international arbitration, is not yet entirely forged and efforts should focus on creating a legal basis for international arbitral adjudication, via the emergence of a transnational unified system of law.[14] Any such harmonization effort, however, should also include some control mechanisms in terms of the process of the creation of a modern *lex mercatoria*. There is a pertinent need for control mechanisms, for an interaction of judges and arbitrators, for the balancing of rules and fairness as well as national interests and arbitral integrity, together with the need for delocalized dispute resolution and judicial control mechanisms, in order to promote the relative predictability of result in international dispute resolution, which is necessary to permit in formed decisions about the legal risks of commercial choices. All of the above, are factors, which will guarantee that, the new *lex mercatoria* develops in a healthy way and that harmonization occurs smoothly.[15]

A combination of normative and institutional approaches to this enormous task, would safeguard its success and, in this way, also guarantee the expansion of the structure of international commercial arbitration.[16]

7.3 A Uniform Rule on Confidentiality in Arbitration

Because of the pressing nature of the confidentiality issue, which demands a pertinent resolution, and because no one can be sure of the scope of confidentiality protections nowadays, it is urgently needed that a uniform rule be adopted. This uniform rule should be a universally accepted default rule, which would be, also, binding in the absence of mutual assent otherwise. A general default rule could be the following:

> In all arbitrations, the arbitrators should require at the threshold that the parties agree on the scope of confidentiality, failing which the arbitrators shall make a protective order on the scope of confidentiality. The parties shall by rule be deemed to have agreed to the terms of that order. Any claim asserting a violation of the parties' confidentiality agreement or protective order accruing during the course of the proceeding shall be resolved by the arbitrators. Any violation of the parties' confidentiality agreement or protective order accruing after the proceedings is terminated shall be resolved by arbitration as per the terms set forth in the parties' arbitration agreement. Arbitrators may impose appropriate damages and penalties on parties found to have breached the confidentiality agreement or protective order.

The proposed rule, has the advantage of not requiring a decision on confidentiality terms at the time of contracting, when, as shown by evidence in practice, parties usually prefer to leave this issue open. It also means that parties agree that

[14] Pechota (1998, pp. 257–263).

[15] Park (1998, pp. 143–172).

[16] Pechota (1998, pp. 257–263).

courts, although avoided altogether as a starting point, will enforce this agreement. Not least, the provision of penalties, in the event of a breach of the confidentiality agreement will deter breaches where damages from a breach may be non-existent or minimal.[17]

Another solution, could be the following uniform rule which provides for a general protection against non disclosure:

> No information concerning an arbitration will be unilaterally disclosed to a third party by any participating party unless required to do so by law or by a competent regulatory body and then only by disclosing no more than what is legally required and furnishing to the arbitrator details of the disclosure and an explanation of the reasons for it.

More detailed provisions regarding discovery and the productions of evidence or other documents or in relation to the award, could be as follows:

> 1. Any documentary or other evidence given by a party or a witness in an arbitration shall be confidential and not disclosed to any party directly involved to the arbitration or any third party without the consent of the parties to the arbitration agreement or an order of a court or arbitral tribunal.
> 2. Written pleadings will not be disclosed to third parties for any purpose save as stated above in 1.
> 3. An arbitrator, when issuing an order for the protection of documentary or other evidence, may in his discretion make such order conditional upon the other party's or parties' special written undertaking not to disclose any of the evidence or details of it to third parties.
>
> Awards should be treated as confidential and not communicated to third parties unless all parties and the arbitrator(s) consent or they fall into the public domain as a result of enforcement actions before national courts or other authorities or they must be disclosed in order to comply with a legal requirement imposed on an arbitrating party or to establish or protect such a party's legal rights against a third party.[18]

The above gives effect to the need for parties to safeguard the duty to observe confidentiality by the introduction of specific terms, as confidentiality of arbitration is not explicitly protected.

---

17 Sarles (2002, pp. 13–14).

18 Paulsson and Raeding (1995, pp. 315–317).

Chapter 8
Conclusions

8.1 A General Critique

8.1.1 An Overview

Both privacy and confidentiality are among the major advantages of arbitration. That having been said, the two concepts differ in their nature significantly. The privacy element, does not presuppose or guarantee that any information, revealed in arbitration, is automatically also confidential. The right to privacy is recognised in English law as an implied right, which attaches to all agreements to arbitrate as an incident of such a contract, unless it is expressly excluded by agreement of the parties. In *Oxford Shipping Co v Nippon Yesen Kaisha [The "Eastern Saga"],*[1] it was held that privacy, albeit implied, was nevertheless a substantive and core element of arbitration. This position, was also adopted in Australia in *Esso/BHP v Plowman.*[2]

Confidentiality has been defined by English courts either as a contractual obligation, or as a legal duty, or from a perspective.[3] In the case where confidentiality is treated as a contractual obligation, it has been traditionally identified as an implied contractual term, as stated in *Associated Electric and Gas Insurance Services (AEGIS) v European Reinsurance Company of Zurich.*[4] Where confidentiality is perceived and treated as an implied contractual term, it can be implied either in fact, as this is regarded as part of the need of the parties to give business efficacy to a transaction, or by operation of law, as demonstrated in *Ali Shipping Co Ltd v*

---

[1]*Oxford Shipping Co v Nippon Yesen Kaisha [The "Eastern Saga"]* [1984] 2 Lloyd's Rep. 373 (QB).

[2]*Esso/BHP v Plowman* (1995) 128 A.L.R. 391, High Court of Australia.

[3]Thoma (2008, p. 300).

[4]*Associated Electric and Gas Insurance Services (AEGIS) v European Reinsurance Company of Zurich* [2003] 1 All E.R. (Comm.) 253, §§ [1]–[22].

K. Noussia, *Confidentiality in International Commercial Arbitration*,
DOI 10.1007/978-3-642-10224-0_8, © Springer-Verlag Berlin Heidelberg 2010

Shipyard Trogir,[5] in which it was recognised as an inherent element of arbitration and where it was established that the duty arose directly from the arbitration agreement, or by custom of a market, trade, or locality, as illustrated in *Hassneh Insurance Co of Israel v Steuart J Mew*.[6]

In relation to the issue of confidentiality in arbitration proceedings, with regards to the arbitral proceedings themselves, the established English practice of consolidating proceedings was initially overturned in *Oxford Shipping Co v Nippon Yesen Kaisha (The "Eastern Saga")*,[7] and later on in *Sacor Maritima v Repsol*,[8] *Aquator Shipping Ltd v Kleimar NV (The Capricorn)*,[9] *Ali Shipping Co. v Shipyard Trogir*,[10] *Laker Airways Inc. v FLS Aerospace Ltd*,[11] *Owners, Master and Crew of the Tug "Hamtun" v Owners of the Ship "St. John"*,[12] *Associated Electric & Gas Insurance Services Ltd. (AEGIS) v European Reinsurance Company of Zurich (Bermuda)*.[13] In the USA, the predominant position is that consolidation would be permitted, as case law, such as *Compania Espanola de Petroleos SA v Nereus Shipping SA*[14] and *Volt Info. Sciences v Board of Trustees*,[15] has demonstrated, although the opposite view has also been followed, in cases such as in *Baesler v Cont'tal Grain Co*[16] and in *Protective Life Ins. Corp. v Lincoln Nat'l Life Ins. Corp.*[17] In Germany, an academic debate exists with regards to the existence or not of an implied duty to observe confidentiality in the absence of an express agreement. The judiciary favours the idea that the obligation to preserve confidentiality exists only in relation to the proceedings themselves and not beyond them.

In relation to the issue of confidentiality in arbitration proceedings with regards to the disclosure (discovery) of documents, in England the existence of the duty of confidentiality, in relation to documents disclosed on discovery in arbitral proceedings, was established in *Dolling-Baker v Merrett*,[18] followed by the decisions

---

[5] *Ali Shipping Co Ltd v Shipyard Trogir* [1998] 2 All ER 136 (CA).

[6] *Hassneh Insurance Co of Israel v Steuart J Mew*, [1993] 2 Lloyd's Rep 243 (Com.Ct.).

[7] *Oxford Shipping Co v Nippon Yesen Kaisha [The "Eastern Saga"]* [1984] 2 Lloyd's Rep. 373 (QB).

[8] *Sacor Maritima SA v. Repsol Petroleo SA* [1998] 1 Lloyd's Rep. 518 (QBD (Comm)).

[9] *Aquator Shipping Ltd v Kleimar NV (The Capricorn)* [1998] 2 Lloyds Rep 379.

[10] *Ali Shipping Co. v Shipyard Trogir* [1998] 1 Lloyd's Rep. 643.

[11] *Laker Airways Inc. v FLS Aerospace Ltd* [1999] 2 Lloyd's Rep. 45.

[12] *Owners, Master and Crew of the Tug "Hamtun" v Owners of the Ship "St. John"*, March 11, 1999, Admiralty Court.

[13] *Associated Electric & Gas Ins. Serv. Ltd. v. European Reinsurance Co. of Zurich (Bermuda)* [2003] UK PC 11 (Jan. 29, 2003) (AEGIS).

[14] *Compania Espanola de Petroleos SA v Nereus Shipping SA*, 527 F2d 966 (2d Cir. 1975).

[15] *Volt Info. Sciences v Board of Trustees* (489 US 468 (1989)).

[16] *Baesler v Cont'tal Grain Co*, 900 F2d. 1193 (8th Cir. 1990).

[17] *Protective Life Ins. Corp. v. Lincoln Nat'l Life Ins. Corp. v. Lincoln Nat'l Life Ins. Corp.*, 873 F.2d 281 (11th Cir. 1989).

[18] *Dolling-Baker v Merrett* [1991] 2 All E.R. 890.

in *Hassneh Insurance Co. of Israel v Mew*,[19] and in *Insurance Co v Lloyd's Syndicate*.[20] Conversely, the decisions of the High Court of Australia, in *Esso Australia Resources Ltd v Plowman*,[21] and of the Swedish Supreme Court, in *Bulgarian Foreign Trade Bank Ltd. v A.L. Trade Finance Inc.*,[22] have shown that the notion of confidentiality is not absolute and may be overturned. However, in *Ali Shipping Corporation v Shipyard Trogir*,[23] the position which supports the duty to observe confidentiality was re-determined, and was further restated in *Glidepath BV and Others v Thompson and Others*.[24] In *Emmott v Michael Wilson & Partners Ltd*,[25] although limits to confidentiality were recognised in occasional circumstances which required confidentiality to be relaxed, it was emphasised that arbitrations in England are private and confidential. In the USA, the ability to obtain pre-arbitral discovery, was demonstrated in *Amgen Inc v Kidney Center of Delaware County Ltd*.[26] Later on, in *United States v Panhandle Eastern Corp.*[27] it was recognised that release of discovery documents was permissible, where no express confidentiality intention existed.[28] The same approach was adopted in *Cont'ship Containerlines, Ltd. v PPG Industries, Inc.*,[29] *Lawrence E. Jaffee Pension Plan v Household International, Inc.*,[30] *Urban Box Office Network v Interfase Managers*,[31] and in *Re Application of Leonard Bernstein et al v On-Line Software International Inc. et al*.[32] However, case law, such as *Industrotech Constructors Inc. v Duke University and Turner Construction Company*[33] and *ITT Educational Services Inc. v*

[19] *Hassneh Insurance Co. of Israel v Mew* [1993] 2 Lloyd's Rep. 243.

[20] *Insurance Co v Lloyd's Syndicate* [1995] 1 Lloyd's Rep. 272.

[21] *Esso Australia Resources Ltd v Plowman (Minister for Energy and Minerals)* (1995) 128 A.L.R. 391.

[22] *Bulgarian Foreign Trade Bank Ltd. v. A.L. Trade Finance Inc.*, Judgment of October 27, 2000, Swedish Supreme Court.

[23] *Ali Shipping Corporation v Shipyard Trogir* [1998] 1 Lloyd's Rep. 643.

[24] *Glidepath BV and Others v Thompson and Others* [2005] 2 Lloyd's Rep. 549.

[25] *Emmott v Michael Wilson & Partners Ltd* [2008] EWCA Civ 184.

[26] *Amgen Inc v Kidney Center of Delaware County Ltd* 879 F.Supp. 878 (N.D.III 1995).

[27] *United States v Panhandle Eastern Corp.* 118 FRD 346 (D.Del. 1988).

[28] Baldwin (1996, pp. 485–486).

[29] *Cont'ship Containerlines, Ltd. v. PPG Industries, Inc.*, No. 00 Civ. 0194 RCCH BP, 2003 WL 1948807 (S.D.N.Y. Apr. 23, 2003).

[30] *Lawrence E. Jaffee Pension Plan v. Household International, Inc.*, No. Civ. A. 04-N-1228 (CBS, 04-X-0057), 2004 WL 1821968 (D. Colo. Aug. 13, 2004).

[31] *Urban Box Office Network v. Interfase Managers* No. 01 Civ. 8854 (LTS) (THK), 2004 WL 2375819 (S.D.N.Y. Oct. 21, 2004).

[32] *Re Application of Leonard Bernstein et al v On-Line Software International Inc. et al*, 232 A. D.2d 336, 648 N.Y.S.2d 602.

[33] *Industrotech Constructors Inc. v Duke University and Turner Construction Company* 1984 67 N.C.App. 741, 314 S.E.2d 272, 17 Ed. Law Rep. 269.

Roberto Arce et al,[34] has demonstrated that confidentiality clauses are enforceable and, thus, should be observed. In France, in *Société True North et Société FCB Internationale v Bleustein et al*,[35] the French Court of Appeal recognised that arbitration, as a private procedure, entails a confidentiality element. In Germany, the issue of disclosure or not of information about the existence of arbitral proceedings, depends on the precise content of the contractual confidentiality obligations.

In relation to the issue of confidentiality in arbitration proceedings with regards to an arbitral award, the English judiciary favours the preservation of confidentiality, as shown in *Department of Economic Policy & Development of the City of Moscow (DEPD) v Bankers Trust Co*[36] and further considered in *Insurance Co v Lloyd's Syndicate*,[37] *Ali Shipping Corp. v Shipyard Trogir*[38] and in *Associated Electrics and Gas Insurance Ltd (Aegis) v European Reinsurance Co of Zurich*.[39] However, courts may allow disclosure of an award, as shown in *Sacor Maritima v Repsol*[40] under certain circumstances, such as where the latter is reasonably necessary, as shown in *Lincoln National Life Insurance Co v Sun Life Assurance Co of Canada*,[41] in *Nesté Chemicals SA v DK Line SA (The Sargasso)*[42] and in *Aegis* v *European Re*.[43] In the USA, the confidentiality of arbitral awards is not implicitly guaranteed or entailed in the parties' arbitration agreement, as case law like *United States v Panhandle Eastern Corp.*,[44] has demonstrated. In France, the position is different, as demonstrated in *Aita v Ojjeh*,[45] and the rule is that there is an implied duty strictly to observe confidentiality of awards. In Germany, the position is that the protection of confidentiality of the arbitral awards should be guaranteed by a detailed express provision by the parties.

---

[34]*ITT Educational Services Inc. v Roberto Arce et al* 2008, 533 F.3d 342; WL 2553998 (C.A. 5, June 27, 2008).

[35]*Societe True North et Societe FCB Internationale v Bleustein et al*, Cour d'Appel de Paris 1999, Rev Arb 2003, 189.

[36]*Department of Economic Policy & Development of the City of Moscow (DEPD) v. Bankers Trust Co.* [2003] EWHC 1337; [2003] 1 W.L.R. 2885.

[37]*Insurance Co v Lloyd's Syndicate* [1995] 1 Lloyd's Rep. 272.

[38]*Ali Shipping Corp. v Shipyard Trogir* [1991] 1 W.L.R. 314, C.A.

[39]*Associated Electrics and Gas Insurance Ltd (Aegis) v. European Reinsurance Co of Zurich* [2003] UKPC 11; [2003] 1 All E.R. (Comm) 253.

[40]*Sacor Maritima SA v. Repsol Petroleo SA* [1998] 1 Lloyd's Rep. 518 (QBD (Comm)).

[41]*Lincoln National Life Insurance Co v. Sun Life Assurance Co of Canada First Instance* [2004] EWHC 343; [2004] 1 Lloyd's Rep. 737, CA; [2004] EWCA 1660.

[42]*Nesté Chemicals SA v DK Line SA (The Sargasso)* [1994] 2 Lloyd's Rep. 6 [1994].

[43]*Associated Electric and Gas Insurance Services Ltd v European Reinsurance Co. of Zurich* UKPC 11, (2003)1 WLR 1041.

[44]*United States v Panhandle Eastern Corp.* 118 F.R.D. 346 (D. Del. 1988).

[45]*Aita v Ojjeh*, Judgment of 18 Feb. 1986, 1986 Revue de l' Arbitrage 583.

8.1.2 Tentative Conclusions

The general rule, as depicted in the case law, is that documents and evidence of in the arbitration are protected by confidentiality, although in *Esso/BHP v Plowman*[46] it was stated that documents or other evidence of the arbitral proceedings are unlikely to remain confidential unless this is expressly and in detail stipulated: Nevertheless, the test for confidentiality of documents, is the one stated in *Ali Shipping v Shipyard Trogir*,[47] where it was held that parties, directly to the arbitration and third parties, are bound by a duty towards the observance of the obligation to confidentiality. However, this test had already been submitted to limitations and exceptions, as shown in *Oxford Shipping Co v Nippon Yesen Kaisha [The "Eastern Saga"]*,[48] *Dolling-Baker v Merrett*,[49] and in *Hassnesh v Mew*,[50] and was further exemplified in *Esso/BHP v Plowman*[51] and *Trade Finance Inc v Bulgarian Foreign Trade Bank Ltd.*[52] In addition, fairly recent case law, such as *Transfeld Philippines Inc & Ors v Pacific Hydro Ltd & Ors*,[53] has shown that the implications of *Esso/ BHP v Plowman*[54] seem to have lessened, and that there is no real difference, anymore, between the English and Australian approach towards confidentiality.[55]

In spite of the disparity in the case law on confidentiality in international commercial arbitration, the general trend still pursues the protection of confidentiality. In the common law world, cases, such as *Associated Electrics and Gas Insurance Ltd (Aegis) v European Reinsurance Co of Zurich*,[56] *Insurance Co v Lloyd's Syndicate*,[57] *Ali Shipping Corporation v Shipyard Trogir*,[58] *United States v Panhandle Eastern Corp. et al*[59] and *Lincoln National Life Insurance Co v Sun Life Assurance Co of Canada*,[60] have demonstrated the need to protect

---

[46]*Esso/BHP v Plowman* (1995) 128 A.L.R. 391, High Court of Australia.

[47]*Ali Shipping v Shipyard Trogir* [1998] 1 Lloyd's Rep 643.

[48]*Oxford Shipping Co v Nippon Yesen Kaisha [The "Eastern Saga"]* [1984] 2 Lloyd's Rep. 373 (QB).

[49]*Dolling-Baker v Merrett* [1990] 1 WLR 1205.

[50]*Hassnesh v Mew* [1993] 2 Lloyd's Rep 243.

[51]*Esso/BHP v Plowman* (1995) 128 A.L.R. 391, High Court of Australia.

[52]*Trade Finance Inc v Bulgarian Foreign Trade Bank Ltd* Case No Y 1092-98, SVEA Court of Appeal.

[53]*Transfeld Philippines Inc & Ors v Pacific Hydro Ltd & Ors* [2006] VSC 175.

[54]*Esso/BHP v Plowman* (1995) 128 A.L.R. 391, High Court of Australia.

[55]In *Transfeld Philippines Inc & Ors v Pacific Hydro Ltd & Ors [2006] VSC 175.*

[56]*Associated Electrics and Gas Insurance Ltd (Aegis) v. European Reinsurance Co of Zurich* [2003] UKPC 11; [2003] 1 All E.R. (Comm) 253.

[57][1995] 1 Lloyd's Rep. 272.

[58]*Ali Shipping Corporation v. Shipyard Trogir* [1998] 1 Lloyd's Rep. 643.

[59]*United States v Panhandle Eastern Corp. et al*, (D.Del. 1988) 118 F.R.D. 346.

[60]*Lincoln National Life Insurance Co v. Sun Life Assurance Co of Canada* [2004] EWHC 343; [2004] 1 Lloyd's Rep. 737, CA; [2004] EWCA 1660.

confidentiality further in order to guarantee its observance. In the continental law world, there is also a strong presumption towards the observance of confidentiality. Thus, in France, in *Aita v Ojjeh*[61] and, more recently, in *Société True North et Société FCB Internationale v Bleustein et al*,[62] the existence of an implied duty of confidentiality was re-emphasised, although other case law such as *Nafimco v Foster Wheeler Trading Company AG*,[63] has demonstrated that there is no absolute guarantee for its existence and subsequent observance.[64] The situation is similar in Germany. The OLG Frankfurt Court, in its decision of 22.10.2004,[65] stated clearly that there is a presumption towards the observance of confidentiality. However, generally speaking, other judgments such as the one in *Bulgarian Foreign Trade Bank Ltd. v. A.L. Trade Finance Inc.*[66] show that in order for the observance of confidentiality to be guaranteed, this need be specifically provided for in the arbitration agreement.

8.2 Ways to Safeguard Confidentiality

The confidentiality problem creates an urgent need for measures to be adopted with the aim of providing a solution to the problems encountered in practice, with regards to the preservation of confidentiality in arbitration.

At first glance, the existence of a consistent judicial approach would be the best way to achieve the observance of the duty of confidentiality.[67] However, the diversity of the established judicial trends and of the judicial reasoning behind them, as illustrated in *Esso/BHP v Plowman*[68] and *Transfeld Philippines Inc & Ors v Pacific Hydro Ltd &* Ors,[69] constitute a vivid proof of the contrasting practical difficulty of achieving and guaranteeing judicial consistency.[70]

Courts have not articulated a general rule on this issue for various reasons, such as the fact that the involvement of courts may reveal that an arbitration will become a public record; or the fact that parties frequently involved in arbitrations, may not be able to withhold the fact of such involvement; or the fact that lawyers and

---

[61]*Aita v Ojjeh* (1986) Revue de'l Arbitrage 583.

[62]*Societe True North et Societe FCB Internationale v Bleustein et al*, Cour d'Appel de Paris 1999, Rev Arb 2003, 189.

[63]*Nafimco v Foster Wheeler Trading Company AG*, Cour d'Appel de Paris, 22.01.2004.

[64]Mueller (2005, pp. 218–219).

[65]OLG Frankfurt, Beschl. v. 22.10.2004 – Case 2 Sch 01/04 (2).

[66]*Bulgarian Foreign Trade Bank Ltd. v. A.L. Trade Finance Inc.*, Judgment of October 27, 2000, Swedish Supreme Court.

[67]Brown (2001, pp. 1015–1017).

[68]*Esso/BHP v Plowman* (1995) 128 A.L.R. 391, High Court of Australia.

[69]*Transfeld Philippines Inc & Ors v Pacific Hydro Ltd & Ors* [2006] VSC 175.

[70]Editorial (1995, pp. 231–233).

arbitrators may disclose their participation to an arbitration; or the fact that financial considerations, ethical duties and public policy issues may detect so; or the fact that third parties participating in an arbitration, such as expert witnesses, may form the grapevine through which information concerning an arbitration is spread.[71] Moreover, in the common-law tradition, the debate on confidentiality in arbitration has been also intensified, in the sense that public interest, on the one hand, may, at times, require arbitration proceedings to remain confidential, but, on the other hand, it may also in some other instances preclude confidentiality. In effect, public policy reasons may require the lifting of the veil of confidentiality. Public interest considerations may also compel the courts to authorise some publicity of the arbitral proceedings.[72]

The above observations show that the solution of a consistent judicial approach is illusionary.[73] In light of the above consideration, it is, therefore, pertinent that a policy be considered in order to establish the best protection of confidentiality within arbitration. What are the factors to be considered when drafting such a policy?

8.3 Policy Means and Considerations

An initial inquiry in crafting a transparent and effective policy which would protect the confidentiality of arbitration agreements, is to determine how such a policy should evolve: i.e. via contract drafting, or via the revision of institutional arbitral rules, or via changes in the substantive law?

Arbitration is a matter of contract, and therefore it would be ideal if parties protected their own and the public's interests in their individual bargains. Bargaining realities, however, often prevent individuals from negotiating confidentiality provisions in arbitration contracts.

Moreover, the public, generally, has no say in parties' private agreements. Legislative or administrative rules may, therefore, be warranted to increase access to information affecting important public interests, without jeopardizing arbitrating parties' legitimate secrecy needs.[74]

8.3.1 Contractual Creation?

Parties to a pre-dispute contract containing an arbitration clause often do not invest time or resources in negotiating privacy and confidentiality rules for possible

[71] Brown (2001, pp. 1000–1004).

[72] Dessemontet (1996).

[73] Brown (2001, pp. 1015–1017).

[74] Schmitz (2006, p. 1241).

proceedings. This, generally, is efficient, because there is no reason for these parties, to waste resources wrangling over details of future arbitration proceedings they never expect to pursue.

Accordingly, it is unlikely that such a reform, to include confidentiality related clauses, will occur solely through parties' contract negotiations, because, on the one hand, companies generally lack the incentive to draft their standard form contracts to require publication of awards, and, on the other hand, individuals usually lack resources or experience, to negotiate successfully for contract provisions protecting the confidentiality of their sensitive information.

8.3.2 Incorporation Through Institutional Arbitration Rules

Institutional or administrative arbitration rules apply when parties incorporate them in their contracts. In other words, these rules may become contract terms by reference. Accordingly, arbitral institutions could reform their rules to cover confidentiality and transparency expressly. This would save contracting parties from having to invest their resources in drafting these provisions. It also may also foster a more balanced approach for the interests of all involved in arbitration, because bargaining and resource imbalances may play less of a role in the development of institutional rules than in parties' contractual negotiations.

Some arbitral institutions have already promulgated transparency rules in order to foster goodwill. However, most institutions that administer arbitrations under parties' private agreements take no position on whether parties should agree to keep information regarding their cases confidential. They may, also, be reluctant to embrace the time-consuming and possibly contentious tasks of developing transparency rules and publishing awards in a systematic manner. Moreover, some administering institutions would be hesitant to risk losing repeat clientele by requiring disclosure of awards. Such rules may cause repeat players to avoid these institutions, or reform their arbitration contracts to require *ad hoc* administration.

8.3.3 Legislative Regulations

As stated above, it may be difficult for parties to draft and mutually accept confidentiality provisions that appropriately protect all parties, as well as the public's interests in access to information because, on the one hand, parties usually do not voluntarily publish arbitration awards that indicate statutory violations, and all disputants do not enjoy equal access and power and, also, because, on the other hand, arbitral institutions are unlikely to act in unison to develop and implement uniform transparency reforms.

Accordingly, legislative regulation may be necessary to foster such reforms. However, this would not be an easy and simple task, in that legislators who draft such reforms would have to consider tensions between contract freedom and fair access to information, in the light of the need to balance the interests of contracting parties as well as the public. Nonetheless, legislators hopefully would pursue that task with balanced concerns and understandings. Legislative rules also allow for greater scope by extending not only to parties to an arbitration agreement, but also to arbitrators, and other third parties who participate in arbitration proceedings.

8.3.4 Considerations with Regards to the Publication and Enforcement of Awards

Although it is suggested that the regulation of the borders of confidentiality will not exclude the publication of arbitration awards, nevertheless, the latter should only occur to a limited extent. In effect, at the same time that publication of awards, affecting important public interests, would occur, default rules, which protect the confidentiality, of individuals' sensitive personal information revealed in arbitration, should also exist. In some cases, this may warrant publication of an arbitration report with careful extraction of individuals' personal information that the public has no right or need to know. Furthermore, it may justify injunctive relief or sanctions to enforce rules precluding non consensual disclosure or use of one's personal information.[75]

Any rules requiring publication of awards should be limited with respect to types of cases covered, substantive writing requirements and means for publishing these awards. Publication rules could also minimise inefficiencies by limiting the substance of reports. Published reports could be limited to the identity of the parties and arbitrators, arbitrator and administrative fees, hearings and disposition dates, a brief description of the claims, and a statement of results. Such limited reports may not further the development of the law to the extent of reasoned and publicly reported judicial opinions, but they would provide more public information than purely private awards or settlement agreements.

Confidentiality protection rules should also prescribe reasonable enforcement mechanisms to prevent parties from leaking information to the press or otherwise revealing sensitive information in order to manipulate or coerce the other party into settlement, or to prevent innocent disclosures, and to minimise the difficulties and inefficiencies which would arise if parties were required to prove actual damages for breach of confidentiality rules. Such rules could also allow for injunctive relief to preclude parties from disclosing information in the first place, and, if disclosure has occurred, monetary sanctions for intentional disclosure of protected information.

---

[75]Schmitz (2006, p. 1245).

Obviously, there is great need for empirical research on all these questions and issues. Confidentiality protection should balance concern for all parties involved in disputes, while not overly intruding on contractual liberty. Regulation should not go beyond proper protection to paternalism, because overly protective measures could backfire by providing repeat players with auxiliary means for hiding information.[76]

8.4 Arguments Against Confidentiality

Those against confidentiality claim that the continued confidentiality of arbitration decisions is short-sighted, in that it reduces the availability of relevant precedent that can benefit both the judiciary and the business community. The inability to publicise a relevant precedent, capable of being used in future proceedings means that only parties directly involved with the contract in question will be affected by it. Parties who are frequent participants in arbitration may greatly benefit from such precedents, as those parties are better able to select arbitrators with prior knowledge of the particular business, a choice which, may be substantially beneficial for the party. Without precedents businesses will be unable to use dispute outcome information to evaluate their risk in filing suit. The ability to examine dispute outcomes is one easy way in which a business can balance the cost of pursuing a claim against the actual loss suffered. However, confidentiality will hide this information from the business community. Moreover, the confidentiality of the arbitral proceeding has a detrimental effect on the use of reputation in contractual choice. Businesses, when choosing a contracting party, frequently consider reputation as one variable to aid in the selection of the appropriate contracting party. Businesses may determine that reputation is highly important in many areas, from sales potential to customer relations, all of which may factor into the contract's value. However, the confidentiality of arbitration awards shields negative and positive outcomes from becoming part of the businesses' identity. Thus, the confidentiality of the arbitral award may have an impact upon a business because it is not allowed to reveal information that may benefit the business by making its contracts more valuable.

Moreover, the risk of not having appropriate information specific to the business's reputation may cause the contracting party to assume a higher level of risk caused by its choice of contracting partner. Policy-making bodies may be unable to develop regulations that mirror current business practices. Policy-making bodies, especially in industries where confidential arbitration is widely used, have to rely partially upon the published decisions, which will be limited, in number, because of confidential awards. This lack of information, may prevent policy-making bodies

[76] Schmitz (2006, p. 1252).

from fully capturing the customs and practices within the industry. Therefore, the policies and regulations developed may become a hindrance to business, as they do not reflect current business practices.

Finally, the current trend of implying a term of confidentiality into the business's contract, where no express term exists, is possibly the most important concern for a business, The imposition of a blanket term of confidentiality in all arbitration clauses clearly fails to recognise the autonomy of the parties, which should allow parties not to have confidentiality in their arbitration agreement. Certainly, the parties should be free to decide the content of the contract, within the noted exceptions of public policy limitations and mandatory laws, and should be able to determine for themselves whether any information is worth protecting as confidential. It is quite possible that neither business will want the outcome of a dispute to be confidential, such as in cases where the outcome has a direct impact on the financial status of one or both the businesses. In such a situation, it may be desirable to release the outcome of the proceedings, and this decision should be honoured by the state and the courts as it in no way impacts, influences, or infringes the authority of the state or the public it is attempting to protect.

In addition to impacting individual businesses, increased protection of the confidentiality of awards would potentially cause damage to international commercial law, as a whole. First and foremost, the *lex mercatoria* is founded on the customs developed by the merchants themselves. Tenets of *lex mercatoria* allow, if not demand, the custom to adapt to the changing environment and commercial practices. However, the use of confidentiality in arbitral proceedings and awards, diminishes the rate of adaptation. As this occurs, the system of *lex mercatoria* will suffer, because it will begin to lag behind the practice of merchants.[77]

8.5 Other Relevant Factors: Legal Cultures and Traditions

Codes, laws and guidelines governing international commercial arbitration developed by various organizations[78] have been drafted against the background of common-law and civil-law values. In balancing these two great legal traditions, it was assumed that together they represent a composite legal tradition, governing international commercial arbitration. The result of that assumption was decades of fine work, enshrining international arbitration doctrines, principles, and rules of law and procedures that blend these two important legal traditions.

How pervasive are the common and civil-law traditions? Are they sufficiently uniform, in nature and operation, to justify their dominant status in formulating

[77]Raymond (2005, pp. 502–516).

[78]Such as the International Court of Arbitration, the International Bar Association and the International Chamber of Commerce.

codes, laws and rules governing international commercial arbitration? And, has international commercial arbitration become unduly reliant upon both the common and civil-law traditions at the expense of other legal traditions that operate against the background of different and changing legal cultures?

A legal culture is distinguishable from, and wider than, a legal tradition. Identifying a legal culture, involves an analysis of the parameters of the nature, source and operation of that culture. The source of a culture may revert back to the social, political and economic roots of that culture. The content of a legal culture, may find formal expression in a legal tradition, such as in codes, statutes and judicial decisions, which are set out in the principles, standards and rules of law governing arbitration. The development of a legal culture may follow religious, political or social patterns, or some combination of all three. A legal culture may also evolve out of market forces that impact upon it differently, over time, place and space. The operation of a legal culture, may be described in the legal literature that outlines how legal rules ought to work, in theory, and how they actually function in practice. A legal culture may also develop, in response to social values that are attributed to law, such as when rendering the operation of law efficient, comprehensible or fair. A legal culture may be described in attitudes towards law, such as the attitudes of the international business community to the cost, impartiality and reliability of national courts of law, or the attitudes of politicians to the regulation of international business through domestic legislation.[79]

A legal tradition is conceived more narrowly than a legal culture and, in some measure, is a subset of that culture. Identifying a legal tradition includes analysing the source, development and operation of a legal system itself. The development of a legal tradition, as it applies to international commercial arbitration, may encompass a particular historical institution, such as the influence of the medieval Law Merchant, upon the evolution of modern international commercial arbitration. The development of an arbitration tradition may also include global traditions, such as the institutionalisation of arbitration in international arbitration codes, laws and guidelines, and the manner in which commercial arbitration is practised in a particular region or global community generally. In some respects, the medieval Law Merchant reflects a legal tradition among merchants that both predated and had an impact upon modern international commercial arbitration. The Law Merchant was cosmopolitan, in incorporating the trading practices of itinerant merchants who travelled across the, then-known, world trading in their wares. In some respects it is in this tradition that international commercial arbitration has evolved into an alternative means of resolving disputes to national courts of law.

International commercial arbitration, is decidedly more complex today when compared to historical variants of dispute resolution, like the medieval Law Merchant.

[79]Trackman (2006, p. 5).

Given that arbitration is grounded in party consent, learning how that consent arises in practice, within discrete business communities, is important in understanding how a culture of international commercial arbitration has evolved. Understanding how law impacts on culture, and culture upon law, also has a significant bearing on the operation of each, in relation to the other in the context of international commercial arbitration. Analysing legal cultures, like those associated with international commercial arbitration, can help to understand not only the attributes of those cultures, but also their disparate application, in a changing global community, including international commercial arbitration.

By considering trends in legal cultures, one can observe the effect of cultural shifts upon the operation of legal institutions, like arbitration. One can observe tendencies, practices, habits and customs that are imputed to a legal culture, as well as perceived changes in those tendencies. Moreover, one can develop measured institutional and non-institutional responses to perceptions of cultural change.

However, because much international commercial arbitration transcends or resists discrete cultural difference, it follows that arbitration is unavoidably affected by disparate legal culture. That influence occurs when international commercial arbitration is grounded in distinct legal cultures, such as when civil-law influences lead to restrictions in the admission of oral testimony in arbitration. Differences in legal culture, among end users, also lead to the development of novel arbitration services.[80] Whether these cultural influences arise by deliberate design or by accretion, they impact on the culture of arbitration itself. As a result, international commercial arbitration consists of a variable amalgam of legal cultures. It is not the product of a single, determinative and pre-existing arbitral culture.

Ultimately comes the question: whether arbitration is the product of cultural pluralism, derived from a blend of civil and common-law traditions and, if so, to what extent? To what extent is this blend itself changing in our global environment?[81] From the perspective of international commercial arbitration legal traditions can also be broken down into local, regional and international traditions. Local legal traditions, encompass the rules and practice of a state or local legal system, such as are embodied in a state's commercial code. Regional legal traditions, include the laws and practices of regional organizations, like the European Union and the North American Free Trade Agreement. International legal traditions include the various institutions adopted by a multitude of states. Thus, a stereotypical conclusion is that international commercial arbitration, along with the lawyer-arbitrators and counsel who serve it, emanates primarily from an amalgam of civil and common-law traditions that are unified by international organizations, like the ICC. However, it should not be blindly assumed, that international commercial arbitration has simply replicated an amalgam of these traditions. As a matter of

[80]Such as the development of uniform, expedited and enforceable procedures to protect the trademarks of established businesses from infringement and from cyber squatters.
[81]Trackman (2006, pp. 7–13).

practice, common and civil-law traditions vary markedly from country to country, as well as over time and space.[82]

A reliance on common and civil-law traditions is also insufficient to serve as the basis for the legal traditions governing international commercial arbitration in the modern era. First, even if civil and common-law traditions were dominant globally and historically, such a dominance has become both "nationalised" and "regionalised" as a consequence of the advent of the modern state, the influence of local custom on the evolution of commercial law and practice, and the development of regional free trade zones. So, too, local legal traditions have evolved, and they are significantly impacted by domestic political, economic and social forces, beyond their early roots in civil or common-law systems.[83] Given the amalgam of different legal traditions, can one detect a distinctively international legal tradition, in commercial arbitration? And, if so, what is the nature and significance of that tradition?

There are different principles by which to gauge the legal tradition of international commercial arbitration. The first principle is consensual, that is to say, the parties choose arbitration. The parties are free to select the nature, form and operation of arbitration, irrespective of whether its nature is *ad hoc* or institutional; or, whether its form is modelled on European, English, American or "other" legal traditions; or whether it is conducted primarily through oral testimony or written submissions; or whether it is impacted by a multi-or bilateral treaty or by discrete customary law influences. The parties to arbitration presumably exercise their choices for distinctive reasons, such as, the existence of a reputation of a preferred arbitration association; or because the particular arbitrators chosen supposedly have commercial expertise beyond that of domestic courts of law; or because international commercial arbitration is perceived to be less costly, more efficient and more "party sensitive" than courts of law; or because of the privacy and confidentiality features, entailed in international commercial arbitration; or simply, to avoid having to rely on the domestic laws and procedures of the legal system and courts of one party. These reasons, for resorting to international commercial arbitration, may be misplaced, but they nevertheless are repeatedly invoked, as bases for resorting to arbitration. A second principle is that parties can make choices which accommodate preferred legal traditions, while still not choosing domestic courts. A third principle is that the manner in which arbitration is conducted may reflect in varying degrees a particular legal tradition and, more broadly, a preferred cultural orientation. A fourth principle is that particular procedures, associated with international commercial arbitration, stand out more starkly when they are modelled on a particular legal tradition. For example, all other factors being constant, one may

[82]English lawyers, ordinarily engage in a more rigorous formulation, of legal doctrine, than American lawyers, who tend to treat the law in a more piecemeal fashion. Civil lawyers, who follow the French tradition of the Code Napoleon, tend to focus less intensively on the scientific analysis of concepts, like "causa" in the law of obligations, than those who adhere to the more recent and scientifically textured German Code, the Bürgerliches Gesetzbuch (BGB).

[83]Trackman (2006, pp. 16–17).

well expect to encounter less reliance on oral testimony before arbitration tribunals, like the ICC, than before an association like the AAA, in which the examination and cross-examination of witnesses, including experts, is often extensive. A fifth principle, is that variations in the services, provided by international commercial arbitration inevitably are influenced by the customer.[84]

A study of the rules of arbitration of different international, regional and local associations reveals that, while commercial arbitration has attributes of a pervasive legal tradition, the rules and procedures through which that tradition are expressed diverge noticeably from one arbitration association to the next. This diversity in arbitral practice, across the global arbitral community does not imply that the legal tradition surrounding international commercial arbitration is either convoluted or a sham. One can debate the nature, extent and value of those differences, but it would be doubtful to insist, as a matter of principle, that rules and procedures, in international commercial arbitration, should be uniform in nature. However, the point is also not that a legal tradition of international commercial arbitration should resist uniformity, any more than it should replicate the already over-generalized traditions of the civil or common law, but that, in as much as international arbitration proceedings transcend proceedings, before national courts, its traditions should differentiate it, from those national law traditions. A further point is that an international arbitration tradition may well warrant having diverse constituent parts, not only because arbitration associations should be free to market their distinct services, but also because parties should be free to choose different arbitration options based on their discrete circumstances and their free choice. Similarly, parties ought to be able to choose among arbitration associations according to their perceptions of the expertise of the association, its reputation, its rules and procedures, the quality of its roster of arbitrators, its costs, and its record of having its awards recognised and enforced in particular foreign jurisdictions. At the same time, the more expansive and complex the choices available to the parties are, the greater is the potential for one party to pressure another to acquiesce in preferred arbitration rules and procedures which closely resemble the dominant party's domestic rules and procedures.

In what respects are the traditions of international commercial arbitration truly global and pervasive in their sphere of application?[85] International commercial arbitration, has evolved, primarily, against the background of two unifying international traditions: the private international legal tradition, directed at the harmonization of laws; and the public international law tradition, committed to reducing global barriers to trade. Despite the fragmentation of global trade along bilateral and regional lines, international commercial arbitration has remained a vital, yet adaptable, constant in the world trade equation. Can international commercial

---

[84]The London Court of International Arbitration states that changes in commercial dispute resolution procedures are, quite properly, driven by the end-user. That is, by the international business community.

[85]Trackman (2006, pp. 20–26).

arbitration adjust culturally to meet the future?[86] Emanating from diffuse economic, social and political environments, parties contemplating international commercial arbitration today can choose from a range of sophisticated instruments which demonstrate what, when, and how, to arbitrate disputes. They can choose arbitration forums and rules based on the perceived stability of the applicable arbitral systems, the development of their jurisprudence, and their record of successfully concluded and enforced arbitrations. Parties can also choose from an increasing number of national and regional arbitration centres that accommodate different legal traditions and respond differently to disparate legal cultures. They can adopt a variety of arbitration clauses, duly adapted to meet their particular needs, i.e. they can opt for the specific protection even of rights that are not explicitly provided for, such as the duty and right to observe confidentiality. In addition, parties are not only able to make choices among different types of international commercial arbitration but they can tailor those choices to their own diverse needs and preferences. International commercial arbitration has also entered the global culture of the Internet. Mainstream local, regional and international arbitration associations also offer various online services, including online resources and the ability to file cases online, carefully protected by sophisticated and password-protected gateway services. There is also evidence that arbitration centres once regarded with suspicion in the international business community are becoming not only more competitive but also readier to provide transparent services and enforceable results. Finally centres directed primarily at providing arbitration education have evolved to assist parties to decide whether and how to use arbitration. These centres vary from advising parties on how to draft arbitration clauses and choose arbitrators to advising them how to form realistic expectations about the time and costs involved in arbitrating disputes.[87]

International commercial arbitration will face ongoing cultural challenges. Again, "localisation" and "regionalisation", as opposed to "internationalisation" of arbitration, is neither good nor bad in itself. In order for the culture, surrounding international commercial arbitration to be non-exclusionary of other cultures, and, wherever for it exclusionary, to be remedied, international commercial arbitration needs be vigilant, so as to avoid being dubbed culturally myopic, in times of change It is important, that arbitrators use modern law merchant practices but scrutinise them, bearing always in mind fairness to the parties involved.

Due to the fact that legal culture surrounding international commercial arbitration have grown both more diffuse and more complicated in operation, while arbitral institutions sometimes have failed to adapt to the demands of changing markets for their services, international commercial arbitration needs to address those legal cultures and traditions once ignored historically, but now carrying far greater political and economic weight. To ignore these legal traditions and cultural influences will be at the peril of arbitration itself. This is not to suggest that

[86]Trackman (2006, pp. 28–30).
[87]Trackman (2006, pp. 34–35).

international commercial arbitration has stood still. Significant progress has been made by local, regional and international arbitration organizations, at demystifying arbitration. Information is increasingly available that explains to parties how arbitration works, and there is also an impressive body of online databases that clarify what, when, how and where to arbitrate, along with the inclusion of a host of conventions, codes, laws, rules and practices on international commercial arbitration. In spite of the existence of such developments, international commercial arbitration is unlikely to be a panacea, but, needs to be able to recognise cultural prejudices and to be sensitive to cultural traditions.[88]

8.6 Future Prospects and Suggested Routes

Alternative dispute resolution should not be dismissed wholesale, because it does not explicitly recognise and protect the need for confidentiality. Instead, it should be recognised as a growing mechanism of dispute resolution. Freedom of contract, or party autonomy, should continue to exist and, within it, businesses and individuals, should be able to secure their ability to create arbitration agreements encompassing their desire to protect the confidentiality aspect of any potential dispute therein involved.

That having been said, there is a growing need to counterweight the disadvantages of confidentiality, before actually proceeding to any widespread legislative measure, to reinforce its protection. Although the business community nowadays widely accepts confidentiality, notwithstanding the term's lack of definition or certainty, it should also consider factors such as, for example, the place and role of confidentiality, within a system that has only a very limited right of appeal. Furthermore, the use of the term confidentiality, which is unsettled and uncertain, is probably short-sighted, in that it removes from the spectrum of general knowledge, not only the establishment of precedent, but also, impacts the gathering of information, the elimination of which could negatively impact the judiciary and the business community.

Thus, the suggestions is made that confidentiality should be observed, but within limits. Although full disclosure and lifting of the veil of confidentiality damages business reputation, publication of certain information at certain stages of the arbitral process, such as the revelation of some information within awards, could be allowed. Parties could still request the protection of information, but would need to demonstrate to the tribunal a need to protect the release of the information, especially the release of information of not so big importance, in terms of secrecy, such as the business names of the parties and nature of the dispute. The availability of this basic information is vital to the business and legal community. Moreover, the confidentiality afforded should be judged on a case by case basis. Blanket

[88]Trackman (2006, pp. 40–43).

confidentiality is an unwise imposition by the judiciary, in light of the need for legal decisions to stand as precedent. Moreover, blanket confidentiality protections may be an unwise agreement for a business, from both a business and public community perception.[89]

Because it is highly probable that parties in international disputes face an uncertain route to the resolution of their dispute, it is important that they take action to smoothen their path, by taking steps such as the drafting of their own dispute resolution clauses. In drafting such clauses, they should consider the required content and length of the clause, the set of dispute resolution rules to be incorporated, as well as the question of their modification or supplementation and the question of the way in which the whole process is to be administered, i.e. whether it will be administered *ad hoc* or via an institution.

More specifically, in drafting arbitration clauses, parties should avoid blindly adopting a wholesale boilerplate clause, but enquire into the possible question of modification or supplementing of the said clause, and in particular they should ensure that they address the *lex arbitri* or *lex fori*; the seat of arbitration, which will determine the procedural applicable laws and will impact on the enforcement procedure; the legal environment, i.e. the laws and courts, of the chosen country, as these may be used to assist the arbitration process; or, in any other way, the enforceability of the agreement to arbitrate, i.e. that fact that local courts, allow parties to enforce the agreement to arbitrate and do not assume jurisdiction over the dispute;[90] the method of appointment of arbitrators; the availability of an interim relief by a court in aid of arbitration; the language of the arbitration proceeding; the currency of the award settlement; and, last but not least, the question of confidentiality and related issues, such as the discovery provisions to be agreed, the availability of punitive damages and the details of the payment of costs.[91] In relation to confidentiality parties should include detailed confidentiality provisions to ensure protection of confidentiality or, even in the case where courts will permit disclosure of information on the basis of public policy or other considerations, safe and precise mitigation of the damages to be incurred from such a disclosure. Also, parties should consider confidentiality concerns when drafting other clauses, such as choice of law clauses, where the extent of protection of confidentiality by a particular country's law should be addressed. In addition, parties may consider requesting a protective order or stipulation in order to ensure confidentiality of the arbitration proceedings, or they may consider obtaining a provisional measure, such as an injunction, to protect confidential information. They may also consider stamping the documents, disclosed on discovery, as confidential, to avoid their further use and, lastly, ask third parties to sign confidentiality agreements, in an effort to deter the latter from disclosing information from the arbitral process,

---

[89]Raymond (2005, pp. 502–516).

[90]A way to check the above is to enquire whether the chosen country has adopted the UNCITREAL Model Law on Arbitration and the New York Convention.

[91]Nolan-Haley et al. (2005, pp. 196–229).

whilst also giving parties to the arbitration a breach of contract remedy in cases of unauthorised disclosure.[92]

8.7 A Final Thought

Courts of justice form part of one of the three pillars of state. Their authority does not rest on consent but on state power. This is so even though a plaintiff is, in a sense, a consenting party, and even though it is possible to point to much litigation where foreign parties have agreed contractually to submit their disputes to the jurisdiction of the courts of a certain state. Once invoked, the jurisdiction is exercised over the parties, not on the basis of their consent, but by virtue of the power of the court as an emanation of the relevant state. So, it is recognised that the activities of courts must be open, so that the proper exercise of that power may be observed, not just by the parties, but by the public at large, which may one day also find itself involved in, or affected by, court decisions. Transparency and answerability, are increasingly, and rightly, stressed as essentials of any court system, in a modern democracy. Arbitration is quite different. Its key theme today is party autonomy. Parties who are free to conduct their affairs by agreement are by agreement also free to opt out of the jurisdiction of the courts, and to decide, how, and before whom, to have any disputes resolved. The force of the case for permitting this, and the virtue of arbitration, are now almost, if not quite, universally accepted.[93] One of the advantages of arbitration, commonly cited, is the privacy or confidentiality of arbitration proceedings. Due to the fact that this is an apparently simple concept, it is strange to find that there is such uncertainty and disagreement about it.[94] Yet, "chaotic", is only one way of describing the law and practice, on confidentiality in international commercial arbitration nowadays.[95]

The meaning and extent of party autonomy are an underlying issue behind arbitration and confidentiality.[96] On the one hand, confidentiality is perceived as one of the fundamental advantages of arbitration. Yet, unlike in the case of privacy, no clear explicit legal framework as to the duty to observe confidentiality exists. Different jurisdictions recognise confidentiality differently, i.e. to varying extents, in spite of the fact that arbitration is a private agreement of parties to submit their dispute to it and, as such, should also be confidential in terms of many aspects. Moreover, even within the jurisdictions where the topic has been most frequently treated judicially, the courts have been unable, or unwilling, to agree on anything more than the bare outlines of a coherent doctrine.

---

[92] Brown (2001, pp. 1017–1024).

[93] Lord Mance (2003, p. 58, §§ 2–3).

[94] Lord Mance (2003, p. 59, § 5).

[95] Sze and Peng Khoon (2007, p. v).

[96] Lord Mance (2003, p. 58, § 1).

The starting point, about which there appears to be no real room for disagreement, is that a consensual arbitration is intended to take place in private. No doubt, it is possible to agree otherwise, but, absent so unusual an agreement, the assumption is one of privacy. The origin of the assumption must rest in either the nature of arbitration itself or some implied term in the parties' agreement. That being so, it can be dispensed with by agreement, but it cannot be regarded as a mere matter of procedure and therefore within the arbitrator's discretion.[97] The fact that something takes place in private will commonly have the consequential effect that others will not learn about it. But, it may be argued that it does not necessarily connote any obligation to keep it secret or confidential. Other suggested problems are the nature and the extent of the obligation to observe confidentiality. Despite the problems of defining the limits of such an obligation, case law accepts that parties to an arbitration agreement undertake obligations of secrecy or confidentiality that are wider than their mere obligation to conduct the proceedings in private.[98]

The difficulty of defining the limits of this duty, has led English courts to accept a general principle of confidentiality, and frequently to examine its limitations.[99] It is right to note that the English case law has not concerned the same situations as in the Australian case law[100] in which any obligation of confidence was held to be excluded. Nor have the English cases been concerned with arbitrations in which government bodies have been parties. Thus, it could be validly argued that the English courts have not had to address explicitly the possible existence of some general "public interest" exception, along the lines that the High Court of Australia would have adopted, had it acknowledged the existence of any duty of confidentiality at all. The High Court's suggestion of a general public interest exception, brings back the issue of the relationship and the contrast between court proceedings and arbitration. If party autonomy is the principle, this is because international and national legal opinions accept that parties should be free both to conduct their affairs and to resolve any disputes in accordance with their own private agreement. The public interest in business affairs may in some cases require the conduct of the affairs to be made public. But, this does not justify or clarify why arbitrations involving a government party should fall into a different category. The logic of the High Court's suggested exception could be applied to any arbitration with a subject-matter of particular public interest. However, this would substantially undermine the practice and purpose of much international arbitration. The rationale of the courts, which is to conduct their affairs in public so as to ensure public confidence in a compulsory system, has no application to consensually chosen arbitration. Thus, it is unclear why the public or press's understandable interest in the subject-matter of a business dispute should override the normal privacy attaching to consensual

[97] Lord Mance (2003, p. 60, §§ 7–8).

[98] Lord Mance (2003, pp. 61–62, §§ 10, 11, 13).

[99] Lord Mance (2003, p. 61, § 17).

[100] In *Esso Australia Resources Ltd v Plowman* (1995) 128 ALR 391 and in *Commonwealth of Australia v Cackatoo Dockyard Pty Ltd* (1995) 36 NSWLR 662.

arbitration. It seems unlikely that English courts, would accept so wide an exception. Nevertheless, there is still room for argument about the scope and basis of the duty of confidentiality.[101]

Many questions are still left unanswered: Is confidentiality truly a reflective characteristic and a defining feature of the arbitral process? Is the duty to observe confidentiality a *prima facie* rule? Or is it the case, as practice has shown, that the exceptions to it formulate the general rule which needs to be followed? What is the doctrinal source and the extent of the exceptions to the duty to observe confidentiality? As the current monograph has shown, there is no clear answer to these theoretical questions, nor clear consensus in the arbitral world, about the importance of the obligation to observe the duty of confidentiality in arbitration. Theory apart, there is sparse quantitative and qualitative data to allow us draw general conclusions as to the real impact of the way in which the present status of confidentiality in arbitration affects the decision of business people in choosing arbitration as a method for resolving their disputes.

It is equally important, by way of conclusion, to look at some of the effects supporting the duty to observe confidentiality. Businessmen like to keep their affairs private, particularly if they have led to dispute, as, in this way, competitors will not learn valuable information and clients and customers will not have their confidence diminished by public disclosure of perhaps embarrassing circumstances. However, a coin has, not only one, but, two sides. The absence of the transparency which assists in ensuring proper standards of behaviour and decision-making in court, may conduce to casual conduct which is prejudicial to fair arbitration. In addition, another pitfall of privacy and confidentiality is that they tend to create a secret world of decision-making, cut off from the mainstream of the law, and highly fragmented of itself. Arbitration embraces whole swathes of specialist commerce and financial dealings, and the persons involved in it value not merely, privacy and confidentiality, but also certainty and predictability. That having been said, private arbitration is inherently unable to develop any body of public jurisprudence and no machinery exists for sanitising awards to enable decisions to be known and followed, or to give guidance to future tribunals.[102] So, where do we stand?

In England, the aim of the Arbitration Act 1996 was to establish the autonomy of arbitration from court intervention, in accordance with the parties' presumed intention when agreeing to arbitration. However, now that some of the disadvantages have had time to manifest themselves, certain quarters have expressed the view that the pendulum has swung too far in favour of party autonomy. For many years the courts have exercised a firm control, over errors of law by arbitrators. The indirect results of this were that many arbitration rulings became public, and that there was much in the way of court precedents to guide arbitrators in future cases.[103] It is also apparent that, although the underlying aim of the observance

[101]Lord Mance (2003, pp. 70–71, §§ 26–27).

[102]Lord Mance (2003, pp. 73–74, §§ 30, 32).

[103]Lord Mance (2003, p. 75, § 34).

of confidentiality is to give effect to party autonomy, the development of the present status of arbitration and confidentiality within it have highlighted the potential problem that privacy and confidentiality deprive the business and legal worlds of a sound body of jurisprudence in important areas of commerce and finance.

In the absence of a way to assess the practical impact of confidentiality in arbitration, there is equally no generally accepted way which can be suggested to tackle the issue and the practical implications involved. Equally, in the absence of a consensus on the origins of the duty to observe confidentiality, no safe guidelines can be drawn as to the directions in which confidentiality should be developed.

There is clearly no golden solution to be found, and the best path lies somewhere in between. The business and financial worlds value the other virtues of confidentiality sufficiently highly to mean that there would probably not be many of those engaging in arbitration, especially in England, who would favour any general relaxation of confidentiality of arbitration and, in this respect, the best solution remains, perhaps, to continue to assess the matter on a case by case basis.[104]

Notwithstanding a proliferation of arbitral disputes, which mirrors a global arbitral world, the age of accelerated economic convergence, in which we live, is not matched by a convergence of national legal systems. Despite the globalisation of arbitration cultural diversity persists, and it is also reflected in arbitration rules and arbitration agreements. As to the future of arbitration, it is bright, provided parties take further, better and more extensive measures in better safeguarding their rights and the whole constitution of arbitration; secondly, provided judges in national courts raise their sights and adopt a trans-national outlook, remembering always the true consensual nature of all international arbitration; and, thirdly, provided that international arbitrators, adjust their sights as well, with robust judgement and a clearer articulation of the decisions made. For a good arbitrator is one who writes acceptable reasons for his stated conclusions, i.e. reasons that satisfy the loser, as well as the winner.

In the future in international arbitration, cultures and legal traditions need converge and co-exist, not in conflict, or distrust, as before, but, in harmony – a symbiotic harmony.[105]

[104]Lord Mance (2003, pp. 76–77, § 37).

[105]Nariman (2004, p. 135).

Bibliography

Ahrend A (1996) Der Zuständigkeitsstreit im Schiedsverfahren. J C B Mohr Siebeck, München

Alexandrow I (2003) Internationale Schiedsgerichtsbarkeit in Deutschland und in den GUS-Staaten. R-U Bochum, Bochum

Arkan S, Yongalik A (2006) Festschrift Liber Amicorum Tugrul Ansay. Kluwer Law International, The Hague

Arnaldez J-J, Derains Y, Hascher D (1997) Collection of ICC arbitral awards 1991–1995, ICC Publishing. Kluwer Law International, The Hague

Ashford P (2006) Documentary discovery and international commercial arbitration. Am Rev Int'l Arb 17:89–131

Audit B (1984) A national codification of international commercial arbitration: the French decree of May 12, 1981. In: Carbonneau TE (ed) Resolving transnational disputes through international arbitration. University Press of Virginia, Virginia

Bagner H (2001) Confidentiality – a fundamental principle in international commercial arbitration? J Int'l Arb 18(2):243–249

Baldwin CD IV (1996) Protecting confidential and proprietary commercial information in international arbitration. Tex Int'l L J 36:451–494

Bamodu G (2001) Extra-national legal principles in the global village: a conceptual examination of transnational law. Int ALR 4(1):6–16

Basedow J et al (2000) Private law in the international arena: from national conflict rules towards harmonization and unification, in Festschrift für Kurt Siehr. TMC Asser, The Hague

Berger KP (1992) Internationale Wirtschaftsshiedsgerichtsbarkeit. In: Horn H (ed) Rechts des Internationales Wirtschaftsverkehrs, Band 10, S 296. M.W.N., Köln

Berger KP (2000a) The new law merchant and the global market: a 21st century view of transnational commercial law. Int ALR 3(4):91–102

Berger KP (ed) (2000b) Understanding transnational commercial law. Quadis, Münster

Berger KP (2001a) The principles of European contract law and the concept of the "creeping codification" of law. Eur Rev Private L 9:21

Berger KP (2001b) The German arbitration law of 1998 – first experiences. In: Briner R, Fortier Y, Berger KP, Bredow J (eds) Law of international dispute settlement in the 21st century. Liber Amicorum Karl-Heinz Böckstiegel. Carl Heymanns, Köln

Berger KP (ed) (2003) The practice of transnational law. Kluwer Law International, The Hague

Berman HJ, Dasser FJ (1998) The "new" law merchant and the "old": sources, content and legitimacy. In: Carbonneau TE (ed) Lex Mercatoria and arbitration. Juris, The Hague

Böckstiegel K-H, Glossner O (1981) Festschrift für Arthur Bülow. Carl Heymanns, Köln

Böckstiegel K-H et al (eds) (1983) Schiedsgerichtsbarkeit in Frankreich, Schriftenreihe des Deutschen Instituts für Schiedsgerichtswesen, Band 3. Carl Heymanns, Köln

Böckstiegel K-H et al (eds) (1985) Schiedsgerichtsbarkeit im deutsch-amerikanischen Wirtschaftsverkehr, Schriftenreihe des Deutschen Instituts für Schiedsgerichtswesen, Band 5. Carl Heymanns, Köln

Böckstiegel K-H et al (eds) (1986) Recht und Praxis der Schiedsgerichtsbarkeit der Internationalen Handelskammer, Schriftenreihe des Deutschen Instituts für Schiedsgerichtswesen, Band 6. Carl Heymanns, Köln

Böckstiegel K-H, Kröll SM, Nacimiento P (2008) Arbitration in Germany, the model law in practice. Kluwer Law International, The Hague

Bonn RL (1972) Arbitration: an alternative system for handling contract related dipsutes. Adm Sci Q 17(2):254–264

Borris C (1999) The reconciliation of conflicts between common law and civil law principles in the arbitration process. In: Frommel SN, Rider BA (eds) Conflicting legal cultures in commercial arbitration: old issues and new trends. Studies in comparative corporate and financial law, vol 4. Kluwer Law International, The Hague

Boyd S (1995) Expert report in Esso v Plowman. Arb Int'l 11(3):273

Briner R, von Schlabrendorff F (2001) Article 6 of the European Convention on Human Rights and its bearing upon international arbitration. In: Briner R, Fortier Y, Berger KP, Bredow J (eds) Law of international dispute settlement in the 21st century. Liber Amicorum Karl-Heinz Böckstiegel. Carl Heymanns, Köln, pp 89–109

Briner R, Fortier Y, Berger KP, Bredow J (2001) Law of international dispute settlement in the 21st century. Liber Amicorum Karl-Heinz Böckstiegel. Carl Heymanns, Köln

Brown AC (2001) Presumption meets reality: an exploration of the confidentiality obligation in international commercial arbitration. Am U Int'l L Rev 16:969–1025

Bruner PL, O'Connor PJ Jr (1989) Bruner and O'Connor on construction law. Thomson West, St. Paul, MN

Brunet E, Speidel RE, Sternlight JR, Ware SJ (2006) Arbitration law in America: a critical assessment. Cambridge University Press, New York

Buehler MW, Webster TH (2008) Handbook of ICC arbitration, commentary, precedents and materials, 2nd edn. Sweet and Maxwell, London

Buhler MR (2002) The clauses of "Confidentalité" in the international contracts. RDAI/IBLJ 3/4:359–387

Bühring U (1996) Arbitration and mediation in international business. Kluwer Law International, The Hague

Buys CG (2003) The tensions between confidentiality and transparency in international arbitration. Am Rev Int'l Arb 14:121–131

Carbonneau TE (ed) (1984a) Resolving transnational disputes through international arbitration. University Press of Virginia, Virginia

Carbonneau TE (1984b) The French jurisprudence on international commercial arbitration. In: Carbonneau TE (ed) Resolving transnational disputes through international arbitration. University Press of Virginia, Virginia

Carbonneau TE (1989) Alternative dispute resolution, meeting the lances and dismounting the steeds. University of Illinois Press, Chicago

Carbonneau TE (ed) (1998) Lex Mercatoria and arbitration. Juris, The Hague

Carbonneau TE (2001) Cases and materials on the law and practice of arbitration, 3rd edn. Juris, The Hague

Carbonneau TE (2005) Cases and materials on international litigation and arbitration. Thomson West, St. Paul, MN

Collins M (1995) Privacy and confidentiality' in arbitral proceedings. Arb Int'l 11(3):321–336

Comite Francais de l'Arbitrage (1986) Revue de l'Arbitrage. ICC, Paris

Comite Francais de l'Arbitrage (2003) Revue de l'Arbitrage, 1. ICC, Paris

Comite Francais de l'Arbitrage (2004) Revue de l'Arbitrage. ICC, Paris

Comment on Decision of 21/09/05 of the Federal Supreme Court, (2005) Schieds VZ, 306

Dalhuisen JH (2007) Dalhuisen on international commercial financial and trade law, 2nd edn. Hart, Oxford

Daly MP (2007) Come one come all: the new and developing world of non-signatory arbitration and class. U Miami L Rev 62:95–128

De Saint Marc Denoix V (2003) Confidentiality of arbitration and the obligation to disclose information on listed companies or during due diligence investigations. J Int'l Arb 20 (2):211

Deck CA, Farmer A (2007) Bargaining over an uncertain value: arbitration mechanisms compared. J L Econ Org 23:547–579

Derrington SC (2007) An illusionary distinction – the Australian and English approaches to confidentiality in arbitration: Transfeld Philippines Inc & Ors v Pacific Hydro Ltd & Ors [2006] VSC 175. A&NZ Mar LJ 21:188–190

Dessemontet F (1996) Arbitration and confidentiality. Am Rev Int'l Arb 7(3–4):299–318. http://www.unil.ch/webdav/site/cedidac/shared/Articles/Arbitration%20&%20Confidentiality.pdf. Accessed 24 August 2008

Devolvé JL (1982) Arbitration in France: the French Law of national and international arbitration. Kluwer Law and Taxation, Deventer

Devolve J et al (2003) French arbitration law and practice. Kluwer Law International, The Hague

Distler W (2000) Private Schiedsgerichtsbarkeit und Verfassung: Eine Rechtsvergleichende Untersuchung zum deutschen und englischen Recht. Peter Lang, Frankfurt am Main

Domke M (1981) Towards an "international" public policy in commercial arbitration. In: Böckstiegel K-H, Glossner O (eds) Festschrift für Arthur Bülow. Carl Heymanns, Köln

Domke M (1999) Domke on commercial arbitration. Thomson West, St. Paul, MN

Duprey P (2005) Do arbitral awards constitute precedent? Should commercial arbitration be distinguished in this regards from arbitration based on investment treaties? In: Gaillard E, Schlaepfer AV, Pinsolle P, Degos L (eds) Towards a uniform international arbitration law? International Arbitration Institute series on international arbitration, no. 3. Juris, New York

Editorial (1995) The decision of the high court of Australia in Esso/BHP v Plowman. Arb Int'l 11 (3):231–233

Editorial (2000) A critique of the Uniform Arbitration Act (2000). World Arb & Mediation Rep 11:326–334

Eisemann F (1981) Zur Rechtswahl in der Schiedsgerichtsbarkeit bei Kaufverträgen. In: Böckstiegel K-H, Glossner O (eds) Festschrift für Arthur Bülow. Carl Heymanns, Köln

Favre Bulle X (2005) Are arbitration proceedings still exclusively reserved for parties? In: Gaillard E, Schlaepfer AV, Pinsolle P, Degos L (eds) Towards a uniform international arbitration law? International Arbitration Institute series on international arbitration, no. 3. Juris, New York

Folberg J, Golann D, Kloppenberg L, Stipanowich T (2005) Resolving disputes: theory practice and law. Aspen, New York

Friel S (2008) Emmot v Wilson and Partners Ltd – confidentiality. Int ALR 11(3):N46–N48

Frommel SN, Rider BA (eds) (1999) Conflicting legal cultures in commercial arbitration: old issues and new trends. Studies in comparative corporate and financial law. Kluwer Law International, The Hague

Gaillard E, Schlaepfer AV, Pinsolle P, Degos L (eds) (2005) Towards a uniform international arbitration law? International Arbitration Institute series on international arbitration, no. 3. Juris, New York

Gallaher N (2003) Legal privilege in international arbitration. Int ALR 6(2):45–49

Gelinas PA (1999) Arbitration clauses: achieving effectiveness. In: Van der Berg AJ (ed) Improving the efficiency of arbitration agreements and awards: 40 years of application of the New York Convention. International Council for Commercial Arbitration Congress series, no. 9. Kluwer Law International, The Hague

Global Legal Group (2006) International arbitration 2006. Global Legal Group, London. http://www.iclg.co.uk. Accessed 13 July 2008

Global Legal Group (2007) The international comparative legal guide to international arbitration 2007: a practical insight to cross-border international arbitration work. Global Legal Group, London

Glossner O (1984) Commercial arbitration in the Federal Republic of Germany. Kluwer Law and Taxation, Deventer

Goldhaber MD (2005) Sneak peek: an inside look at more than 100 major disputes from the secret world of arbitration. Focus Europe 22. http://www.americanlawyer.com/focuseurope/scorecard0605.html. Accessed 12 June 2008

Gunter PY (2005) Transnational rules on the taking of evidence. In: Gaillard E, Schlaepfer AV, Pinsolle P, Degos L (eds) Towards a uniform international arbitration law? International Arbitration Institute series on international arbitration, no. 3. Juris, New York

Günther K (2000) Einshränkungen der Erhebung von Dokumentenbeweisen aufgrund von Vertraulichkeit und Gaschäftsgeheimnissen. In: Berger KP et al (eds) Festschrift für Otto Sandrock. Recht und Wirtschaft GmbH, Heidelberg

Guyon Y (1995) L'Arbitrage. Economica, Paris, pp 7–8

Handelskammer Hamburg (2007) Schiedsgerichtsbarkeit und Wirtschaftsmediation in Hamburg. Handelskammer Hamburg, Hamburg

Haynes JR (1999) International arbitration may not be as confidential as you think – or want. In: Frommel SN, Rider BA (eds) Conflicting legal cultures in commercial arbitration: old issues and new trends. Studies in comparative corporate and financial law, vol 4. Kluwer Law International, The Hague

Heaps J, Taylor C (2006) Legal privilege and confidentiality in England and Wales. In: Koehnen M et al (eds) Privilege and confidentiality: an international handbook. IBA, London

Henry M (2005) The contribution of arbitral case law and national laws. In: Gaillard E, Schlaepfer AV, Pinsolle P, Degos L (eds) Towards a uniform international arbitration law? International Arbitration Institute series on international arbitration, no. 3. Juris, New York

Herbert Smith Newsletter (2008) Confidentiality in arbitration: an update. Herbert Smith Newsletter No 71, London

Herzog PE (1984) Introductory remarks: the need for a comparative perspective. In: Carbonneau TE (ed) Resolving transnational disputes through international arbitration. University Press of Virginia, Virginia

Higet K (1998) The enigma of the Lexy Mercatoria. In: Carbonneau TE (ed) Lex Mercatoria and arbitration. Juris, The Hague

Hilaire J (2000) L' Arbitrage dans la Periode Moderne (XVIeme-XVIIeme siècle). Rev Arb 2:187–226

Hill R, Fletcher S (2004) Confidentiality of arbitration in court proceedings. Int ALR 7(4): N48–N50

Hochstrasser D (2005) Public and mandatory law in international arbitration. In: Gaillard E, Schlaepfer AV, Pinsolle P, Degos L (eds) Towards a uniform international arbitration law? International Arbitration Institute series on international arbitration, no. 3. Juris, New York

Hodges P (2007) The relevance of Article 6 of the European Convention on Human Rights in the context of arbitration proceedings. Int ALR 10(5):163–169

Hoettler P (2007) Das fingierte Schiedsverfahren, Schriftenreihe des Deutschen Instituts für Schiedsgerichtswesen, Band 20. Carl Heymanns, Köln

Hollander C, Adam T (2000) Documentary evidence, 7th edn. Sweet and Maxwell, London

Horn H (ed) (1992) Rechts des Internationales Wirtschaftsverkehrs, Band 10, S 296. M.W.N., Köln

Jacot-Guillarmond O (1988) L'Arbitrage Privé Face a l'Article 6(1) de la Convention Européene des Droits de l'Homme. In: Matscher F, Petzold H (eds) Protecting human rights: the European dimension. Liber Amicorum Gérard J Wiarda. Carl Heymanns, Köln

Jagusch S (2005) Recent codification efforts: an assessment. In: Gaillard E, Schlaepfer AV, Pinsolle P, Degos L (eds) Towards a uniform international arbitration law? International Arbitration Institute series on international arbitration, no. 3. Juris, New York

Jarrosson C (1989) L' Arbitrage et la Convention Européene des Droits de l'Homme. Rev Arb 4:573

Kalavros KF (1992) Dietisia-Syllogi Keimenon & Nomothesia, 2nd Ed., Sakkoulas, Athens-Komotini

King DB (2005) Consistency of awards in cases of parallel proceedings concerning related subject matters. In: Gaillard E, Schlaepfer AV, Pinsolle P, Degos L (eds) Towards a uniform international arbitration law? International Arbitration Institute series on international arbitration, no. 3. Juris, New York

Klammaris K (ed) (2009) Fetschrift für Prof K.D. Kerameus. Sakkoulas-Bruylant, Athens

Koehnen M, Russenberger M, Cowling E (eds) (2006) Privilege and confidentiality: an international handbook. International Bar Association, London

Kouris S (2005) Confidentiality: is international arbitration losing one of its major benefits? J Int'l Arb 22:127

Kratky-Dore L (2006) Public courts versus private justice: it's time to let some sun shine in on alternative dispute resolution. Chi-Kent L Rev 81:463–520

Kroell S (2002) Recognition and enforcement of foreign arbitral awards in Germany. Int'l Arb L R 5:160–177

Lachmann P (2002) Handbuch für die Schiedsgerichtspraxis, 2nd edn. Oceans, New York

Laeuchli UM (2007) Civil and common law: contrast and synthesis in international arbitration. Disp Resol J 62:81–85

Lando O (2000) The principles of European Contract Law and the Lex Mercatoria. In: Basedow J et al (eds) Private law in the international arena: from national conflict rules towards harmonization and unification, Festschrift für Kurt Siehr. TMC Asser, The Hague

Lazareff S (1999) Towards a common procedural approach. In: Frommel SN, Rider BA (eds) Conflicting legal cultures in commercial arbitration: old issues and new trends. Studies in comparative corporate and financial law, vol 4. Kluwer Law International, The Hague

Leahy ER, Bianchi CJ (2000) The changing face of international arbitartion. J Int'l Arb 17 (4):19–61

Lew JDM, Mistellis L (eds) (2007) Arbitration insights: twenty years of the annual lecture of the School of International Arbitration. International arbitration law library series, no. 16. Kluwer Law International, The Hague

Lindahl M, Avokatbyra A (1983) International commercial arbitration under the rules of the Arbitration Institute of Stockholm Chamber of Commerce. In: Papers presented to the American Bar Association section of litigation, where? how? American Bar Association, Chicago

Lord Mance (2003) Lecture on confidentiality of arbitrations. In: Proceedings of the 2nd conference on dispute resolution, India, 13 Sept. 2003, pp 58–77

Lord Mustill MJ (2008) The history of international commercial arbitration – a sketch. In: Newman L, Hill RD (eds) The leading arbitrator's guide to international arbitration, 2nd edn. Juris, New York

Lord Mustill MJ, Boyd SC (1989) Commercial arbitration, 2nd edn. Butterworths, London

Lord Neil QC (1996) Confidentiality in arbitration. Arb Int'l 12:287

Lord Parker of Waddington (1959) The history and development of commercial arbitration. In: The Hebrew University of Jerusalem, Lionel Cohen lectures fifth series, Jan. 1959. Magnes, Jerusalem

Lowenfeld AF (1998) Lex Mercatoria: an arbitrator's view. In: Carbonneau TE (ed) Lex Mercatoria and arbitration: a discussion of the new law merchant. Juris, New York

Mantilla-Serrano F (2005) Towards a transnational procedural public policy. In: Gaillard E, Schlaepfer AV, Pinsolle P, Degos L (eds) Towards a uniform international arbitration law? International Arbitration Institute series on international arbitration, no. 3. Juris, New York

Matscher F, Petzold H (eds) (1988) Protecting human rights: the European dimension. Liber Amicorum Gérard J. Wiarda. Carl Heymanns, Köln

Mbaye K (1999) Arbitration agreement: conditions governing their efficiency. In: Van der Berg AJ (ed) Improving the efficiency of arbitration agreements and awards: 40 years of application of the New York Convention. International Council for Commercial Arbitration Congress series, no. 9. Kluwer Law International, The Hague

Mentschikoff S (1961) Commercial arbitration. Colum L Rev 61:846
Merkin R (2000) Arbitration Act 1996, 2nd edn. LLP, London
Merkin R (2004) Arbitration law. LLP Informa, London
Misra J, Jordans R (2006) Confidentiality in international arbitration: an introspection of the public interest exception. J Int'l Arb 23:39–48
Mueller C (2005) La Confidentialite en Arbitrage Internationale Commerciale: Un Trompe-l'Oeil? ASA Bull 2005:216–240
Nappert S, Cooke T (2003) The privy council on confidentiality and the enforcement of awards. Int ALR 6(2):43–44
Nariman F (2004) East meets west: tradition, globalization and the future of arbitration. Arb Int'l 20(2):123–138
Neil P (1996) Confidentiality in arbitration. Arb Int'l 12(3):287
Newman L, Hill RD (eds) (2008) The leading arbitrator's guide to international arbitration, 2nd edn. Juris, New York
Nolan-Haley J, Abramson H, Chew PK (2005) International conflict resolution: consensual alternative dispute resolution process. Thomson West, St. Paul, MN
Noussia K (2009) Confidentiality in arbitration revisited: John Foster Emmott v Michael Wilson & Partners Ltd [2008] EWCA Civ 184. ZZPInt 14:1–37
Ong CYC (2005) Confidentiality of arbitral awards and the advantage for arbitral institutions to maintain a repository of awards. Asian Int'l Arb J 1(2):169–180
Park WW (1984) The influence of national legal systems on international commercial arbitration: recent developments in English arbitration law. In: Carbonneau TE (ed) Resolving transnational disputes through international arbitration. University Press of Virginia, Virginia
Park WW (1998) Control mechanisms in the development of a modern Lex Mercatoria. In: Carbonneau TE (ed) Lex Mercatoria and arbitration: a discussion of the new law merchant. Juris, The Hague
Paulsson J, Raeding N (1995) The trouble with confidentiality. Arb Int'l 11(3):303–320
Pechota V (1998) The future of the law governing the international arbitral process. In: Carbonneau TE (ed) Lex Mercatoria and arbitration: a discussion of the new law merchant. Juris, The Hague
Peltzer OM (2000) Die Dissenting Opinion in der Schiedsgerichtsbarkeit. Peter Lang, Frankfurt am Main
Petrochilos G (2004) Procedural law in international arbitration. Oxford private international law series. Oxford University Press, Oxford
Petsche MA (2005) The growing autonomy of international commercial arbitration. Sellier, München
Pongracic-Speier M (2002) Confidentiality and the public interest exception: considerations for mixed international arbitration. http://cfcj-fcjc.org/clearinghouse/drpapers/2001-dra/monique_pongra.html. Accessed 24 August 2008
Prechac J (2003) Seneca: conversations, beneficial actions. In: Devolve J et al (eds) French arbitration law and practice. Kluwer Law International, The Hague
Pruetting H (2001) Vertraulichkeit in der Schiedsgerichtsbarkeit und in der Mediation. In: Briner R, Fortier Y, Berger KP, Bredow J (eds) Law of international dispute settlement in the 21st century, Liber Amicorum Karl-Heinz Böckstiegel. Carl Heymanns, Köln
Pryles M (2008) Confidentiality. In: Newman L, Hill RD (eds) The leading arbitrator's guide to international arbitration, 2nd edn. Juris, New York
Rabinovitch-Einy O (2002) Going public: diminishing privacy in dispute resolution in the internet age. Va J L Tech 7(4):1–26. http://www.vjolt.net/vol7/issue2/v7i2_a04-Rabinovitch-Einy.pdf. Accessed 15 September 2008
Raeschke-Kessler H, Lehre HK (1989) Aktuelle Rechtsfragen der Schiedsgerichtsbarkeit. Verlag Kommunikationsforum, Carl Heymanns, Köln
Raeschke-Kessler H, Berger KP, Lehne HK (1995) Recht und Praxis des Schiedsverfahrens, 2nd edn. Verlag Kommunikationsforum, Carl Heymanns, Köln

Rawlings N, Seeger K (2003) Aegis v. European Re and the confidentiality of arbitration awards. Arb Int'l 19(4):483–490
Raymond AH (2005) Confidentiality in a forum of last resort: is the use of confidential information a good idea for business and society? Am Rev Int'l Arb 16:479–516
Redfern A, Hunter M (2004) International commercial arbitration, 4th edn. Oxford University Press, Oxford
Reimann M, Zekoll J (2005) Introduction to German law. C.H. Beck, München
Reuben RC (2006) Confidentiality in arbitration: beyond the myth. U Kan L Rev 54:1255–1300
Robb A (2004) Confidentiality and arbitration. In: 39 Essex Street Chambers, London. http://www.39essex.co.uk/index.php?art_id=228. Accessed 10 June 2008
Robert J, Carbonneau TE (1983) The French law of arbitration. Mathew Bender, New York
Rützel S, Christ M (2006) Legal privilege and confidentiality in Germany. In: Koehnen M, Russenberger M, Cowling E (eds) Privilege and confidentiality: an international handbook. International Bar Association, London
Rützel S, Wegen G, Wilske S (2005) Commercial dispute resolution in Germany – litigation arbitration mediation. C.H. Beck, München
Sachs G (2008) Verhaltensstandards für Schiedsrichter, Schriftenreihe des Deutschen Instituts für Schiedsgerichtswesen, Band 23. Carl Heymanns, Köln
Sanders P (1981) Harmonisation of arbitartion laws: a model law? In: Böckstiegel K-H, Glossner O (eds) Festschrift für Arthur Bülow. Carl Heymanns, Köln
Sarles J (2002) Solving the arbitral confidentiality conundrum in international arbitration. American Arbitration Association's Annual Volume, 18th edn. ADR & the Law, New York. http://www.appellate.net/articles/Confidentiality.pdf. Accessed 23 September 2008
Schiedsgericht Berlin (1990) Schiedsgerichtsordnung des Schiedsgerichts Berlin. Schiedsgericht Berlin, Berlin
Schmitz AJ (2006) Untangling the privacy paradox in arbitration. U Kan L Rev 54:1211–1253
Schroeder HP (2007) Die lex mercatoria arbitralis, Struktuelle Transnationalität und transnationale Rechtsstrukturen im Recht der internationalen Schiedsgerichtsbarkeit. Sellier, München, pp 449–455
Schuetze RA (2005) Ausgewaehlte Probleme des deutschen und internationalen Schiedsverfahrensrechts. Carl Heymanns, Köln
Schuetze RA, Tscherning D, Wais W (1990) Handbuch des Schiedsverfahrens: Praxis der deutschen und internationalen Schiedsgerichtsbarkeit, 2nd edn. Walter de Guyter, Berlin
Schultz T (2006) Human rights: a speed bump for arbitral procedures? An exploration of safeguards in the acceleration of justice. Int ALR 9(1):8–23
Schwab HCKH, Walter G (1990a) Schiedsgerichtsbarkeit Kommentar, vol 4. C.H. Beck, München
Schwab HCKH, Walter G (1990b) Schiedsgerichtsbarkeit Kommentar, vol 5. C.H. Beck, München
Schwarz EA (1999) Choosing between broad clauses and detailed blueprints. In: Van der Berg AJ (ed) Improving the efficiency of arbitration agreements and awards: 40 years of application of the New York Convention. International Council for Commercial Arbitration Congress series, no. 9. Kluwer Law International, The Hague
Secomb M (2000) Confidentiality and privacy in arbitration: the lessons of Ali. VJ 4:89–94
Seriki H (2006) Confidentiality in arbitration proceedings: recent trends and developments. JBL 2006(5):300–311
Shackleton SR (1999) Global warming: milder still in England, Part 2. Int ALR 2(4):117–136
Shany Y (2003) The competing jurisdictions of international courts and tribunals. Oxford University Press, Oxford
Sheppard A (1998) Ali Shipping Corp v Shipyard Trogir [1999] 1 W.L.R. 314 (CA (CIV DIV)). Int ALR 1(3):N53–N54
Sindler M (2008) Litigation, dispute resolution and arbitration: privacy matters. Olswand Law Firm Newsletter, 3 July 2008. http://www.legalweek.com/Company/360/Navigation/18/Articles/1141052.html. Accessed 15 August 2008

Stouthuysen AR (2006) Belgium: how effective are nondisclosure agreements? ACC Docket 25 (7):144–147
Straatmann K, Timmermann FH (1984) Handelsrechtliche Schiedsgerichts-Praxis, Band 3. Handelskammer Hamburg, Hamburg
Straatmann K, Ulmer P (1975) Handelsrechtliche Schiedsgerichts-Praxis, Band 1. Dr Otto Schmidt KG, Köln
Straatmann K, Ulmer P, Timmermann FH, Wiesner G (1982) Handelsrechtliche Schiedsgerichts-Praxis, Band 2. Dr Otto Schmidt KG, Köln
Sturges WA (1953) Cases on arbitration law. Mathew Bender, New York
Sturges WA (1960) Arbitration – what is it? N Y U L Rev 35:1031
Sumampow M et al (eds) (1992) Law and reality: essays on national and international procedural law in honour of Cornelis Carel Albert Voskuil. M Nijhoff, The Hague
Sze QL, Peng Khoon EL (2007) Confidentiality in arbitration: how far does it extend? Academy, Singapore
Thoma I (2008) Confidentiality in English arbitration law: myths and realities about its legal nature. J Int'l Arb 25(3):299–314
Thompson R, Derains Y (1974) Cour d'Arbitrage de la Chambre de Commerce Internationale – Chronique des Sentences Arbitrales. JDI 101:876
Thompson CR, Finn AMK (2007) Confidentiality in arbitration: a valid assumption? A proposed solution. Disp Resol J 62:75–79
Trackman LE (2002) Confidentiality in international commercial arbitration. Arb Int'l 18(1):1–18
Trackman L (2006) "Legal traditions" and international commercial arbitration. Am Rev Int'l Arb 17:1–43
Uff K, Noussia K (2009) On the protection of confidentiality of arbitral proceedings: a comparative approach of the position in England, Australia, U.S.A. and Canada. In: Klammaris K (ed) Fetschrift für Prof. K.D. Kerameus. Sakkoulas-Bruylant, Athens, pp 1428–1449
Van der Berg AJ (ed) (1999) Improving the efficiency of arbitration agreements and awards: 40 years of application of the New York Convention. International Council for Commercial Arbitration Congress series, no. 9. Kluwer Law International, The Hague
Van Dijk P, Van Hoof GJH (1990) Theory and practice of the European Convention of Human Rights, 2nd edn. Kluwer, Deventer
Vlas P (1992) The principle of fair trial in international civil litigation. In: Sumampow M et al (eds) Law and reality: essays on national and international procedural law in honour of Cornelis Carel Albert Voskuil. M Nijhoff, Leiden
Von Breitenstein D (2000) Rechtsordnung und "Lex Mercatoria" – Zur vergeblichen Suche nach einem "anationalen" Recht für die internationale Arbitrage. In: Berger KP, Ebge WF, Elsing S, Großfeld B, Kühne G (eds) Festschrift für Otto Sandrock. Recht und Wirtschafte, Heidelberg
Ware SJ (1999) Default rules from mandatory rules: privatizing law through arbitration. Minn L Rev 83:703–732
Wilkey M (1999) The practicalities of cross-cultural arbitration. In: Frommel SN, Rider BA (eds) Conflicting legal cultures in commercial arbitration: old issues and new trends. Studies in comparative corporate and financial law, vol 4. Kluwer Law International, The Hague
Woolhouse SP (2004) The effect of an arbitration award on subsequent arbitration between different parties – an English law perspective. Int ALR 7(5):150–156
Yates GT (1984) Arbitration or court litigation for private international dispute resolution: the lesser of two evils. In: Carbonneau TE (ed) Resolving transnational disputes through international arbitration. University Press of Virginia, Virginia
Zamboni M (2003) Confidentiality in mediation. Int ALR 6(5):175–190

Table of Cases

A. England

B. USA

C. France

D. Germany

E. Sweden

F. Australia

G. European Cases

H. Arbitral Awards

Table of Statutes

A. International

B. England

C. USA

D. France

E. Germany

Index

Kolibri 360 GmbH
Ferdinand-Jühlke-Straße 7
99095 Erfurt, Deutschland
produktsicherheit@kolibri360.de